THE POLITICS OF FEAR

How Republicans Use Money, Race, and the Media to Win

Manuel G. Gonzales
and
Richard Delgado

Paradigm Publishers
Boulder • London

10076788

Copyright © 2006 by Paradigm Publishers

Published in the United States by Paradigm Publishers, 3360 Mitchell Lane, Suite E, Boulder, Colorado 80301 USA.

Paradigm Publishers is the trade name of Birkenkamp & Company, LLC, Dean Birkenkamp, President and Publisher.

Library of Congress Cataloging-in-Publication Data

Gonzales, Manuel G.
  The politics of fear: how Republicans use money, race, and the media to win / Manuel G. Gonzales and Richard Delgado.
     p. cm.
  Includes bibliographical references and index.
  ISBN–13: 978-1-59451-241-4 (hardcover : alk. paper)
  ISBN–10: 1-59451-241-8 (hardcover : alk. paper)
  1. Conservatism—United States.   2. United States—Politics and government—1989-
I. Delgado, Richard.   II. Title.
  JC573.2.U6G656 20906
  320.520973—dc22

                                                                2006004357

Printed and bound in the United States of America on acid-free paper that meets the standards of the American National Standard for Permanence of Paper for Printed Library Materials.

Designed and Typeset by Straight Creek Bookmakers.

10 09 08 07 06 1 2 3 4 5

Dedicated to our mentors,
Roger L. Williams, David J. Weber, and Henry McGee

Gonzales and Delgado document the stunning success of a network of wealthy donors and corporations in creating and sustaining a set of think tanks, legal action groups, and media strategies. These institutions have provided an agenda and very well-supported consistent advocacy for a powerful and effective conservative movement and drastically changed the agenda of American politics.

Although there are many institutions with important resources that are not part of this movement, the moderate and progressive forces in U.S. society have no similarly articulated national strategy. Many of them eschew work on big ideas and fundamental change in favor of short-term funding of community organizations or minor technical experiments, ignoring the basic structure of society or the economy, which usually defeats those efforts.

If we are to have a full democratic debate in the United States, we need to understand what has happened. Those with different values must realize that they are shooting random arrows in many directions while the right wing, which now controls all three branches of the federal government, is coming at them fast in a tank.

—*Gary Orfield,* Harvard University

Contents

Preface and Acknowledgments

Political commentator Joe Conason begins his 2003 book *Big Lies: The Right-Wing Propaganda Machine and How It Distorts the Truth* by giving a long list of ways that liberalism has dramatically improved the lives of American citizens during the twentieth century. These include Medicare, Social Security, and a host of other popular and far-reaching reforms. As impressive as it is, however, this list is far from complete. *Brown v. Board of Education,* the Peace Corps, and the struggle for women's rights are just a few of the most significant omissions. The contributions of conservatism to social progress, on the other hand, have been modest at best. Indeed, as critics have noted, conservatives have consistently opposed democratic reform at every turn. Obsessed with preserving the privileges of political and economic elites, they have fought tooth and nail to block efforts to promote the rights of workers, consumers, women, minorities, and other disenfranchised segments of the population. Yet, in spite of this poor record, conservative candidates have won election time and again during the past thirty-five years, a period of Republican ascendancy that has culminated with a near-monopoly on political power. Our book is an attempt to explain this paradox.

Using the Republican Party as a vehicle, conservatives have dominated the political life of the United States since the seventies by employing a host of scare tactics to win elections. While the fear of racial minorities (and preservation of white privilege), as we argue, has remained the most effective tool in the GOP arsenal, from time to time other groups—Communists, gays, immigrants, and terrorists, just to name the most obvious—have served as convenient scapegoats. Thus, the GOP has won popular support despite a political agenda that works against the interests of the great majority of the citizenry, including the bulk of the middle class. Beset by fear, Americans have been willing to support a party that promises them security even at the expense of their liberties and economic well-being.

"The politics of fear" have figured prominently in the writings of other students of the Republican ascendancy—Dan T. Carter, Alan Crawford, Thomas Edsall, Michael Lind, Godfrey Hodgson. In our study, however, racial politics takes center stage. Moreover, while most of the journalists and scholars mentioned emphasize the role of blacks, Spanish-speaking minorities generally receive short shrift. This work will help to correct that deficiency. Although conservatives have begun to court the Latino voter, fear of brown people, and the political manipulation of this fear, will undoubtedly continue into the future given the heavy immigration from Latin America and the transformation of Latinos from a regional into a national minority.

During the past twenty years, a great deal has been written on the rise of conservatism, so much so that it is almost impossible to keep abreast of the latest findings. Works of synthesis are sorely needed. Our study, which addresses this void, systematically reviews this voluminous literature and tries to make sense of it.

A prevalent theme in these new studies, written mostly by progressive scholars, is that the conservative resurgence was primarily a reaction to the excesses of the sixties. According to this popular interpretation, the advances of the "rights revolution" came at the expense of the white middle class, notably the hardworking lower-middle class. While this view contains an element of truth, it is important to give the achievements of the sixties their due. Reading most accounts today, one would think that the turbulent decade was dominated by drug-taking hippies, opportunistic minorities, their misguided liberal allies, and a variety of other "losers." But people didn't march and die in the streets because they were bored. We forget today what conditions were like at midcentury for the underprivileged. Racial oppression was rampant; the plight of blacks, in particular, dire. We have short memories. Look again at the photograph of the nine beleaguered black children attempting to enroll at Little Rock's Central High School in 1957. They are surrounded by a segregationist mob. See the hatred in those white faces. Without federal protection, the children most likely would have been injured or even killed. *That's* what the sixties were about. Yes, wage-earning whites would ultimately pay a price. But, their anger has surely been misplaced—to the immense political and material advantage of the rich and the superrich.

Nor have minorities gained as many advantages as their detractors would have us believe. According to the 2000 U.S. census, Huron, California, the hometown of one of us, has 6,306 residents. Mostly immigrants (53.7 percent), 98.3 percent of the residents of this San Joaquin Valley community are Latino, predominantly Mexican. The median household income is $24,609. No one—not a single person—living there in 2000 had a college degree. As the late Marc Reisner pointed out in *Cadillac Desert,* an award-winning PBS documentary based on his 1986 environmental study of the same name, Huronites toil throughout most of the year from sunrise to sunset on the factory farms of the Westside, America's most productive agricultural region. Yet, he marveled, almost all of them remain in a state of chronic poverty. Many farmworkers own nothing more than a secondhand car or truck. Huron, it is clear, is not exactly the epitome of the American Dream.

A multitude of problems—drugs, alcohol, and domestic abuse, to name a few—haunt the town. Many residents rely on welfare, especially during the winter, when unemployment skyrockets as high as 28.8 percent. Yet the meager government handouts to farmworkers are practically nothing compared with the welfare—public subsidies and tax breaks—provided to their employers, the factory farms and their corporate allies, collectively known as agribusiness. The poverty in places like Huron is not just a product of structural deficiencies characteristic of the national and global economies. Public policies have a great deal to do with it.

Needless to say, raised in this culture of poverty, we see a different America than most of our compatriots. Moreover, once we left for the university—where we ultimately earned a Ph.D. in modern Italian history (in the case of Gonzales) and a law degree (in the case of Delgado)—we encountered an entirely different world. Our universities in the sixties and seventies seemed to be more like country clubs than college campuses. Wealth abounded. The student body was lily-white. We have thus experienced an unusually large swath of the entire socioeconomic spectrum. Few people can make a similar claim in a society that is still largely segregated. Having lived with both the haves and the have-nots, we bring to this study of Republican ascendancy a unique perspective, and a highly critical one.

The Republican Party, conservative critics will argue, receives harsh treatment in the pages of this book. It does—and rightly so. People, after all, need to be judged not according to what they say but for what they do. The Democrats come in for criticism as well, especially the leadership of the party. However, this study is not about "The Strange Death of the Democratic Party," a much-needed book. Rather it is an explanation of the triumph of conservatism, especially the GOP, and an analysis of its meaning. It is the Republicans that rule today. Why spend much time on their rivals? Democrats seem to be largely irrelevant in the current political process.

Several years ago, during a moment of temporary insanity, as one of us was in the midst of a tirade about how many of his colleagues were perpetrating a series of myths that distorted the reality of minorities in the United States, one of his daughters, then a doctoral candidate at the University of California-Berkeley, stopped him short. "Dad," Vanna interjected, "why are you criticizing people who have absolutely no power at all? Ethnic studies departments are fighting for their lives. Why don't you tackle the heavyweights, the people who *do* have the power?" In retrospect, he considers his daughter's words the best advice he ever received.

His daughter is only one of many people we want to thank. Despite busy schedules, colleagues and friends have been generous with their time. Their suggestions have been much appreciated. Since few of them completely endorse our political perspectives, our debt is so much the greater. We authors, of course, bear sole responsibility for any errors found in our study.

Jean Stefancic was kind enough to look over drafts of our work, offer helpful suggestions, and provide encouragement for the completion of this project. The same applies to Michael Parenti, whose Marxian perspectives have significantly shaped our own views on politics and history.

Our views on the media benefited greatly from the input of Jeff Perlstein, director of Media Alliance in San Francisco, and Marc Sapir, codirector of Retropoll, both of whom were kind enough to look over parts of the manuscript and offer useful comments.

Many colleagues have contributed valuable criticisms from a variety of academic perspectives. These include Laurie Fischer, Maria Giuili, Katherine Graham, Mickey S. Huff, Dori Mazzone, Scott MacDougall, Matthew Powell, Jim Rawls, Michael Steinberg, Greg Tilles, and David Vela. Several of our students, too, came to our aid with timely suggestions as well as key bibliographical materials, among them Marlanee Emigh, Jason Harvey, Gilbert LoCoco, Jay Meadows, Mayu Nakamura, Rob Reggiardo, Doug Ruthnick, Katy Sater, Steven Schneider, Merrill Tan, Willie Tanoto, and Scotti Zablackis. Of our students, Gary Lyons, Jesse MacKinnon, and Kristina Rizga, in particular, proved to be assiduous and dependable collaborators.

Brenda Chodroff and Rick Mitchell, longtime friends and soul mates, were generous with both their time and effort.

We are deeply indebted to the editors at Paradigm Publishers, and especially to Dean Birkenkamp, who wholeheartedly supported our efforts at every turn. Our production editor, Julie Kirsch, was a model of efficiency, and her assistance was invaluable.

Finally, our families deserve special mention, not just because of their moral support but also because of their insights on the political process. In addition to Vanna, thanks go to her husband Curtis and to Gonzales's second daughter, Amalia. His wife Cindy, as always, was his main critic and supporter. Indeed, this book would not have been written had it not been for her passionate love of American politics. Delgado's daughters Maya and Lisa and his brother Cesar provided constant inspiration, and UC Berkeley's Center for the Study of Law and Society provided him with a supportive setting for completing this book.

INTRODUCTION

Since the Vietnam War, the United States has witnessed the emergence of a powerful right-wing political movement that differs significantly from its predecessors. This New Right (or New Conservatism) has proven remarkably successful, first under Ronald Reagan and more recently under the two Bushes.[1] "Conservatism," the British journalist-historian Godfrey Hodgson once observed, "has always been reactive, a response to political movements which the conservative feared and wanted to halt."[2] The new variety is true to this pattern. Consisting of a religious and a secular wing—and finding its home in the Republican Party, which it now dominates—this movement largely represents a defensive reaction to two perceived threats arising in the sixties: (1) a growing secular humanism and (2) the progress, real and imagined, of women and racial and other minorities.[3] It is their repugnance for the sixties that helps to explain the deep animosity of conservative diehards toward Bill and Hillary Clinton, whom they see as symbols of the tumultuous decade.[4] Far from dead, the "old white guys" are back with a vengeance.

Conservatism, of course, has always been a powerful force in American politics.[5] After all, political views usually mirror socioeconomic status, and from the very outset, most white Americans owned property. Today, the United States is the most affluent society in history: The median U.S. household income in 2004 was $44,389.[6] During the past fifty years, as they have benefited from greater educational and economic opportunities, the majority of Americans have come to identify themselves as middle-class.[7] ("The idea of the middle class," one scholar has noted, "became the defining feature of American society in the 1950s.")[8] This class identity accounts, in large part, for the continued success of the GOP in modern times even though since the forties, the party affiliation of registered voters has consistently favored Democrats.[9] However, by itself the traditional conservative bent of the American people fails to completely explain Republican dominance.[10] Equally important, as we hope to illustrate, is the ability of conservatives to marshal financial resources and to capitalize on popular discontent. The conservative ascendancy reflects both the power of money—the pervasive influence exerted by corporate interests—and the use of fear as a tactic to mobilize mass support.

1

Today's conservative consensus is in large part a product of a concerted ef-fort by a relatively small number of individuals, mostly members of the political and economic elite, to dictate public policy. The origins of this movement lie in the Vietnam era. Like the Radical Left, the Radical Right emerged during the turbulent sixties. Repelled by the excesses of the counterculture, young conservatives began to mobilize on college campuses. Mostly disaffected youths, militant right-wingers, for all their energy, were at first powerless to effect change. This state of affairs changed dramatically in the seventies, when they found financial sponsors in the business community. In a very real sense, the New Right, as a political movement rather than simply a vague youthful aspiration, was a creation of corporate elites. Thanks to their friends' deep pockets, the small militant core was able to work out and propagate its ideas while transforming itself into a widespread movement.

Today the New Right consists of a myriad of well-funded conservative organizations led by a cadre of committed free-market ideologues. Firmly in control of the Republican Party, the movement has achieved remarkable suc-cess, culminating in the two-term presidency of George W. Bush. In power, conservatives are in the process of bringing about a profound revolution. Their ultimate aim is to dismantle the welfare state constructed by liberals during the Depression. Claiming to be champions of a new moral order, triumphant conservatives are busy enacting a radical probusiness agenda, a reflection of the degree to which the corporate elite has co-opted the movement. That the bulk of the middle class has backed the Right and its elitist program is puzzling to most scholars. Inimical to their interests, the GOP platform has nonetheless garnered popular support among voters.

That Americans would behave irrationally—that they would vote against their own self-interest—has been labeled the Great Paradox by a variety of pundits and scholars. What accounts for it? Some students of politics believe it is a matter of religious beliefs. Others emphasize moral values. Still others find the key in a profound insecurity that haunts life as Americans enter the twenty-first century. Certainly much evidence suggests that Americans are in the midst of a religious revival, a cyclical occurrence in the nation's history. Undoubtedly these explanations have something to do with voting patterns. It is the quest for security, however, that we find most compelling. A survey of the history of the New Right indicates that while its popularity has many sources, the one that stands out is *fear*. Over and over again, it is this sentiment that New Right lead-ers emphasize. Writing in 2005, one critic of President George W. Bush notes that "fear is the currency of this president, and his administration and his allies dole it out on a daily basis."[11] Republicans have dominated the ballot box since the time of Richard Nixon not by appealing to voters' altruistic sentiments—as Democrats have done until recently—but rather by appealing to their worst instincts, particularly their fear of those dif-ferent from themselves.

→ CHAPTER ONE ←

THE NEW RIGHT

Birth of a Movement

The early sixties found American conservatism in the throes of a crisis; "the liberal consensus," the late historian John A. Andrew III recalls, "appeared to reign supreme."[1] Under President John F. Kennedy, the Democrats, with their liberal ideology, seemed to be the party of the future. Democrat-backed programs—the Great Society, the welfare state, the civil rights movement—threatened to permanently alter the political and social landscape of the republic, particularly after 1964, when the party registered spectacular electoral victories. In that year, when Lyndon Johnson won the presidency with a whopping 61 percent of the popular vote, "an ascendant liberalism reached its postwar zenith."[2] More than twice as many Americans registered as Democrats than as Republicans,[3] yet the promise of long-term ascendancy by the Democrats never came about.

President Johnson and his party, despite Herculean efforts, were unable to resolve the intractable problems of the inner cities. Their efforts to create the Great Society suffered a further setback when the war in Vietnam dragged on. Disillusionment was most profound among the middle class. Perfectly willing to wave the flag so long as the battles were fought by the nation's poor people—blacks, Latinos, southern whites—middle-class patriots underwent a sudden change of heart after the termination of college deferments in 1969, when they and their sons were ordered to the rice paddies of Southeast Asia to protect the American Way. Of the three million soldiers who served in the war, only 20 percent came from the ranks of middle- and upper-class families.[4] The elites, of course, were never in much danger: Of the 29,701 men who graduated from Harvard, MIT, and Princeton in the years from 1962 to 1972, only twenty died in Vietnam.[5]

The civil rights movement and the attempt to create the Great Society inspired fear among the propertied classes, as efforts to challenge

3

the status quo always do.[6] But they also created a near-panic among some working- and middle-class males, who saw their prerogatives slipping away. The assassinations of President Kennedy, Malcolm X, Dr. Martin Luther King Jr., and Robert Kennedy in the turbulent sixties are a testimony to this fear. (In the United States, it seems, the haves are much more likely to employ violence to preserve their privileges than the have-nots are willing to pursue insurrection to abolish those privileges.)

Thus, the election of Richard Nixon (1913–1994) in 1968 and Ronald Reagan (1911–2004) twelve years later signaled the reemergence of conservatism as the dominant political ideology. The early rise of the New Right, generally dated about 1973–1974, was both a cause and a reflection of this ideological triumph.[7] Ensconced in the Republican Party from the very outset, the New Right (a term coined by Lee Edwards, a movement activist who later became a professional historian) was a broad coalition composed of disparate elements. The core of the movement consisted of a generation of youthful discontents who emerged from the probusiness elements that had controlled the GOP since the time of Reconstruction. The immediate roots of the emerging consensus, however, date back to the post–World War II conservatives whose formative experience was the Cold War. The New Right evolved naturally out of the Old Right; the sociologist Jerome L. Himmelstein rightly concludes that no sharp break separated the two.[8]

The chief organ of the older mainstream conservatives—themselves divided into a number of factions—had been the *National Review,* the influential journal founded in 1955 and edited for the next thirty-five years by William F. Buckley (b. 1925). The Yale graduate and ex-CIA agent received able assistance from a small but dedicated staff, including publisher William Rusher (b. 1923), a college classmate. James Burnham (1905–1987) and Frank S. Meyer (1909–1972), both renegades from Marxism, were two other key contributors to the publication.[9]

During this early period, Roman Catholics, as the historian George Nash points out, were heavily represented in the ranks of American conservatism,[10] with anticommunism as a dominant thread.[11] A devout Catholic, Buckley was representative of this alliance. "The Cold War may be over," a friend noted in 1999, "but it remains Buckley's foremost political preoccupation."[12] Buckley is the godfather of the New Right, the "paterfamilias," as one student of the movement aptly describes him, the link between the old and new conservatism.[13] "Bill Buckley," Godfrey Hodgson concluded, "is probably the most important single figure in the whole history of the revival of conservatism in late twentieth-century America."[14]

It was a younger generation of Catholics, however, who provided the primary impetus for the new brand of conservatism that budded in the sixties, before blossoming into a full-fledged movement in the mid-1970s.[15]

Reacting to the excesses of the counterculture, these young activists were influenced as much by Barry Goldwater (1909–1998) as they were by Buckley.[16] The most committed of these youthful conservative Catholics were Houston lawyer Richard A. Viguerie (b. 1933); Wisconsin journalist and radio news director Paul Weyrich (b. 1942); and John T. (Terry) Dolan (1950–1986), who came from a fiercely conservative Irish American background (his brother Tony became President Reagan's chief speechwriter). Together with Howard Phillips (b. 1941), a secular Jew who converted to Christianity in the mid-1970s, these Catholic militants would provide dynamic leadership for the emerging New Right. Ultimately, Viguerie, who pioneered the techniques of direct-mail fund-raising, would easily become the most influential of these ambitious firebrands. Decades of untiring efforts on behalf of the cause earned him widespread recognition among his colleagues as "the symbolic leader of the New Right."[17]

In addition to its more dynamic leadership, the New Right is distinguished from the Old Right, according to Himmelstein, by strategy and organization.[18] Although repelled by the methods of the radical civil rights activists, the generation that came of age in the seventies was quick to use these tactics for its own ends.[19] New Right leaders realized that, like their opponents, they needed to mobilize mass support. If the Republican Party was ever going to successfully challenge the Democratic Party for power and stem the liberal tide, it needed to shed its country club image by creating a popular base, a lesson that gained force from the enormous support elicited by the insurgent third-party presidential candidacy of George Wallace in 1968. The GOP, these strategists determined, needed to attract both working-class ethnics and white southern constituencies.

This conservative revolution began with the creation of a multitude of associations. In the beginning, the most important of these were Phillips's Conservative Caucus (TCC) and Weyrich's Committee for the Survival of a Free Congress (CSFC), both established in 1974.[20] Dolan's National Conservative Political Action Committee (NCPAC), another key organization, sprang up a year later. And the American Conservative Union was created during this period as well.[21]

Funding the New Right

To win back America from the forces that, from their perspective, threatened to destroy it, the Young Turks needed benefactors with deep pockets. They found them in the corporate community. As mentioned earlier, business interests had formed the backbone of Republicanism since Reconstruction. During the post–World War II boom, however, corporate political donations to both major parties had been rather modest. This changed dramatically in the mid-seventies, when the U.S. economy, after thirty years of prosperity, underwent a precipitous decline.[22] While its share of the world gross national product (GNP) stood at about 40 percent in the fifties, by the seventies the United States' share had dropped to less than 30 percent.[23] Deindustrialization hurt traditional industries, especially in the northern Rust Belt metropolitan centers, where both unemployment and underemployment soared. Double-digit inflation eroded purchasing power and discouraged investment throughout the country. Both the trade and the federal deficits ballooned.

When economic dislocations continued into the eighties, many businessmen blamed the government for the downturn. Panicked, they were now willing to contribute large sums to the coffers of the GOP and its affiliates. "The most important element of the big-business mobilization," one scholar avers, "was the flow of corporate money to expand existing conservative research organizations and create a host of new ones."[24] William E. Simon Sr. (1927–2000), an archconservative Wall Street entrepreneur, played the key role in getting the corporate community to open up its wallets and contribute to the GOP beginning in the late seventies. The alliance between wealthy businessmen and New Right operatives is epitomized by the well-documented relationship between Paul Weyrich and multimillionaire beer mogul Joseph Coors (1917–2003). These men maintained close personal and ideological ties from the time they met in Colorado in the early seventies until the powerful philanthropist's death.[25]

Funding also came from individual contributions. New Right operatives were awash in these donations. This was especially true of Richard Viguerie, whose smashingly successful direct-mail fund-raising provided the economic foundation for many of the key institutions of the movement.[26] Tagged "the Funding Father" of the revitalized conservative movement by protégé Morton Blackwell (b. 1939), the tireless Viguerie has mailed some two billion letters soliciting political contributions.[27] Individual and corporate contributions to the GOP soon reached staggering proportions as the rich in America became richer. Globalization and the new information and communication technologies—notably the computer and the Internet—developed toward the end of the twentieth century boosted American economic production to unprecedented levels, with the wealthiest segments of the population monopolizing most of the profits.[28] From 1986 to 2001, according to the Internal Revenue Service (IRS), total personal income expanded by more than $3.8 trillion, of which more than $2 trillion went to the richest 10 percent.[29]

New Recruits

Meanwhile, the Republican Party and the movement that was coming to dominate its apparatus were benefiting not only by a massive infusion of money but by an influx of new recruits, especially from the South. The genesis of this trend antedated the rise of the New Right. Beginning during the Vietnam War, Republican ranks swelled with ex-Dixiecrats (the segregationist States Rights Democratic Party that sprang up briefly after 1948), who found the Democrats' progressive stance on civil rights unpalatable.[30] "For a substantial segment of the white South," recalled Thomas Byrne Edsall, the veteran *Washington Post* reporter, "conservatism became a cloak with which to protect racial segregation."[31] In 1964, South Carolina senator Strom Thurmond (1902–2003) became a key convert when he switched parties in order to support Barry Goldwater's bid for the presidency. (The Arizonan was one of only eight GOP senators to vote against the landmark 1964 Civil Rights Act.)

Conservatives were only too glad to encourage these defections—even if it meant sanctioning racism. In 1962, Young Americans for Freedom, a right-wing student group, awarded Thurmond, a champion of white supremacy, its "Freedom Award."[32] This alliance proved a fortuitous event. "In fact," the journalist Sanford D. Horwitt recalled, "Lyndon Johnson was the last Democratic presidential candidate to win a majority of the white vote" in the Old South.[33] Today the Republican Party enjoys its staunchest support in the Sun Belt and more particularly in the old Confederacy. Ronald Brownstein, a liberal columnist, discovered that by 2002, the eleven ex-Confederate states plus Oklahoma and Kentucky provided the GOP's margin of majority in the House and Senate.[34] As is well known, the most loyal backers of President George W. Bush are those who most identify with him: white Protestant males from the South.

The Role of Values

If it was the rise of blacks and other ethnic minorities that most alarmed southerners, it was the emerging feminist movement—notably its support of legalized abortion—and the sexual revolution that galvanized the Christian (or Religious) Right into action by the end of the seventies.[35] The Creighton University historian Bryan Le Beau pinpoints 1976 as the beginning of what he and others call the New Christian Right.[36] Although many Roman Catholics were and remain staunch conservatives (right-wing Catholic groups include the Cardinal Mindszenty Foundation, the Catholic League for Religious and Civil Rights, and Catholics United for the Faith), the rank and file of the Christian Right (a coalition of organizations that includes the Moral Majority, the Religious Roundtable, and the Christian Voice) consist almost exclusively of Protestants, especially members of evangelical denominations, mainly pentecostal-charismatics and fundamentalist Baptists.[37] Although not strictly a part of the New Right, the Unification Church, founded by the Reverend Sun Myung Moon

(b. 1920), certainly shares its politics. Most Christian Right activists were and remain fundamentalists (Christians who interpret the Bible literally), who numbered forty-five million by 1980—one of every five Americans.[38] Overwhelmingly, fundamentalists live in the South.

Under Billy Graham and other older leaders, conservative Protestants calling for a return to traditional values had tended to shy away from direct political action. However, the apparent collapse of Christian morality—symbolized by the 1972 Equal Rights Amendment (ERA) campaign, the 1973 Supreme Court abortion rights decision, *Roe v. Wade,* and the gay rights movement—called for a drastic change in direction. Led by televangelists such as Jim Bakker, Jimmy Swaggart, Pat Robertson, and Jerry Falwell, Christians launched a new religious crusade, one that would revolutionize U.S. politics. The GOP was only too happy to accommodate conservative Christians—Catholics as well as Protestants—whose ideas were highly compatible with the Republican agenda. Sara Diamond, arguably the leading authority on religious conservatives, summarizes the movement's agenda:

> Were the Christian Right to achieve its wish list of policy goals, things would certainly be different. For starters, abortion would be illegal. Homosexuals would be, if not invisible, then certainly unprotected from all types of discrimination. Children would pray in the schools, which would be run privately or by local school districts, with no government-mandated curricula. The entertainment media would voluntarily eliminate profanity from the airwaves and movie scripts. The range of ideas and images accessible in bookstores, libraries, magazines, and art exhibits would be sharply curtailed.[39]

The strength of the Christian Right has always resided in the South, the most avowedly religious of all the country's regions—as well as the most illiterate, violent, and impoverished.[40] In 1979, the Reverend Jerry Falwell (b. 1932), the foremost champion of evangelical Republicanism, founded the Moral Majority, a political pressure group promoting capitalism, anti-communism, and traditional Christian values. Falwell received aid from Catholic GOP operatives who hoped to create a popular base for their party, including Paul Weyrich, "a man some call the father of the Christian Right," his faithful comrade-in-arms Richard Viguerie, and Phyllis Schlafly (b. 1926), research director of the St. Louis–based Cardinal Mindszenty Foundation and the leading anti-ERA crusader.[41] Within two years, Moral Majority spokespeople claimed a membership of four million.

In 1989, when the fundamentalist-dominated Moral Majority shut down, following several financial and sex scandals centering on wayward televangelists, faith healer Marion G. (Pat) Robertson (b. 1930), a graduate of Yale Law School and an ordained Southern Baptist minister, founded the

Christian Coalition. Illustrating their effective use of the mass media—particularly Robertson's Christian Broadcasting Network (CBN) in Virginia Beach, Virginia—Christian conservatives built vast electronic ministries and scored solid electoral victories, especially south of the Mason-Dixon line. By the mid-1980s, Robertson's weekday *700 Club,* the most popular program on CBN, boasted an estimated audience of one million.[42] Among the greatest beneficiaries of Christian support was North Carolina senator Jesse Helms (b. 1921), who joined the GOP in 1970.[43] The evangelical movement, which returned to the fold after briefly supporting Robertson's third-party bid for the presidency in 1988, undoubtedly "has become the most powerful grassroots component of the Republican Party."[44] The key to its success, according to Diamond, is that the Religious Right benefits from a vast evangelical culture and the myth, perpetrated by its leaders, that it is a persecuted minority.[45] (The perpetration of a victim mentality, and the inculcation of fear, as the following chapters will illustrate, have been strategies fostered by the entire leadership of the conservative Right, not just its Christian wing.) Needless to say, the popular Robertson himself has not done badly: "The combination of Christianity and cash has [given] Dr. Robertson a . . . net worth . . . estimated at somewhere between $200 million and $1 billion."[46]

The Neocons

Another influential element within the reconstructed Republican Party consisted of neoconservatives (neocons), disaffected liberal and socialist intellectuals, many of them Jews, who now provided the GOP with a cadre of intelligent and committed ideologues.[47] Disillusioned with the Stalinist terror in the USSR at the time of the Depression, they gradually shifted their political allegiance. Becoming champions of liberal democracy during the Cold War, they came to affiliate with the Democratic Party. Ultimately, according to Godfrey Hodgson, their fundamental tenet became the belief that America was "morally superior to other societies," a concept historians term *American exceptionalism.*[48]

However, the rise of the New Left and what they perceived as its excesses finally drove neoconservatives into the Republican fold.[49] The student rebellions of the sixties, with their attack on the university, forced many of these middle-class intellectuals, especially the professors, into a grim reassessment. The sociologist Barbara Ehrenreich explains: "They began to think of themselves, however dimly, as members not of a formless, all-inclusive middle class, but of an *elite.* And a self-conscious elite, no matter how inclined to noblesse oblige, has a stake in maintaining the inequalities that define the status quo."[50] Displaying the zeal so typical of the recently converted, these true believers, never very numerous—their movement "remains what it always was," a critic observed in 2004, "a largely inside-the-Beltway phenomenon"[51]—but heavily subsidized by right-wing foundations, would exert a powerful influence on Republican policies beginning in the mid-1970s.

By the middle of the following decade, however, neocons, now staunch supporters of Ronald Reagan, were beginning to be estranged from the rest of the GOP establishment.[52] Superpatriots, neocons too feared the specter of communism. Nevertheless, they disagreed with other Republicans on a number of issues, including foreign policy and immigration.[53] Moreover, neocon influence on the Reagan administration sparked much resentment from more traditionally minded members of the GOP, the Old Right, as well as some New Right leaders.

Obsessed with maintaining a strong stance against international communism, neocons were also concerned with domestic issues. More specifically, they feared the apparent decline of American morals, which they attributed to the "rights revolution" initiated by the social movements of the sixties. Like evangelical Christians—from whom they differed in many other ways—and GOP traditionalists, neocons saw such social issues as abortion, gay rights, and drug use as symptoms of spiritual decay. In the "cultural wars," they came down firmly on the side of traditional values.

Leading the neocon crusade were two Jewish intellectuals from New York City, Irving Kristol (b. 1920) and Norman Podhoretz (b. 1930), godfathers of the movement.[54] Kristol, who once famously defined a neoconservative as "a liberal who has been mugged by reality," announced his political transformation from a Trotskyite to a right-winger in the columns of the journal *Encounter,* which he cofounded with Stephen Spender and edited in 1953–1958. (Later, it came to light that the left-leaning journal had received funding from the CIA.)[55] Eventually, his conservative views found full expression in *The Public Interest,* which he and the sociologist Daniel Bell (b. 1919) cofounded in 1965 (the journal ceased publication in 2005), and in *The National Interest,* which he published after 1985. These journals received heavy subsidies from Wall Street bond trader William E. Simon Sr., secretary of the treasury under both Nixon and Ford—the very same William Simon who had issued the clarion call for a conservative revolution a few years before.[56]

Married to the celebrated historian Gertrude Himmelfarb (b. 1922), Kristol has been affiliated with several right-wing think tanks, including the American Enterprise Institute, the Hudson Institute, and the Manhattan Institute.[57] Their son, William Kristol (b. 1952), formerly an adviser to Vice President Dan Quayle and now editor of Rupert Murdoch's *Weekly Standard,* is among the most respected of neocon pundits.[58] Indeed, the young Harvard-trained political philosopher may be "the most influential Republican/neoconservative publicist in America today."[59]

Norman Podhoretz, at one time a Fulbright Scholar at Cambridge, served as editor of *Commentary,* the leading journal of the neocon movement, from 1960 to 1995. Considered the movement's "most representative figure," Podhoretz has been active in a variety of anticommunist organizations, including the Committee for the Free World, the Committee on the Present Danger, and the Coalition for a Democratic Majority, which he helped found.[60] Now a senior fellow at the Hudson Institute and a favorite of the Bush administration, Podhoretz received a Presidential Medal of Freedom in 2004.

Other liberal apostates were Herbert Stein (1916–1999), Seymour Martin Lipset (b. 1922), Nathan Glazer (b. 1923), Ben Wattenberg (b. 1933), Norman Podhoretz's wife, the social critic Midge Decter (b. 1927), and their son-in-law, Elliot Abrams (b. 1948).[61]

Influential gentiles also joined neocon ranks, among them academic and political stalwarts Jeane Kirkpatrick (b. 1927), Michael Novak (b. 1933), and Daniel Patrick Moynihan (1927–2003). (Like Daniel Bell, Moynihan never fit comfortably into the neocon category given his continued espousal of progressive ideas.) Other well-known intellectuals sometimes considered neocons include Paul Johnson, Diane Ravitch, George Gilder, Francis Fukuyama, Roger Kimball, Michael Ledeen, Martin Peretz, James Q. Wilson, Thomas Sowell, Richard Pipes, and William Bennett.[62] Neocon perspectives dominate most right-wing think tanks, Rupert Murdoch's *New York Post,* the Reverend Moon's *Washington Times,* the editorial page of the *Wall Street Journal,* and the journals cited earlier.

The Collegiate New Right

In contrast to the neocons, who mainly came from the working class (at least the first generation) and the Republican Old Guard, including Buckley, who came from privileged homes, leaders of the secular New Right generally emerged from middle-class backgrounds. Typical was Richard Viguerie, whose father was a Houston petrochemical engineer. (Son of a working-class German immigrant, Paul Weyrich is a notable exception.) Attending college, often at elite universities, in the sixties and seventies, they reacted to the chaos they associated with campus antiwar and civil rights protesters by embracing right-wing causes.

A small minority, these youths sought fellowship in tight-knit conservative student associations. Among the oldest of these were College Republicans, founded in 1892, and Young Republicans, founded in 1931. Several of these youth-oriented associations arose after World War II. One was Campus Crusade for Christ, the first Christian youth group to focus on college students, founded at UCLA in 1951 by Bill Bright (1922–2003). A Fuller Seminary student, Bright was deeply influenced by the evangelical revival then sweeping the country. Organized in military fashion, Campus Crusade was conceived as a bulwark against communism. When he died, Bright left behind a $374-million-a-year empire staffed by 26,000 employees in 191 countries.[63]

Another promising youth group was the Intercollegiate Society of Individualists (ISI). Founded in 1953 by libertarian Frank Chodorov (1887–1966), this small group of young conservative intellectuals later changed its name to the Intercollegiate Studies Institute.[64] Its first president was William Buckley, a Chodorov disciple. Other prominent members included M. Stanton Evans, who went on to become a syndicated columnist and author, and Garry Wills, then a Jesuit seminarian, now a celebrated historian with liberal proclivities.

The most successful organization in spreading the conservative gospel to college students, however, was Young Americans for Freedom (YAF), founded by ex-communist Marvin Liebman (1924–1997) and friends in 1960. Inspired by William Buckley and founded on his Sharon, Connecticut, estate, YAF has been described as "a network of conservative organizations on college campuses that served as training grounds for virtually the entire movement leadership."[65] Most of the key New Right leaders were indeed YAFers, among them Viguerie, who served as its first executive secretary; Phillips, one of the original founders, at the time student body president at Harvard; Dolan, who died prematurely of AIDS; Patrick Buchanan (b. 1938), the nativist firebrand and three-time presidential contender; L. Brent Bozell III (b. 1955), Buckley's nephew, currently active in a variety of right-wing initiatives; and R. Emmett Tyrrell Jr. (b. 1943), an influential though somewhat eccentric journalist. Joining their numbers was college dropout Paul Weyrich (a member of the Young Republicans while at the University of Wisconsin).

Ratfucking

Honing their skills in student government, the youthful Republicans who came out of YAF and other right-wing student organizations were pioneers in establishing the aggressive, take-no-prisoner style that has characterized the Republican Party and the conservative mass media in recent decades. It is this militant element within the GOP, more than any other, even the neocons, that has transformed the current political debate into a war of ideas. Their coming of age, appropriately, occurred under Richard M. Nixon. "The men who made Nixon president," critics charge, "routinely resorted to vicious pranks, spying, and underhanded personal attacks against the Democrats, those dirty tricks that the boyish Watergate trickster Donald Segretti memorably called 'ratfucking.'"[66]

The foremost exponent of dirty tricks was political strategist Lee Atwater.[67] A former intern under Strom Thurmond, the brilliant and brash southerner enjoyed a meteoric rise, serving as executive director of the College Republicans, South Carolina field director for Nixon's Committee to Reelect the President (CREEP), and chairman of the Republican National Committee. Campaign director for George H. W. Bush, Atwater reached the pinnacle of his political career with the election of the wealthy Texan to the White House in 1988. Before his premature death three years later from a brain tumor, the guru of dirty politics trained a whole generation of leaders in the Machiavellian strategies that have come to characterize the GOP, especially after the Reagan years.[68] One obituary, written by journalist Sidney Blumenthal, recalled Atwater's most enduring legacy particularly well:

> It must be said that every campaign in which Lee Atwater played a role was marked by low tactics and lies. Even polling for anti-Semitism in a congressional race was not beneath him. But his special genius lay in manipulating the status anxieties of the white middle and working classes, territory he knew instinctively. He helped to turn contemporary Southern politics away from the possibility of a genuine populism uniting blacks and whites around common economic issues. The outrageous antics of the bluesman who made "Bad Boy" his signature song [Atwater was a talented blues guitarist] were quietly appreciated in the boardrooms of the new glass skyscrapers.[69]

Among the most successful practitioners of the no-holds-barred, win-at-any-cost approach are Atwater disciples Mary Matalin (b. 1953) and Karl Rove (b. 1951), influential members of the George W. Bush team and undoubtedly among the chief supporters of the "compassionate conservatism" that the president claims to represent.[70] "Lee Atwater," Matalin recalled fondly, "was a genius, a best friend, and one of the most wonderful people the world has known."[71] Apparently she was serious. Though he never graduated from college, Rove, currently Bush's senior political adviser and (after March 2005) deputy chief of staff, was appointed national executive director of the College Republicans in 1970–1972 and elected chairman in 1973–1974, when, with Atwater's help, he beat out Terry Dolan. His first mentor was Donald Segretti.[72] Apparently, he learned the tricks of the trade quickly, for before long he was conducting "training sessions for College Republicans on the nuance and technique of Nixon-style dirty tricks."[73] Next to the president, Rove, a self-made man who seems to idolize his boss, is probably the most powerful man in the nation's capital.[74] George W. Bush himself worked closely with Atwater on his father's 1988 campaign as "senior adviser" (the two fraternity men had much in common) and presumably learned a thing or two about the use of chicanery and obfuscation from his colleague. The younger Bush, it has been observed, is "the only President with functional experience of being a White House staffer."[75]

War by Other Means

Another prominent young Republican in the eighties, and onetime George W. Bush political adviser, is Ralph E. Reed (b. 1961), a leading evangelist organizer, sometimes called "the Christian Lee Atwater" because of his aggressive campaign tactics. (Reed once described his modus operandi in this fashion: "I do guerilla warfare. I paint my face and travel at night. You don't know it's over until you're in a body bag. You don't know till election night.")[76] In 1983–1985, as a student at the University of Georgia, Reed served as executive director of College Republicans. Later, Reed founded Students for America, which focused on recruiting religious students into right-wing politics. He became the preeminent Religious Right strategist in the nineties, when he served as the executive director of Robertson's Christian Coalition. Reed resigned his post in 1997, when the organization was beset by declining memberships and legal challenges, to form his own Atlanta-based political consulting firm, Century Strategies, and serve as an Enron lobbyist.[77] Apparently, it was Rove who found Reed the job with the Houston-based energy company.[78]

   Reed's mentor in College Republicans was Newt Gingrich protégé Grover Norquist (b. 1957), a Harvard graduate who had preceded him as executive director of the organization in 1981–1983. Even more than his early associates—both Reed and Gingrich earned doctorates in history—Norquist, the son of a Polaroid executive, was and remains consumed with politics. "Like his fellow radical conservatives," a disgruntled colleague later recalled, "Norquist believed politics was an extension of war by other means."[79] He continued, "There was nothing traditionally conservative in Grover's approach. As I conformed myself to the movement, I was being inculcated into a radical cult that bore none of the positive attributes of classical conservatism—a sense of limits, fair play, Tory civility, and respect for individual freedom."[80] Today, Norquist leads the foremost antitax organization in the country, the corporate-funded Americans for Tax Reform (ATR), where he continues to use the search-and-destroy tactics he and Reed honed in the early eighties.[81] The ultraconservative Norquist has been described as the most powerful Republican operative outside the White House.[82]

Strains Begin to Appear

It would seem impossible to keep these disparate elements of the "new and improved" Republican Party working together after the seventies.

At times the constituent factions appeared to have conflicting agendas. In spite of untiring efforts by consensus builders such as Paul Weyrich, constant tension arose between the religious and the secular wings, "the party's Christian social conservatives and its business-rooted money men."[83] An issue such as abortion was bound to strain the relationship between the "values-oriented" religious conservatives and their libertarian-minded counterparts who opposed any kind of state intervention, especially one violating the sanctity of the individual. For their part, the neocons have had to surmount the nagging suspicion of being careerists and opportunists, as well as ward off the anti-intellectualism and anti-Semitism of old-line party members.[84]

By the nineties, neoconservatives, who advocated an aggressive U.S. foreign policy, came under fire from a small group of Republicans who championed American isolationism in the aftermath of the Cold War, an internal conflict that first surfaced in 1981.[85] These self-styled "paleoconservatives," who found their intellectual spokesman in Russell Kirk (1918-1994), a Catholic convert, were especially put off by the vehement and unremitting pressure neocons exerted on U.S. foreign policy in favor of Israel. Led by ex–Spiro Agnew speechwriter Pat Buchanan—"who may have done more than almost any other individual to popularize white supremacy and Christian nationalist ideas in America"[86]—the isolationists also opposed a liberal immigration policy, which neocons tended to support. By the middle of the decade, thanks in part to an infusion of Rupert Murdoch money, the ascendancy of neoconservatives in the movement was secure—even the *National Review* had been won over to their views.[87]

Saved by the War

Isolationists had good reason to fear neocon foreign policy initiatives. The primary intellectual architects of George W. Bush's foreign policy would be Richard Perle (b. 1942) and Paul Wolfowitz (b. 1943), recently appointed by the president to head the World Bank.[88] Together with their neocon colleagues, these strategists would be the most vociferous proponents of preemptive war in the Middle East. American domination of the region, with its vast oil reserves, drew attention as early as the presidency of the elder Bush.[89] The war on terrorism, in the aftermath of the Al Qaeda attacks of September 11, 2001, provided the opportunity for this design to go into operation. Beset by corporate scandals and economic problems, Bush was only too happy to be bailed out by his father's advisers. The destruction of the Al Qaeda terrorists and the Taliban government in Afghanistan that protected them was of secondary importance; the real goal was toppling the Saddam Hussein regime. Using the transparent excuse that Iraq, which supposedly had a vast arsenal of weapons of mass destruction and maintained close links with Al Qaeda and other international terrorist organizations, posed a military threat to the United States and that the Iraqi people would welcome their liberators with open arms, the Bush administration launched Operation Iraqi Freedom in March 2003.[90] As Scott Ritter, a former United Nations weapons inspector, puts it, "This war is about political ideology. It's about a bunch of neo-conservatives in Washington, D.C., who have hijacked the national security of the United States for the pursuit of their own politically driven ideological objectives."[91]

Clearly, the Republican Party was beset by factionalism, especially after the Reagan years. Yet, as the new millennium opened, the GOP had succeeded beyond anything its opponents could have imagined. "On January 20, 2001," political reporter Nina Easton notes, "the most conservative new president in two decades took the oath of office."[92] Despite a contested election, President George W. Bush and the New Right coalition ascended to power intent on bringing about a conservative revolution. Almost immediately they benefited from what must have seemed to them a providential event—the terrorist attacks of 2001, which unexpectedly opened up vast possibilities for a great social and political transformation under the banner of fear and insecurity. If the Bush administration has made sweeping "reforms" since the tragic events of September 11, however, continuity has been more apparent than change. In retrospect, the GOP has merely resumed its traditional role, which is, according to political analyst Kevin Phillips, a disaffected Republican, "not simply to revitalize U.S. capitalism but to tilt power, policy, wealth and income toward the richest portions of the population."[93]

→ CHAPTER TWO ←
CONSERVATIVE FOUNDATIONS

The Best Government Money Can Buy

"The chief business of the American people is business," President Calvin Coolidge declared in 1925. The Republican president was describing a state of affairs, the intimate nexus between politics and economics, that historian Charles Beard traces back to the Founding Fathers.[1] In fact, this economic influence was even more apparent in the late nineteenth century, the age of the robber barons, than in Coolidge's own day. As Mark Twain noted at the time, government during the Gilded Age, a term he coined in 1873, was at the beck and call of the captains of industry.

Nothing was neutral about a government supposedly dedicated to laissez-faire principles. After all, it was not the Vanderbilts, the Mellons, and the Carnegies who were regularly clubbed over the head by state and federal authorities who intervened to put an end to management-labor confrontations. As Kevin Phillips puts it, "Corporate growth and momentum after the Civil War occurred not because of laissez-faire, but in considerable measure because railroads and other behemoths were big enough to methodically take over and dominate state legislatures, thereby taking control of the U.S. Senate and much of the federal and state judiciary."[2] Truly, as Godfrey Hodgson reiterates, "Pro-business governments are the default in American political history."[3] This is not to be marveled at if, as both Alexis de Tocqueville and John Stuart Mill observed, the glorification of wealth has been the outstanding feature of American life.

With some exceptions, the country has generally been run by spokesmen for vested interests, from Alexander Hamilton to Richard Olney to Elihu Root to John Foster Dulles to Cyrus Vance to William Casey (all of them prosperous corporation lawyers, as indeed were Presidents Abraham

17

Lincoln and Rutherford B. Hayes). Whether Democrat or Republican, the business historian Ferdinand Lundberg observed in 1968, administrations during the first two-thirds of the twentieth century were completely under the thumb of Wall Street.[4] Today it is corporations that largely fund political campaigns—not many private citizens can afford $2,000-a-plate fund-raisers. In Washington, D.C., spurred on by industry lobbyists, the people's representatives, whether Democrats or Republicans, champion the big business agenda, especially low corporate taxes and gigantic military budgets. And, upon leaving political office they often retire to high-level corporate positions where they rub elbows with ex-Pentagon senior officials.

Opportunities abound. For example, Robert Rubin, President Clinton's secretary of the treasury (and former cochair of Goldman Sachs), received offers of thirty to forty board memberships upon leaving public office, according to a spokeswoman for his current employer.[5] Less fortunate ex-officeholders settle for jobs as business consultants and lobbyists. This revolving door linking the congressional-military-industrial complex has dominated political life for decades, to the delight of the Fortune 500.

Today, big business has done even better in the nation's capital. It is the captains of industry, commerce, and finance themselves, rather than their stand-ins and proxies, who govern the American people. Both George W. Bush (b. 1946) and Dick Cheney (b. 1941) are ex–oil company executives. The first Bush cabinet included a dozen members who have sat on the boards of directors of more than thirty corporations, including AT&T, Microsoft, Monsanto, GM, Philip Morris, Lockheed Martin, and Boeing; not to mention the national security adviser, now secretary of state, Condoleezza Rice (b. 1954), who is a former director at Chevron, Charles Schwab, and Transamerica.[6] When President Bush picked John Snow, chairman of CSX Corporation, the nation's largest railroad company, to replace Paul O'Neill as treasury secretary, the nominee was forced to divest himself of stock holdings in sixty-one companies to gain Senate confirmation.[7] Counting Snow, three ex–chief executive officers held cabinet-level positions in the first Bush II administration (and two dozen ambassadors were former CEOs or company chairmen).[8] The net worth of the individual members of that cabinet, according to the Center for Public Integrity, a citizens' watchdog group, ranged from $9.3 to $27.3 million, almost ten times more than their immediate predecessors on the Clinton cabinet.[9] Describing their election in 2000, Texas progressive Jim Hightower concludes, "It's the penultimate corporatization of the White House."[10] Former U.S. secretary of labor Robert B. Reich adds, "There's no longer any countervailing power in Washington. Business is in complete control of the machinery of government."[11]

Right-Wing Foundations

To understand how Republican ascendancy has been so complete, one has to follow the money. The trail ultimately leads to right-wing foundations.[12] "Foundations are tax-free institutions created to give grants to both individuals and nonprofit organizations," according to G. William Domhoff, a sociologist at the University of California at Santa Cruz. "They provide," he explains, "a means by which wealthy people and corporations can in effect decide how their tax payments will be spent, for they are based on money that otherwise could go to the government in taxes."[13] Conservative foundations have become more numerous and influential since the early seventies,[14] when "a handful of traditionally conservative foundations redefined their programs with the aim of reshaping the public agenda and constructing a network of conservative institutions and scholars."[15] Jean Stefancic and Richard Delgado documented the existence of at least sixty conservative foundations in 1997.[16] Today many more dot the landscape. Five of them have stood out from the rest in terms of wealth and influence since the seventies: the Lynde and Harry Bradley Foundation (now defunct), the Koch Family foundations, the John M. Olin Foundation, the Scaife Family foundations, and the Castle Rock Foundation—controlled by members of the Coors family—which has replaced the Adolph Coors Foundation. Collectively, the aim of these groups is to promote a far-right agenda. How specifically do they carry out this ambitious mission? According to People for the American Way, a liberal watchdog organization:

> They fund national conservative "think tanks" [see chapter 3, this volume] to package and repackage conservative issue positions; state think tanks to lend a local flair to these issues; national political groups to lobby in Washington and shape national media coverage; state-based groups to do the same in the states; grassroots organizations to stir up local activism; national and state media to report, interpret and amplify these activities; scholars to record the history of such activities and push the intellectual boundaries of the issues; graduate students to form the next wave of scholarship and movement leadership; and college newspapers to shape the milieu in which America's next generation of political leaders comes to their political awakening.[17]

In the late seventies, conservatives began attempting to coordinate the activities of the various right-wing foundations, under the aegis of the Institute for Educational Affairs, with the Bradley Foundation taking the initiative. These efforts culminated in 1991 with the creation of an independent Philanthropy Roundtable. According to its Web site, the national organization coordinated the funding of over six hundred individual donors and foundations by 2005.[18]

Scaife

The most conservative of the foundations are probably those administered by philanthropist Richard Mellon Scaife (b. 1933), great-grandson of the famous Pittsburgh financier, Thomas Mellon. Next to William Buckley, it has been said, Scaife may be "the single most important private citizen in the contemporary conservative movement."[19] Heir to a banking fortune and publisher of the *Pittsburgh Tribune-Review,* the secretive tycoon is the most generous benefactor of the New Right. With an inherited fortune now estimated to be about $1 billion, Scaife reportedly donated at least $340 million to right-wing causes before 1999 through his family's Carthage, Allegheny, and Sarah Scaife foundations.[20] His favorite beneficiary is the Heritage Foundation, but he also contributes large sums to the American Enterprise Institute and a host of other right-wing think tanks.[21] A recovering alcoholic with a checkered past, Scaife sits on the board of trustees of both the Heritage Foundation and the Hoover Institution. The network of Scaife-funded organizations includes media watchdogs, taxpayer unions, legal foundations, and college campus groups. "Name a major right-wing institution," writes one investigative reporter, "and the odds are that Scaife is a principal funder."[22]

The free-spending multimillionaire has lavishly funded the Republican Party and its candidates to public office. "In history's measure, though, Scaife is likely to be remembered most for his role in largely bankrolling the opposition to Bill Clinton that resulted ... in the second impeachment trial of a president of the United States," according to the historian Haynes Johnson.[23] Harboring a profound animosity toward Bill Clinton, he generously supported investigations of the president's personal life and family finances using a variety of vehicles, one of which was the ultraright-wing magazine, the *American Spectator.*[24] Edited by R. Emmett Tyrrell Jr., the Washington, D.C.–based publication spent some $2.4 million of Scaife's money on this fruitless personal vendetta.[25] The failure of the so-called Arkansas Project led to the rapid decline of the *Spectator,* which had once aspired to displace the *National Review* as the nation's premier conservative magazine. "[B]y concentrating his giving on a specific ideological objective for nearly 40 years, and making most of his grants with no strings attached," the *Washington Post* concluded in 1999, "Scaife's philanthropy has had a disproportionate impact on the rise of the right, perhaps the biggest story in American politics in the last quarter of the 20th century."[26]

The John M. Olin Foundation

Another conservative foundation, Olin, has been a leading funder of conservative think tanks, such as the American Enterprise Institute, the

Washington Legal Foundation (which sues various defendants for being overly liberal), the Center for Individual Rights (which sues colleges and universities for the same transgressions), and the Heritage Foundation (which uses the money for a host of right-wing programs). Olin has also supported the Hoover Institution and Manhattan Institute, two other purveyors of conservative ideas, and through them a panoply of conservative scholars. Few top right-wing writers have not, at some point, received Olin money to write books and articles calculated to advance the conservative agenda. Over the years, Olin has supported Robert Bork (who once held the Olin chair in legal studies at the American Enterprise Institute), Dinesh D'Souza (whose *Illiberal Education* accuses American colleges and universities of being dens of wild-eyed leftism), and Ben Wattenberg's newscasting career.

With an eye to the future, Olin has also generously funded college students interested in conservatism. It provides scholarships for law students and stipends for law professors specializing in conservative law and economics and has given generously to start conservative student newspapers and journals. It has also underwritten the National Association of Scholars, a group of conservative academics, and the Center for the Study of Popular Culture, a right-wing organization established by disillusioned leftists. Olin is not the only conservative organization to invest lavishly—spending so freely that it may soon go out of business[27]—in developing the next generation of leaders. In a recent issue of the *New York Times,* Jason DeParle drew attention to the cushy summer internship program the Heritage Foundation had established for young conservative students and intellectuals. One, Katherine Rogers, a junior at Georgetown, was "working in donor relations, which she thinks will be useful in her intended career as a pharmaceutical lobbyist."[28] Another foundation, the Earhart Foundation, along with Scaife, also funds right-wing college campaigns, such as efforts to abolish affirmative action.[29]

Smart ALEC

A good example of the kinds of organizations right-wing foundations fund is the American Legislative Exchange Council (ALEC), one of the most powerful and least understood political bodies in the country. A brainchild of Paul Weyrich, ALEC is a corporate lobby that drafts business-friendly bills for state legislators across the country. The money to fund the lobby initially came from John Birch Society member Joseph Coors. Today it comes from corporations such as R. J. Reynolds and Koch Industries and business groups such as the American Petroleum Institute, as well as foundations. Not surprisingly, the legislative bills often favor the groups that sustain the organization. Reportedly, "ALEC played a critical role in pushing Enron's fifty-state utility deregulation agenda."[30] Roughly a third of the nation's 2,400 state lawmakers belong to ALEC.[31]

Training the Next Generation

Another function of these right-wing foundations, as indicated, is funding youth training. Among the major reasons for their success, one scholarly study finds, is that "conservatives have adopted a grow-your-own approach, funding law students, student editors, and campus leaders with scholarships, leadership training, and law-and-economics classes aimed at ensuring that the next generation of academic leaders has an even more conservative cast than the current one."[32] The practice of cultivating a new generation of right-wing leaders was well established even before the advent of the New Right.[33]

The foremost organization in this regard at present is the Leadership Institute (LI), founded in 1979, with Coors financial backing, by Paul Weyrich's good friend Morton C. Blackwell. The youngest Goldwater delegate at the Republican convention in 1964, Blackwell served as state chair of both the College Republicans and the Young Republicans in Louisiana. Later he worked in direct-mail fund-raising with Richard Viguerie. Presided over by Blackwell, LI—classified, for tax purposes, as a nonprofit, nonpartisan educational foundation—has enjoyed phenomenal success in training political activists. By the mid-1990s, LI had graduated over ten thousand students, among them Ralph Reed and Grover Norquist.[34] By 2004, the number of graduates was up to forty thousand.[35] "Morton Blackwell," Norquist affirms, "is a Johnny Appleseed of politics, spreading activists all around."[36] Many graduates of LI, which one writer called a "boot camp for young conservatives," end up taking staff positions with Republicans in Congress. But others have gravitated toward journalism and broadcasting. "We teach political technology," said Blackwell in a recent interview. His institute's classes, which are virtually free to students, include seminars on public speaking, including the advice to elongate words when simulating compassion and biting them off to show anger. They also show students how to face down skeptical media and emulate the communication skills of their hero, Ronald Reagan.[37]

On the eve of the twenty-first century, Blackwell's acolytes occupied key positions throughout the Republican Party apparatus. Trained in the politics of fearmongering, their influence ranges far and wide. Though hardly a household name, Morton Blackwell remains one of the most powerful leaders of the New Right.

His legacy extends well beyond youth education. In 2000, he served as executive director of the Council for National Policy (CNP), a highly secretive policy organization founded in 1981 by the Reverend Tim LaHaye. The council's membership is a veritable who's who of the New Right.[38] In 2004, Blackwell was elected to the Republican National Committee.[39]

Right-wing foundations may not possess the vast financial resources of the largest philanthropic foundations in the country, but by coordinating their efforts, they have focused on achieving their general objectives rather than simply concentrating on single issues. Thus they have been extraordinarily effective in pushing their probusiness agenda. Beneficiaries of this largesse, the New Right has been able to tap into a powerful war chest that has given them a clear edge on their Democratic opponents. Republicans may constantly caution the public against "throwing money at problems," but this strategy has done wonders for *their* political fortunes. It was not until Howard Dean pioneered innovative methods of fund-raising via the Internet that the funding gap began to narrow.

In the meantime, conservative money has indeed, as a recent book put it, "shaped America's social agenda."[40] One investment that has paid off handsomely has been the funding of quasi-academic think tanks devoted to causes dear to the conservative heart. (For a list of these and other key conservative institutions, see appendix A.) Consider, now, the roles that these policy organizations have played in recent times.

⇢ CHAPTER THREE ⇠

RIGHT-WING THINK TANKS

Scholarship for Sale

The chief beneficiaries of foundation money are think tanks. "Think tanks," social historian G. William Domhoff explains, "are nonprofit organizations that provide settings for experts in various academic disciplines to devote their time to the study of policy alternatives free from the teaching and departmental duties that are part of the daily routine for most members of the academic community."[1] In fact, *think tank,* first used around 1900, "is an imprecise term that refers to all sorts of private research groups."[2]

Despite the generic label, these policy research institutes are a varied lot. Ideologically, for example, they span the political spectrum. Sparked by fear of a looming liberal ascendancy, conservative think tanks—that is, those that avow a right-wing agenda—began to surface in the post–World War II era (an exception is the Hoover Institution, which was founded in 1919 by Herbert Hoover). It was only in the seventies and eighties that they experienced any real success. Several of them, however, now wield awesome influence.[3] Of the twenty-five think tanks and policy discussion organizations cited most often in the national media in 2002, ten were conservative or center-right (six were progressive or center-left, and nine were centrist).[4] In rank order, the right-wing groups cited most often were the Manhattan Institute, the Hoover Institution on War, Revolution, and Peace (Hoover Institution), the Washington Institute for Near East Policy, the Heritage Foundation, the American Enterprise Institute (AEI), the Center for Strategic and International Studies (CSIS), the Cato Institute, the RAND Corporation, the Family Research Council, and the Hudson Institute. The most influential of these centers in terms of public policy are probably the AEI, the Heritage Foundation, the Hoover Institution, and the CSIS (which is technically a "policy discussion organization" rather than a think tank). Altogether, conservative think tanks outspent their liberal counterparts at least four to one in the late nineties.[5]

Corporate Funding

Think tanks receive financing not only from foundation grants but also private and corporate donations. This has been the case especially since 1978, when with the publication of his influential book, *A Time for Truth,* leveraged-buyout king William Simon Sr., fearing for the future of the capitalist system, initiated a concerted effort to get big business to fund right-wing projects. By the mid-1980s, financial support for the Heritage Foundation came from eighty-seven of the five hundred biggest companies in the country.[6] Instrumental in funneling corporate funds to think tanks—as well as conservative college newspapers—has been the Institute for Educational Affairs (IEA), founded in 1978 by Simon and Irving Kristol to channel corporate dollars to free-market organizations.[7] As early as 1982, IEA could count on 145 corporate donors.[8] In 1990, the institute merged with the Madison Center—founded by William Bennett and University of Chicago professor Allan Bloom two years before—to become the Madison Center for Educational Affairs (MCEA).[9]

Strange Charity

Think tanks have managed to acquire tax-exempt status as charities. When most Americans think of charitable organizations, they envision groups such as the Red Cross, the United Way, or the March of Dimes. Many conservatives, however, prefer to contribute to the Heritage Foundation and other right-wing "charities."

Individuals often use tax-exempt foundations as a means of funneling money to think tanks. Donald Rumsfeld (b. 1932) is among the most recognizable names employing this strategy. In 1985, the current secretary of defense, who possesses a personal fortune estimated at between $35 million and $135 million, created a private charitable organization, D.H.R. Foundation, to which he and his wife have donated at least an estimated $5 million to $10 million.[10] In 1998, the Center for Public Integrity reported, the Rumsfeld foundation "paid out $261,420 in grants, largely to conservative think-tanks such as the Leadership Institute, Freedom House and the Heritage Foundation and government affiliated think-tanks, such as the RAND Graduate Institute, which received $21,000."[11]

A prime example of a corporate-backed think tank is the Manhattan Institute for Policy Research, founded in 1978 by William Casey (1913–1987), who later became CIA director under President Reagan. For its size, legal scholars Jean Stefancic and Richard Delgado observe, this institute published more op-ed articles than any other think tank.[12]

Among its most prominent authors have been George Gilder, Thomas Sowell, and Linda Chavez. Along with subsidies from leading right-wing foundations, the New York City–based organization has received funding from such corporate sources as the Chase Manhattan Bank, Citicorp, Time Warner, and Procter & Gamble. Boosted by these and other major firms, the Manhattan Institute's annual budget reached $5 million by the early nineties.[13]

What Do Conservative Think Tanks Do?

What is it that these right-wing think tanks try to accomplish with these donations? Their primary objective is the triumph of conservative principles. Like the foundations that fund them, these groups ultimately wish to turn the clock back to a "golden age," before the advent of the welfare state. They pursue this objective by a variety of means, including writing books and position papers, conducting training sessions for policymakers and politicians, and sending their own affiliates, both fellows and board members, directly into government service. Right-wing think tanks have enjoyed phenomenal success in accomplishing the last goal: In President Reagan's first term alone, fifty high-level appointees reportedly came from the Hoover Institution, thirty-six from the Heritage Foundation, thirty-four from the AEI, and eighteen from the CSIS.[14]

The Heritage Foundation

A prime example of a well-financed and well-connected policy center is the Washington, D.C.-based Heritage Foundation, "considered the leading conservative think tank in America."[15] Since its founding in 1973—with seed money from Richard Scaife and Joseph Coors—by thirty-one-year-old Paul Weyrich, who served as first president, the organization has received millions in financial support from the Bradley, the Sarah Scaife, and the Olin foundations.[16] Moreover, the institute, "true to its 'New Right' origins, also relied on direct-mail fundraising."[17] Concerned over what it saw as President Nixon's abandonment of true Republican principles, the Heritage Foundation aimed to revitalize the conservative Right. Its self-professed mission, according to its Web site, "is to formulate and promote conservative public policies based on the principles of free enterprise, limited government, individual freedom, traditional American values, and a strong national defense."[18]

Advocacy rather than abstract theorizing has been its focus from the very beginning. "Our role," a Heritage vice president candidly asserted, "is to provide conservative public-policymakers with arguments to bolster our side."[19] For this reason, pure scholars have been less prominent in its ranks than practical politicians with real power. Fellows include ex–secretary of education William Bennett (b. 1943), a leading voice in neocon circles, who also sits on the board of directors of the Sarah Scaife Foundation.[20] The apogee of its influence occurred during the eighties, when, led by Dr. Edwin J. Feulner Jr., a Rhodes Scholar who had helped fellow congressional aide Paul Weyrich to start the organization, the Heritage Foundation "served as the intellectual mother-ship of the Reagan administration."[21] The institute's one-thousand-page volume, *Mandate for Leadership,* proved highly influential among policymakers throughout the Reagan presidency.

The American Enterprise Institute

Perhaps the best-known conservative think tank today is the American Enterprise Institute for Public Policy Research. Founded in 1943 as a business research group, an adjunct of the Chamber of Commerce of the United States, the AEI made rapid strides after the fifties under the leadership of W. Glenn Campbell (1925–2002) and William J. Baroody (1916–1980). During this early period, reacting to what its directors saw as a vast liberal monopoly of America's leading institutions, a fear it shared with like-minded organizations, AEI focused on assembling an all-star cast of conservative social scientists, especially economists, who would combat their ideological opponents in the academic arena. The Washington, D.C.-based institute only became the staunch right-wing defender of big business it is today after 1977, when William Baroody Jr., succeeding his father, assumed leadership.

Although, in contrast to the Heritage Foundation, AEI continues to emphasize a scholarly rather than a public policy agenda, by the mid-1980s, most of its budget came from corporate donations.[22] It has subsequently established close ties with the Business Roundtable. Founded in 1974, this group is a militant lobbying organization consisting of the chief executive officers of some two hundred Fortune 500 companies. A rich endowment from these firms permits the Business Roundtable to subsidize "resident scholars loyal in their opposition to the tax and antitrust laws."[23] In 2000, now headed by Christopher C. DeMuth, the AEI received seven donations of $1 million or more, the highest being $3.35 million.[24] The corporate connection is impossible to miss. In the late nineties, seventeen of its twenty-eight directors held forty directorships at thirty-seven corporations.[25] A cabinet member in two Republican administrations, William Simon Sr., who became president of the Olin Foundation in 1976, sat on the AEI board of directors. Other foundation officials eventually reaching high-level status in the Reagan administrations included Jeane Kirkpatrick, Murray Weidenbaum (b. 1927), Antonin Scalia (b. 1936), and James C. Miller III (b. 1942). Past and present AEI fellows and other associates include right-wing luminaries Robert Novak, Ben Wattenberg, Richard Perle, Irving Kristol, Dick Cheney, his wife Lynne Cheney (b. 1941), Robert Bork (b. 1927), Charles Murray (b. 1942), and Dinesh D'Souza (b. 1961)—all of them frequent guests on the major political talk shows (as is David Gergen, an ex-AEI employee).[26]

The Hoover Institution

Situated at Stanford University, the Hoover Institution, too, has wielded a significant impact on government policy in recent years under Republican administrations. Before the sixties, the Hoover Institution, while politically conservative (mirroring the views of its founder and leading patron, President Herbert Hoover),[27] was primarily known for its excellent library and archives. Subsequently, it developed into a major policy research center under Baroody's ex-colleague, W. Glenn Campbell, a Harvard-trained economist who was born in Canada. Called "the most effective institution builder in the conservative movement" during its ascendancy, the uncompromising right-winger served as director of the prestigious institute from 1960 to 1989.[28] The organization's influence is most pronounced today in foreign policy. Eight members of the twenty-eight-member Defense Policy Board—the powerful Pentagon advisory panel that Defense Secretary Rumsfeld regularly consults—come out of the Hoover Institution, including George Schultz (b. 1920), Pete Wilson (b. 1933), and Newt Gingrich (b. 1943).[29] Richard Perle, who served as panel chairman until he was forced out of that position in 2003 and resigned altogether the following year, is another prominent member of the Hoover family. And ex–Stanford provost Condoleezza Rice, now secretary of state, has Hoover ties.

Social Insecurity? The Role of the Cato Institute

Another think tank that has seen its stock rise sharply under Bush II is the Cato Institute. Founded in 1977, the libertarian think tank began with a $500,000 gift from David and Charles Koch, two brothers from Wichita who made their fortune in oil. The influence of the Cato Institute and its president, Ed Crane, on current public policy is most evident in the administration's push to dismantle the Social Security system, called by economist Paul Krugman "America's most successful program."[30]

The centerpiece of FDR's New Deal, Social Security has come under attack by the political Right from the very beginning.[31] Leading the crusade, beginning in 1980, have been the libertarian scholars affiliated with Cato.[32] A champion of the free-market system, President Bush has always endorsed their position, but it was only after the "mandate" he received from his reelection that he felt confident enough to move against the enormously popular retirement program. Predictably, an administration that has amassed as much power as it has by encouraging and playing on people's fears, especially after September 11, initiated the assault with a massive scare campaign. Social Security, Bush and supporters charged, was now unworkable, and it was only a matter of time before it would collapse. The solution, they claimed, was to partially privatize the system. The GOP-dominated Congress, right-wing pundits, and even Federal Reserve chairman Alan Greenspan, a staunch libertarian, quickly joined the choir.[33] In the meantime, a series of right-wing front groups with such innocuous names as For Our Grandmothers, Progress for America, Freedom Works, and Alliance for Retirement Prosperity gave the campaign the appearance of a mass movement.

Critics, indeed virtually everyone except diehard Republicans, pointed out that Social Security was in no immediate danger.[34] Moreover, plenty of other options could forestall a real crisis. Cynics suspected that the whole campaign was a scheme to put money in the pockets of Wall Street bankers, who had invested so heavily in Bush's reelection campaign. Opposition came from Democrats and a coalition of liberal groups, with strong backing from a variety of powerful nonpartisan organizations, including the fifty-five-million-member American Association of Retired Persons (AARP).[35]

Early indications are that the Republican administration may have been overzealous, underestimating the resolve of the American public to maintain liberal entitlements, not only Social Security but also Medicare and Medicaid, LBJ programs also under assault by the hard Right. Whether George W. Bush can succeed in destroying the welfare state, something that even the popular Ronald Reagan ultimately balked at doing, remains to be seen. The outcome of this battle will also provide a good gauge of the power of right-wing think tanks.

The Federalist Society and Pacific Legal Foundation

The conservative impact on government is most evident in the executive and legislative branches. While more subtle, however, right-wing influence has also been pervasive in the judicial system. Conservative foundations and think tanks have contributed heavily to law schools, endowing chairs and providing student scholarships in an effort to imbue the legal system with their principles. Ivy League schools, the University of Chicago, and George Mason University in Fairfax County, Virginia, near Washington, D.C., have found particular favor among right-wing groups.

A major force in influencing the legal establishment has been the Federalist Society for Law and Public Studies, which has received almost $750,000 from Scaife.[36] Funded by the IEA and the Olin Foundation, the low-profile association was founded in 1982 by law students Lee Liebermann (Yale), later a prominent attorney, and Spencer Abraham (Harvard), the future senator from Michigan and energy secretary in George W. Bush's first administration. A Washington, D.C.-based organization of conservative lawyers, the Federalist Society counts among its members President Reagan's private lawyer and later George W. Bush's solicitor general Theodore Olson (b. 1940), ex-independent counsel Kenneth W. Starr (b. 1946), Utah senator Orrin Hatch (b. 1934), ex-attorney general Edwin Meese III (b. 1931), would-be Supreme Court justice Judge Robert Bork, and Supreme Court associate justices Antonin Scalia and Clarence Thomas (b. 1948).[37] Targeting lawyers, judges, and law professors, the Society, according to its Web site, "has created a conservative and intellectual network that extends to all levels of the legal community."[38]

The ubiquitous Meese, who resigned as President Reagan's attorney general after accusations of financial improprieties and is now affiliated with the Hoover Institution, founded the Pacific Legal Foundation in San Francisco and serves as vice chairman of the Kansas City-based Landmark Legal Foundation (its board of advisers has included Rush Limbaugh). These foundations are two of the most prominent of a tightly connected network of law firms supported by conservative donors to champion right-wing causes, including the recent (failed) campaign to end affirmative action. The Pacific Legal Foundation's parent organization, the National Law Center for the Public Interest, and its regional affiliates received almost $8 million in Scaife contributions from 1988 to 1996.[39]

Litigating for the Lord

A growing number of Christian legal firms sustain evangelical litigants in their court battles, among them two powerful Virginia-based groups: the Rutherford Institute, founded in 1983, and the American Center for Law and Justice (ACLJ), founded in 1991 by Pat Robertson. By the late nineties, under the auspices of George Mason University, judges were receiving regular invitations to free seminars sponsored by right-wing public policy groups.[40]

Bring Your Checkbook

The cultivation of the legal sector brought immediate benefits. As Kevin Phillips points out, by the end of the nineties, legal scholars working closely with the business community and right-wing think tanks were busy polishing "arguments that writing a check to a political campaign was a form of free speech protected by the First Amendment."[41] Indeed, this is the very argument that a federal appellate court on May 2, 2003, used to declare unconstitutional most of the major provisions of the McCain-Feingold campaign finance reform law (signed into law on March 27, 2002, it is formally known as the Bipartisan Campaign Reform Act of 2002), which eliminated the "soft money" donations that could be made to political parties and affiliated groups.[42] Conservatives continued to oppose restrictions on campaign funding on constitutional grounds even when the Supreme Court, voting 5–4, overturned the lower court's ruling in December 2003. Chief Justice William Rehnquist (1924–2005) and Associate Justice Scalia, using the free-speech argument, were passionate opponents of the campaign reform law. Right-wing columnist Cal Thomas agreed: "Money cannot corrupt politicians. Politicians corrupt themselves."[43] Apparently, graft has become a constitutional right.

Installing Right-Wing Judges

The failure to curb the power of money has facilitated the great influence that corporations today wield on the judicial system. A measure of their leverage has been their success in persuading that system to protect corporate interests from "greedy lawyers." As journalist Michael Scherer has argued, big business, intent on tort reform, is quietly funding what amounts to a legal revolution.[44] Since 1998, Scherer asserts, working through front groups, major corporations have contributed over $100 million to make the state and federal judicial systems more business-friendly.[45] By courting judges and ousting targeted attorney generals, corporations are gradually decreasing their vulnerability to lawsuits and increasingly eroding consumer protections.

Conservatives have unapologetically made control of the federal judiciary one of their main goals and have enjoyed notable success. The twelve years of Republican ascendancy in the White House beginning in 1980, according to progressive historian Howard Zinn, "transformed the federal judiciary ... into a predominantly conservative institution. By the fall of 1991, Reagan and Bush had filled more than half of the 837 federal judgeships, and appointed enough right-wing justices to transform the Supreme Court."[46] The push continues under the present Bush administration.[47]

The Payoff Begins

The consequences have been momentous. That Kenneth Starr, a corporate lawyer and dyed-in-the-wool conservative who was a steadfast opponent of virtually the entire Clinton program, was selected to investigate the chief executive as "independent counsel"—a Republican vendetta that cost U.S. taxpayers $70 million before the Senate finally acquitted the president on February 12, 1999—was not entirely fortuitous.[48] Starr is a senior partner in the law firm of Kirkland and Ellis, which represents right-wing foundations such as Landmark Legal as well as corporations including Philip Morris and General Motors. It was William Rehnquist, an ultraconservative ideologue appointed chief justice by Ronald Reagan, who selected the Special Division, the panel of three federal appeals judges that ultimately nominated Starr to fill the post of independent counsel. All of this confirms President Clinton's view of Starr: "His bias against me was the very reason he was chosen and why he took the job."[49] It would seem, then, that the Clinton impeachment crusade was as much a creation of a cabal of Federalist lawyers as it was of the Christian Right.

Of course, the blame for turning the impeachment into a circus goes beyond a few zealous prosecutors. If the hunt for the president was not, as Hillary Clinton charged, a product of a vast right-wing conspiracy, it came awfully close. One knowledgeable student of the impeachment and the events that led up to it, attorney and journalist Jeffrey Tobin, not a great fan of the former president, concludes:

> The most astonishing fact in this story may be this one: in spite of his consistently reprehensible behavior, Clinton was, by comparison, the good guy in this struggle. The president's adversaries appeared literally consumed with hatred for him; the bigger the stakes, the smaller they acted. They were willing to trample all standards of fairness—not to mention the Constitution—in their effort to drive him from office. They ranged from one-case-only zealots in the cause of fighting sexual harassment to one-defendant-only federal prosecutors, and they shared only a willingness to misuse the law and the courts in their effort to destroy Bill Clinton.[50]

Stealing an Election

A few years later, it was the Rehnquist Court—or, more specifically, the five most conservative judges on that body[51]—that overturned a state court ruling calling for a hand count of the Florida votes during the hotly disputed 2000 presidential election, thus ensuring the election of George W. Bush to the White House. Supporting the majority position were judges

Thomas and Scalia, who both refused to abstain from the voting even though the former was married to a consultant to the Bush campaign and the latter had two sons employed by law firms representing Bush in the Florida legal proceedings.[52] That Florida governor Jeb Bush and his secretary of state, Katherine Harris—George W. Bush's brother and his campaign manager in the Sunshine State, respectively—had erroneously purged 57,700 voters, mostly blacks (who overwhelmingly vote the Democratic ticket), from the voting registries in the months preceding the presidential election on grounds that they were convicted felons was not even a consideration.[53]

"They have selected a president," the respected journalist Daniel Schorr concluded, referring to the judges who engineered the "judicial coup."[54] Since these very individuals, especially Rehnquist himself, had previously been staunch and consistent champions of states' rights and opponents of the expansion of federal power, their landmark decision now struck their many critics as outrageously partisan.[55] Whatever the merits of this view, the transformation of the U.S. Supreme Court from a relatively liberal institution under Earl Warren to a staunchly conservative one under William Rehnquist represents the most far-reaching legacy of the Conservative Revolution.

We Have the Umpires

In an old joke, the Devil challenges St. Peter to a baseball game: his all-stars versus those of the saint. Peter is incredulous. "How could you possibly compete," he asks, "when we have all the great players, like Christy Matthewson, Honus Wagner, Ty Cobb, and Babe Ruth?" "Ah," the Devil replied with a twinkle in his eye, "we have the umpires." The Republicans undeniably have the umpires.

Firmly in control of the judiciary since the Reagan years, right-wingers have been quick to use the courts as a tool to muzzle and discredit their ideological foes. During the long investigation (1994–1999) instituted to remove Bill Clinton, Starr and his team of prosecutors received invaluable help from Judicial Watch, a right-wing watchdog group led by Larry Klayman. "Judicial Watch," Haynes Johnson reports, "used Scaife money to sue members of the administration in at least eighteen separate matters, forcing everyone named in dragnet subpoenas, from secretaries and interns to top officials, to pay extensive legal bills out of their own pockets."[56] These initiatives were not mere nuisance suits meant to inflict personal and financial hardship, adds Johnson; they aimed at nothing less than to nullify the results of Clinton's presidential election.[57]

Another example of the calculated use of litigation as a right-wing political tool was the concerted effort in mid-2004 to stop the release of director Michael Moore's anti-Bush documentary *Fahrenheit 9/11.* Despite a multitude of legal and other obstacles, the controversial film finally opened to great acclaim, but all too often the mere threat of legal action by right-wing groups with access to plenty of money and legal expertise is enough to discourage all but the most committed of opponents.

Spoon-Fed Intellectuals

Right-wing think tanks and advocacy groups also reach out directly to the public in an effort to effect political and policy change. Between 1990 and 1993, for example, conservative institutions provided over $2,730,000 to four right-of-center periodicals: the *National Interest,* the *Public Interest,* the *New Criterion,* and the *American Spectator.*[58] Aside from popular journals, these groups subsidize scholarly studies that sustain their ideological positions. These works are generally written by resident fellows whose research is financed, and often published, by the think tanks. Among the most familiar of these heavily funded scholars are William Bennett (Heritage), Charles Murray (AEI), Linda Chavez (Manhattan), Thomas Sowell (Hoover), Shelby Steele (Hoover), and 1976 Nobel Prize winner Milton Friedman (Hoover).

"The authors," a perceptive critic has noted, "even when on the payroll of avowedly conservative research institutions, are always referred to as 'scholars,' a term that suggests objectivity. In fact, while many of these neoconservative social scientists have plausible qualifications, for these purposes they often write not in their capacity as scholars, but as practitioners of that very 'advocacy journalism' conservatives used to denounce so fiercely in liberals."[59] It is indeed ironic that some of these foundation-sponsored intellectuals have been among the most vociferous critics of liberal "scholar-activists" representing women's studies, African American studies, and other academic disciplines spawned by the civil rights movement of the sixties. In fact, as the same critic suggests, these right-wing academics themselves are even more adamant than their ideological opponents in pushing an agenda—and much better funded.[60]

Defending the privileged, rather than the underprivileged, is a highly lucrative enterprise. Indeed, the desire for material advantage may well explain why Irving Kristol and other like-minded intellectuals embraced the rightward ideological shift in the first place. As Barbara Ehrenreich writes: "If the federal government and the universities were no longer expanding, it was time to find a new patron for the intellectual vanguard of the professional middle class, and the neoconservatives hoped to find one in an obvious place—the corporate elite."[61] Moreover, playing on popular fears, these spoon-fed intellectuals are forever calling for the freedom of the individual from the restraints imposed by the state—*liberty* is their favorite word—but they conveniently forget that the greatest threat to individualism in today's society is not the government, even with George W. Bush and his attorney general Alberto Gonzales at the controls, but the very corporate culture that they are paid to defend.[62] ("We have always put up with restrictions inside a corporation which we would never put up with in the public sphere," remarks an urban affairs expert. "But what many do not realize is that life within some sort of corporation is what the future will increasingly be about.")[63] If ever a parasitic class thrived divorced from everyday life, this think tank elite is it.

The number of hired guns is considerable. The Web site of one right-wing think tank, the Hoover Institution, listed 130 fellows and 12 visiting fellows in mid-2004.[64] Its scholars include not simply academic types but several politicos, past and present, including Condoleezza Rice, Ed Meese, George P. Schultz, Pete Wilson, and Newt Gingrich. These and other subsidized scholars publish through their associated institutions, so, as one can well imagine, the "scholarly" output of these think tanks is prodigious.

Not all of the publications are obscure policy studies and manuals. Conservative turncoat David Brock, who received the grandiose title of John M. Olin Fellow in Congressional Studies at the Heritage Foundation even without having an advanced degree, received $11,000 from the Olin and Bradley foundations to research and write *The Real Anita Hill,* a hatchet job on Clarence Thomas's accuser, a 1994 best seller that was warmly embraced by the conservative set.[65] (Brock was not very impressed by the intellectual vigor displayed in the position papers, written by nominally independent researchers, that the Heritage Foundation churned out: "Essentially, the papers backed up an already fixed ideological viewpoint, dictated directly by a tier of Heritage executives who decided the organization's position on a given issue, and indirectly by the outside foundations that held Heritage's purse strings.")[66]

Or consider *Illiberal Education: The Politics of Race and Sex on Campus,* a 1991 book by Indian immigrant Dinesh D'Souza, "a fervent advocate of free enterprise whose livelihood has depended heavily on right-wing foundation grants almost from the moment he set foot on these shores."[67] As its title suggests, the controversial volume is one long diatribe against liberal ideas on college campuses. The author, an ex–John M. Olin Research Fellow at the AEI, is currently Robert and Karen Rishwain Research Fellow at the Hoover Institution. Among his conservative credentials, the hardworking immigrant served as editor-in-chief, during his college years, of the ultraright-wing *Dartmouth Review,* where he collaborated with future GOP pundit Laura Ingraham. (This publication was heavily bankrolled by the Olin Foundation, which was a major source of funding for Ben Wattenberg's television show, *Think Tank.*) Later D'Souza served as the editor of *Policy Review,* the Heritage Foundation's widely distributed journal, and as a policy adviser under President Reagan. Like other right-wing pundits, D'Souza feeds on fear—in his case, fear of the liberal intelligentsia.

An even more prominent example of a pseudo-academic book that has been heavily subsidized by the New Right is *America in Black and White: One Nation, Indivisible,* by the husband-wife team of Stephan (b. 1934) and Abigail Thernstrom (b. 1936). This 1997 best seller, an attack on affirmative action, received support from the Carthage, Bradley, Smith Richardson, Earhart, and Olin foundations, the latter of which reportedly shelled out $180,000.[68] A $100,000 advance came, too, from the Manhattan Institute, where Abigail Thernstrom is presently a fellow.[69]

Upholding Academic Standards

Ex-liberals, the Thernstroms are major players in the National Association of Scholars (NAS), a network of conservative university professors dedicated to combating "liberal bias" on college campuses. By 1996, nine years after its creation, the organization boasted four thousand members, including graduate students.[70] Heavily funded by conservative groups, the NAS board of advisers is littered with luminaries affiliated with right-wing think tanks, among them Jeane Kirkpatrick, Irving Kristol, and Seymour Martin Lipset.[71] The NAS political agenda is not difficult to divine: fear-mongering about a liberal takeover and declining standards. "What betrays NAS' professed concern with academic 'standards' more than anything else," notes researcher Sara Diamond, "is the PC hunters' neglect of the universities' bottom-line crisis. California's crown jewel UC and Cal State campuses are falling apart before our eyes, and the organized defenders of Western Civilization are busy counting how many deconstructionists can dance on the head of a pin."[72]

Exposing "the idiocies and viciousness of radical leftism in the universities" is also the mission of ex-radical David Horowitz (b. 1939), who in 1988 founded and still runs the Center for the Study of Popular Culture (CSPC), a Los Angeles–based nonprofit organization, another major beneficiary of right-wing largesse.[73] President of a spin-off organization, Students for Academic Freedom, Horowitz has embraced a novel form of affirmative action: Charging that conservatives are systematically excluded from faculties, he has launched a campaign, using the coercive power of the state, to force colleges to hire more professors of his political persuasion. "The intent," according to Roger W. Bowen, general secretary of the American Association of University Professors, "is to take away academic freedom."[74]

A similar organization to the CSPC, in terms of scope and funding, Accuracy in Academia (AIA) is a right-wing student group established in 1985 to monitor liberal college professors, take secret notes in their courses, and file complaints with the administration. Still another academic watchdog group heavily funded by the Right, the American Council of Trustees and Alumni (ACTA), founded in 1995 by Lynne Cheney, former chair of the National Endowment for the Humanities, has been waging an aggressive and well-financed campaign recently to discredit academics who refused to condemn the September 11 terrorist bombings.[75] By compiling a list of these "fifth columnists" and sending it to three thousand college trustees across the country, the ACTA agenda is obvious: to encourage dismissal of intransigent liberals on college faculties—this from an organization that ostensibly opposes "political correctness" and champions "free speech." ("Liberty for wolves," as the Oxford political philosopher Isaiah Berlin aptly observed, "is death to the lambs.")[76]

Not Conservative? You're Fired!

The counterpart of these campus-oriented watchdog organizations in the field of mass communications is Accuracy in Media (AIM), founded in 1969 by Reed Irvine (1922–2004), and now headed by his son Don, to monitor television and newspapers and expose "liberal lies." (Accuracy in Academia was in fact a spin-off of the Irvine group.) "Much of AIM's work," in the view of two observers, "is dedicated to getting those they disagree with fired."[77] The same mission characterizes the work of the right-wing Media Research Center, founded in 1987 and headed by L. Brent Bozell III, former director of Terry Dolan's NCPAC.[78] Both organizations hector editors, columnists, and publishers that they disagree with and threaten them with boycotts, attacks on their advertising revenue, and other measures to tone down expression that they consider too liberal.

Conservatism prevails today not just as a political movement but also as an intellectual mood. Clearly, in the battle of ideas, right-wingers have more than held their own. American society has not fared as well. Not the least of the casualties of the conservative ascendancy has been the co-optation of a significant part of the nation's intelligentsia. Journalist Michael Lind explains why:

> Chiefly because of the *Gleichshaltung* (coordination) carried out in the past several decades by the conservative foundations and a few well-placed fixers like Irving Kristol and his son William, there is no longer an independent conservative intellectual movement in the United States. What passes for intellectual conservatism is little more than the subsidized propaganda wing of the Republican party.[79]

Next: The Media

Conservatives have not stopped with creating pseudoscholarship. They also actively and energetically deploy strategies to turn the mass media to their favor. This approach, as will be seen in the next chapter, is twofold: policy papers and books for the world's elite (editors, members of Congress, departmental chairs), and op-ed columns, shock jocks, and slanted news releases for busy journalists and, through them, for the rest of us. Furthermore, the right-wing media are no less reliant on the politics of fear than are other organs of the conservative machine.

→ CHAPTER FOUR ←

CONSERVATIVES AND THE MASS MEDIA

Crucial to the conservative goal of swaying voters and policymakers is the manipulation of the mass media. Right-wing perspectives today dominate much of both the print and the electronic media (see appendix B). Michael Parenti, one of America's leading progressive thinkers, observes:

> Media bias usually does not occur in random fashion; rather, it moves in the same overall direction again and again, favoring management over labor, corporations over corporate critics, affluent whites over inner-city poor, officialdom over protestors, the two-party monopoly over leftist third parties, privatization and free-market "reforms" over public-sector development, U.S. dominance of the Third World over revolutionary or populist social change, investor globalization over nation-state democracy, national security policy over critics of that policy, and conservative commentators and columnists . . . over progressive or populist ones.[1]

Media critic Michael Massing makes many of the same points: The media are timid, fearful of appearing liberal, especially prone to give government the benefit of the doubt, and sensitive not to paint business in a bad light. "Of all the internal problems confronting the press," he concludes, "the reluctance to venture into politically sensitive matters, to report disturbing truths that might unsettle and provoke, remains by far the most troubling."[2]

Who Owns the News?

Ideological direction comes from the very top. In 2002, according to *Forbes* magazine, more than one-third of the fifty wealthiest citizens in the United States gained the preponderance of their fortunes in

41

media-related industries.[3] Massively wealthy, the owners of the major networks and newspapers are staunchly conservative (as are their corporate sponsors)—it is not likely that many billionaires this side of Ted Turner and George Soros vote the Democratic ticket.[4] Not surprisingly, during the 2000 presidential election, 48 percent of the daily newspapers in the country endorsed Bush, while only 23 percent supported Gore.[5]

There is no better example of right-wing bias at the top of the corporate ladder than media mogul Rupert Murdoch (b. 1931), who owns one of the handful of conglomerates that control virtually the entire industry in the United States. (The other major media conglomerates are Time Warner, Disney, Viacom, Seagram, Sony, General Electric, and AT&T.) A diehard conservative who sits on the board of directors of the libertarian Cato Institute, the Australian-born publisher (he became a U.S. citizen in 1985) exerts massive influence on political discourse through his media empire, which in addition provides employment for hundreds of conservative commentators. Murdoch's conglomerate (News Corporation) owns the Fox television network; Fox News Channel, a twenty-four-hour cable network launched in 1996 that is fiercely partisan (and virtually lily white); Twentieth Century movie studio; several publishing houses, including HarperCollins; 130 daily newspapers, including *The Times* of London and the *New York Post*; and a multitude of other media outlets in the United States and abroad.[6] Murdoch has recently expanded onto the Internet and satellite television, as well as the sports industry (News Corp. paid $311 million for the Los Angeles Dodgers in 1998 and sold the struggling team six years later for $430 million).[7]

General Electric (Ronald Reagan's former employer) is one of the Pentagon's leading contractors. Its many holdings include three news networks, including NBC. What are the odds that NBC will ever run an exposé of the military-industrial complex or that its news department will provide balanced coverage of an antiwar protest? As has been observed, News Corp., General Electric, and "the handful of global conglomerates that dominate America's media system have about as much interest in challenging the status quo in America as elephants have in challenging the status quo in the jungle."[8]

Right-Wing Dominance

Predictably, media employees mirror the views of their employers and advertisers. Who dominates the political talk show format on radio? For most Americans, the name Rush Limbaugh (b. 1951) remains virtually synonymous with talk radio, and with good reason. Aired on more than six hundred radio stations, his views are impossible to ignore: "You can drive almost anywhere in the United States on any weekday and get a three-hour, undiluted, un-rebutted and often persuasive advertisement for President Bush and the Republican Party."[9] (In 2001, Premiere Radio Networks awarded Limbaugh an eight-year, $285 million contract.)[10] Limbaugh has lots of company; New Right luminary Paul Weyrich has estimated that some fifteen hundred conservative talk show hosts hold forth on radio.[11] They dominate "attack" radio, and nothing is sacred to them—except big business. Prominent right-wing radio commentators with large followings include G. Gordon Liddy, Michael Reagan, and Ollie North.

Conservatives dominate the airwaves throughout the country. In Portland, Oregon, to cite what is admittedly an extreme case, listeners of the city's two local commercial political talk and news stations, KUGN and KPNW, are subjected to eighty hours per week (over four thousand hours per year) of Limbaugh and other conservative commentators, "with not so much as a second programmed for a Democratic or liberal perspective."[12]

Who are the syndicated columnists one sees over and over in the major newspapers? By the mid-1990s, George Will (b. 1941), ex–Washington editor for the *National Review,* and Cal Thomas, an evangelical Christian, ranked one and two in terms of visibility.[13] They both continue at or near the top of the rankings today. Thomas Sowell, Charles Krauthammer, William Rusher, and other archconservative writers also have little trouble finding sympathetic editors and owners to pick up their syndicated columns. Editorial pages of major newspapers seem to feature two William Safires for every one Paul Krugman.

And who are the most visible political commentators on television, the most powerful opinion molder of all? Little is progressive about recent Catholic convert Robert Novak, ex–disc jockey Sean Hannity, born-again Christian Fred Barnes, or the bombastic John McLaughlin, ex-Jesuit priest and another former Washington editor of the *National Review.* Bill O'Reilly (b. 1949) claims to be "fair and balanced"—"the most ingeniously cynical slogan in the history of media marketing," according to *New York Times* executive editor Bill Keller[14]—but there's a reason why 72 percent of viewers tuning in to *The O'Reilly Factor,* the most popular show on Fox News, described themselves as conservatives in a 2004 Pew Research Center study.[15] According to one noted critic, "the most prominent talking heads are all white males. The public is not even hearing policy recommendations from a significant segment of the body politic."[16]

High-Paid Darlings

These media darlings are not exactly working for minimum wages. Media scholar Robert McChesney reports that a 2002 survey of the forty largest-circulation newspapers in the U.S. indicates that, on average, journalists made almost twice as much as a typical worker.[17] Salaries among journalists in the electronic media are as high as those of their colleagues in the print media, if not higher. The marquee names, of course, earn much more. With salaries rivaling those of star athletes—themselves products of the communication revolution—members of the elite media living in affluent neighborhoods in and around New York City and Washington, D.C., can hardly be expected to be sympathetic to antiestablishment views.[18] "Journalists at the dominant media," McChesney avers, "are unlikely to have any idea what it means to go without health insurance, to be unable to locate affordable housing, to have their children in underfunded and dilapidated schools, to have relatives in prison or on the front lines of the military, to face the threat of severe poverty."[19]

Given their background, Eric Alterman finds that while his fellow journalists working for prestigious media outlets may be liberal on social issues, their "views on economic matters are generally consistent with their privileged position on the socioeconomic ladder, and hence, well to the right of most Americans."[20] Moreover, he adds, celebrity journalists can supplement their lofty salaries with generous stipends for corporate appearances:

> Journalists are not being paid tens of thousands to give a single speech by public school children, welfare mothers, individual investors, health-care consumers, or even (in most instances) unions. They are taking it from banks, insurance companies, investment houses, and all manner of unindicted CEOs. If they want to continue to be invited, they had better not write anything that might offend these people.[21]

What Liberal Bias?

Conservatives are fond of citing the liberal credentials of university professors, as ex-radical David Horowitz has done recently in supposedly proving the liberal bias of Ivy League academics,[22] but it would be interesting to poll media pundits in terms of *their* political orientation. Don't hold your breath; it is about as likely to happen as that Vice President Cheney will reveal the beneficiaries of his charitable contributions or the names of the business executives who helped him formulate the Republican energy policy at the secret October 2002 meetings.[23] (Except for fellow Republican Tom DeLay, whose transgressions are well documented, it is difficult to find a public figure whose personal ethics are as questionable as those of the vice president.)[24] Most members of the television media may well be registered Democrats. However, their politics are moderate or slightly right of center. In his memoirs, Bill Clinton recalls a discussion he had in this regard with Senator Alan Simpson, a conservative Republican from Wyoming, who observed about the elite media: "Most of them voted for you, but they think more like your right-wing critics do, and that's more important."[25]

Certainly this is true of the most influential members of the television media, the Beltway political commentators. These talking heads, on both network and cable channels, are assuredly more conservative than the population at large, particularly on economic issues. If elections were left to them, the GOP candidate would win by a landslide. Listening to their commentary one would never guess that Bill Clinton was twice elected president of the United States and that Al Gore was the people's choice during the 2000 presidential election, despite being outspent by over $60 million by a Republican opponent who raised a whopping *$193 million.*[26]

Recall what the mainstream media did to Gore in 2000. Taking their cue from right-wing pundits, whose strategy was to call into question Gore's honesty and even his mental stability—a strategy later used against Howard Dean—the major media participated in character assassination, enthusiastically portraying Gore as stiff, self-aggrandizing, and kooky, when in fact his mind was more flexible than that of his opponent and his ideas close to the American mainstream.[27]

Despite all of this, one of the most vociferous and outrageous of conservative charges is that the media establishment is controlled by liberals, an allegation first made forcefully by the late Reed Irvine and most recently by media insider Bernard Goldberg.[28] Bear in mind that the Right constitutes an ideological movement, and members of such groups—"true believers," as the American political philosopher Eric Hoffer referred to them—tend to interpret the world in absolute terms. As secular as well as religious right-wingers see it, the struggle is one between Good and Evil. Neutrality is impossible: "You're either with us or against us." This means that the majority of media reporters who strive to remain impartial—for example, Tom Brokaw and Dan Rather, both now retired—are reckoned by right-wing ideologues to be among the enemy, a rather idiosyncratic method of tracking.[29]

Moreover, as the journalist-historian Eric Alterman demonstrates, the alleged media bastions of liberalism that conservatives love to hate—*The New Yorker, Harper's, Atlantic Monthly, New Republic, Washington Post,* and even the much-maligned *New York Times*—are packed with articles by conservatives, including Andrew Sullivan, P. J. O'Rourke, William Safire, George Will, Robert Novak, and Charles Krauthammer.[30] Books by well-known right-wing authors, such as Ann Coulter and Bernard Goldberg, receive regular reviews in the so-called liberal press. This ideological toleration is rare, to say the least, in major right-wing publications.

Nevertheless, the criticism of liberal media bias is made so often and with such vehemence that it is difficult not to see the charge as orchestrated by right-wing zealots, a point emphasized by David Brock in his 2004 best seller, *The Republican Noise Machine: Right-Wing Media and How It Corrupts Democracy.* (So concerned was Brock with right-wing influence on the media that he founded and became CEO of the progressive Media Matters for America, a media watchdog group.) Once again, it may not be a conspiracy, but it seems highly suspect. Conservatives seem to be popping up everywhere. During the past two or three years, for some obscure reason, right-wing hacks such as Dennis Miller and Rush Limbaugh, who know little more than the average fan, have surfaced on sports programs as "commentators." What's this about?

On the other hand, the entire left wing of the U.S. political spectrum is virtually missing in the media. Twenty years ago a frustrated critic lamented, "There are few progressives and no socialist commentators in the mass media. In contrast, reactionaries, militarists, and ultra rightists have a multimillion dollar yearly propaganda budget donated by business firms."[31]

This political bias is even more apparent today. On television, for example, where are the liberal counterparts of the ultraconservative Bill O'Reilly, who hosts a *daily* program? Where is a left-wing network to balance off Fox News, now headed by GOP hardball strategist Roger Ailes and "operate[d] as an adjunct of the Republican Party"?[32] The best that liberals can come up with is a modest for-profit talk radio network, Air America, featuring satirist Al Franken, which initiated operations in March 2004. According to a study by Fairness & Accuracy in Reporting (FAIR), a bipartisan media watch group, covering the first nineteen weeks of 2001, 89 percent of the guests with a political affiliation on Fox's signature political news show, *Special Report with Brit Hume,* were Republicans.[33]

During the Afghanistan war, Fox correspondents wore U.S. flag pins, and anchor Brit Hume dismissed civilian deaths in the war-torn country as unworthy of coverage.[34] Embedded journalists went even further in uncritically justifying the unprovoked attack on Iraq in March 2003. While some 90 percent of western Europe opposed the war against Saddam Hussein, who allegedly harbored weapons of mass destruction, polls indicate that about three-quarters of the American population backed their government's decision to invade, even in the absence of credible evidence to support the administration's case. This wide discrepancy in public opinion had more than a little to do with the U.S. media's jingoistic slant. According to Robert McChesney, an expert on media studies, news coverage of the Iraq war ranks "among the very darkest moments in U.S. journalism history."[35] With few exceptions, the mainstream media enthusiastically supported the war.[36]

Conveyor Belt for the Administration

Interviewed early in 2005, Amy Goodman, host of Pacifica Radio's *Democracy Now!*, remarked, "Bush not finding weapons of mass destruction exposed more than the Bush administration—it exposed the media that acted as a conveyor belt for the lies of the administration. It's not just Fox that was alleging it, it was CNN, it was MSNBC, it was NBC, ABC, it was the *New York Times,* it was the *Washington Post,* day after day, front page, above the fold, lead stories in the newspapers and television about weapons of mass destruction."[37] Rather than focusing on the transparent pretexts for the six-week war, American journalists had a field day reporting the official versions of the largely fictitious saga of Private Jessica Lynch and the heroic May 1 jet landing by George Bush, in full gear, on the USS *Abraham Lincoln,* a costly publicity stunt.[38] In September 2003, President Bush was forced to admit that no discernible evidence linked Saddam Hussein and Al Qaeda, yet his admission received no coverage in the *Wall Street Journal* or Rupert Murdoch's *New York Post.*[39] The media were slow, too, to provide coverage a year later of American atrocities committed against insurgents during the pacification campaign.[40] Moreover, but for the extraordinary sleuthing of one veteran journalist, Seymour Hersh, the press might well have completely missed one of the biggest stories of 2004: American torture at Abu Ghraib prison.[41]

Not surprisingly, the most biased coverage of the war appeared on Fox News.[42] When newsman Peter Arnett, working for cable rival MSNBC, gave an unflattering assessment of the U.S. military during an interview on state-run Iraqi television, Fox News labeled the New Zealand–born journalist a traitor, par for the course for "the flag-wrapped, star-spangled tenor of its coverage."[43] That American television coverage of the war was so one-sided reflects, too, the extensive use of former U.S. admirals and generals as military analysts, many of them employees of defense firms and advisers for groups promoting the invasion—a clear conflict of interest.[44]

If CNBC could find a weekly slot for the ultraconservative editorial board of the *Wall Street Journal,* why can it not do the same for journalists representing the other side of the political spectrum? If a right-wing crusader like Pat Buchanan can spend years on CNN's *Crossfire* and *The Capital Gang,* as well as NBC's *The McLaughlin Group,* why can't a progressive thinker like Michael Parenti or Noam Chomsky get airtime? When panelists do ideological battle on these kinds of shows, as media critic Mark Hertsgaard wryly notes, the leftist position usually goes to former Clinton administration officials, hardly wild-eyed radicals.[45] Quite aside from intellectuals from the militant left such as Parenti and Chomsky, first-rate critics of the politics of greed are not in short supply: Kevin Phillips, William Greider, and Robert Reich, to name only a few. These liberal-minded pundits express themselves powerfully and eloquently.

Unfortunately, most Americans read little, preferring to watch television, where antiestablishment points of view get short shrift. If academia is so full of "reds," as right-wingers charge, why are they invisible in the media? Why do so few liberal professors get the opportunity to write syndicated columns, host radio talk shows, or appear on television as guest commentators? Instead, defenders of the status quo abound.

Treating the White House with Kid Gloves

Right-wing media bias is most evident in coverage of the White House. Compare, for example, media coverage of Presidents Clinton and Reagan: The Democrat was widely maligned; the Teflon president—blame never stuck to him—received kid gloves treatment.[46] The media jumped on the bandwagon, almost to a person, when conservatives launched their vituperative campaign to impeach the Democratic president for lying about his sexual transgressions. Right-wing columnists lost all sense of balance, as they went after anyone associated with the White House. William Safire of the *New York Times* went so far as to accuse the First Lady of being a "congenital liar."[47] The suicide of Clinton aide Vince Foster may well have been precipitated by personal attacks from the media, the *Wall Street Journal* in particular.[48] But when the aging Reagan lied about trading arms for hostages in clear violation of the law—thus committing not only a sin but a crime as well—the national press chose to ignore the elephant in the room. The weeklong coverage of his death in June 2004 by all the major networks, and their gushing admiration for his dubious legacy, only confirmed the media's love affair with him.

Maintaining less cordial relations with journalists than the Great Communicator, the Bushes, both father and son, have nonetheless received far more favorable media treatment than they deserve. When Bush the elder invaded Panama in 1989 and arrested the elected head of state, General Manuel Noriega, on drug charges—arrogance bordering on the extreme—the U.S. media were completely uncritical. One might have thought the invasion was a routine military exercise. Nor did the media find it strange that the United States threatened in 2004 to bring drug trafficking charges against deposed Haiti president Jean-Bertrand Aristide, who had fallen out of favor with the Bush administration.[49] But what else can one expect from what public intellectual Bill Moyers describes as "a media oligarchy whose corporate journalists are neutered and whose right-wing publicists have no shame"?[50] Is it any wonder that young people are increasingly turning to *Saturday Night Live* and to *The Daily Show with Jon Stewart* (on Comedy Central) for their news?[51]

A particularly egregious example of media bias and irresponsible journalism occurred in the summer of 2003. Noted Clinton basher Robert

Novak, acting on information he received from two senior White House officials, exposed the classified identity of a CIA operative to the public on July 14. The incident was all the more curious since the agent, Valerie Plame, was the wife of a former U.S. ambassador, Joseph Wilson, who had run afoul of the Bush administration.[52] Sent to Niger to investigate whether Saddam had attempted to buy material that could be used to manufacture nuclear weapons, Wilson found no such evidence. Despite his own emissary's report, President Bush, attempting to build up support for the coming war in Iraq, went ahead and made the link before the American public in his State of the Union address in January 2002. After Gulf War II, Wilson denied the White House claim and criticized the invasion, drawing the administration's ire. Why was the ex-ambassador's wife exposed as a CIA operative? Were the Bush crowd punishing the recalcitrant emissary? Was Karl Rove, the president's chief political strategist, implicated in some way? Now here was a story that begged to be told. But the media, apparently still in a patriotic mood, were strangely hesitant. They practically had to be cajoled into following up with some good old-fashioned investigative reporting.

Had the Clinton White House been suspected of such a breach of national defense, media pundits would surely have howled for special prosecutors and impeachment. But these public servants were almost as reticent to investigate as was Attorney General Gonzales. (When the government was finally forced to launch an investigation, it was innocent journalists who refused to identify their sources who were threatened with prosecution rather than Novak, who at the time of writing continued to lead a charmed life.)[53] By and large, the media have bent over backward to accommodate the president; "George W.," *Newsweek* columnist Anna Quindlen charges, "has developed a Teflon coating slicker and thicker than that of Ronald Reagan."[54]

Sesame Street Moves to the Right

Republican policies have rarely received the careful media scrutiny that Democratic policies do. Why should they? After all, these policies generally reflect the views of the media establishment. As progressive gadfly Jim Hightower points out, media conglomerates "all *love*" George Bush II and his deregulation agenda "because it's their agenda, too."[55]

Indeed, even the Public Broadcasting Service (PBS) exhibits a conservative bias, if one judges by the programming (e.g., fifteen hundred hours of William Buckley's *Firing Line*), which is not difficult to fathom given its heavy reliance on corporate funding.[56] A 1989 study on PBS's *MacNeil/Lehrer Newshour,* for example, found its guest list dominated by representatives of two right-wing Beltway think tanks, the Center for

Strategic and International Studies and the American Enterprise Institute. The report concluded, *"MacNeil/Lehrer*'s virtual exclusion of public interest leaders is a sad commentary on public TV."[57] One has only to check out the lineup of corporate sponsors—they prefer to be known as "underwriters"—to realize that the piper calls the tune.

Given their powerful influence on PBS, how ironic that conservatives have waged a vast and unrelenting campaign, spearheaded by AIM and the Committee on Public Integrity (COMINT), a David Horowitz media watchdog, to defund the network, part of a broader strategy to deny public monies to those institutions that in the slightest way refuse to go along with their right-wing agendas.[58] In parallel fashion, noncommercial Christian radio stations are doing everything they can to crowd National Public Radio (NPR) affiliates off the airwaves.[59] Apparently, these champions of free speech will be satisfied with nothing less than complete suppression of liberal views on the airwaves. And they are halfway there: A FAIR study conducted in June 2003 of the guest lists of four NPR news shows—*All Things Considered, Morning Edition, Weekend Edition Saturday,* and *Weekend Edition Sunday*—"shows the radio service relies on the same elite and influential sources that dominate mainstream commercial news, and falls short of reflecting the diversity of the American public."[60] The study counted 2,334 quoted sources. In terms of party affiliation, GOP guests took the top seven spots among the most frequently cited sources; altogether, Republican guests outnumbered Democrats 61 to 38 percent.

Conservatism for the College Set

Just as corporate America owns the major news media, vast amounts of Republican money have gone into supporting conservative newspapers on college campuses. For example, the aforementioned Institute for Educational Affairs, the corporate philanthropy institute founded by William Simon and Irving Kristol, provided funding for over seventy campus newspapers by the mid-1980s through its Collegiate Network.[61] The network's first member, in 1980, was the ultraconservative *Dartmouth Review,* which received $15,000 from IEA during its first ten years (and over $295,000 from the Olin Foundation in the same period).[62]

Around 1998, conservatives began taking the ideological war to another realm favored by the young—the Internet. As one media critic reports:

> With increasing speed, conservative think tanks, policy institutes, religious groups, and grassroots organizations are turning the Internet into a vast conservative neighborhood where everyone knows each other. In

fact, most of the groups crudely lumped together as "the right"—from neo-nazi, white supremacist, and militia organizations to Christian right, conservative, and libertarian groups—are extremely active on the Internet and are regularly updating and building their sites.[63]

The key Web sites are Townhall.com (www.townhall.com) and the Heartland Institute (www.heartland.org), the major conservative policy portals.[64] Founded in 1993 as a project of the Heritage Foundation and the *National Review,* the former claims to be the nation's leading right-wing online service, uniting over fifty-five publications and organizations, including Americans for Tax Reform, the Federalist Society, and the Traditional Values Coalition. Founded in 1984 by Joseph Bast, the Heartland Institute has become the Right's paramount information clearinghouse. The progressive Left operates many Web sites but nothing remotely approaching Townhall.com and the Heartland Institute in scope and complexity.

We should remember, too, the role of conservative think tanks (the subject of the previous chapter) in manufacturing what Americans read, what legislators hear, and how and what students learn.

The conservative attack on the media as an instrument of liberal ideology is part of a broader right-wing strategy to use fear as a means of advancing its own agenda, as we shall soon see. The tactic of fearmongering figures prominently among media outlets themselves. Fox TV's stock-in-trade, for example, is crime, indignation, and fear of immigrants, and CNN is not far behind.[65] The Muslim threat to Americans has been another cable TV staple, an exaggerated fear exploited years after September 11 by Rupert Murdoch and other media moguls (at a time, in reality, when a U.S. resident was more likely to be hit by lightning than to be struck down by Islamic fanatics).

The reader who has come this far has learned about the birth of the right-wing juggernaut, its funding, some of its major institutions, and how it gets its point of view before the American people. Now it is time to focus on that point of view and the contents of conservative ideology in greater detail.

CHAPTER FIVE

MODERN CONSERVATISM
Ideology and Agenda

The Main Ideas

Republicans often indignantly reject the suggestion that they came to power as a result of a clever, somewhat disingenuous, and well-funded campaign of tricks, public relations manipulations, and clever catchwords, insisting that the public chose them because of the superiority of their ideas. Just what is it that the New Right believes?

The New Right's main ideas are simply stated. They include small government, fiscal responsibility, patriotism, merit, spreading democracy, family values, quietist judges and original intent, free trade, supply-side economics, privatization, federalism and states' rights, and compassionate conservatism. Some of these ideas, such as patriotism, spreading democracy, and fiscal responsibility, are ones that many liberals share, at least in the abstract. But others—small government, quietist judges, supply-side economics, privatization, and federalism—are the conservatives' stock-in-trade.

How have these fared in the real world? Many have proved to be spectacular failures. For example, the ideology that supply-side economics and deregulation will spur the economy, produce more jobs, and "raise all boats" has turned out to be an illusion.[1] The rich have simply pocketed their gains and invested little in producing jobs for U.S. workers. Trickle-down economics under Reagan produced few gains for the middle class and a generally stagnant economy, while the Clinton years saw robust job growth and reduction in the national debt. Earlier, during the sixties, under Democratic presidencies, black family income rose 53 percent; black employment in professional, technical, and managerial occupations doubled. The proportion of blacks in poverty fell from 55 percent to 27 percent. Black unemployment decreased 34 percent.[2] Today, poverty haunts the ghettoes once again. Under Bush II, the federal deficit has grown rapidly, while the economy as a whole has stagnated and jobs have dwindled or left for overseas. A million more people became poor in 2004, and poverty has increased in each of the last four years.[3] Working people were earning about $53 more a week in 1972 than they did in 2004—19 percent more back then than today.[4] Some forty-five million Americans currently lack health insurance. All of these dismal socioeconomic trends, economists from the Economic Policy Institute concluded in late 2005, have only gotten progressively worse during the past four years of GOP rule.[5]

Other conservative ideas, such as promoting democracy in the rest of the world, have likewise produced few gains. Nothing, of course, is wrong with trying to set a good example of responsive, open government at home in hopes that developing countries will emulate it. But the aggressive way in which neoconservatives have sought to superimpose a U.S. version of free-market governance—in Latin America and the Muslim world, for example—has cost us friends as well as lives, and today those regions seem even less sympathetic to us than they were before.

Still other conservative ideas, such as fiscal and judicial restraint, have suffered a different fate—quiet abandonment. After trumpeting them in the early years of their ascendancy, the Republicans, without announcing that they were doing so, retired them when they proved inconvenient. The budget, which in the Clinton years showed a large surplus, now is mired in the largest deficit in our country's history because of massive tax cuts for corporations and the wealthy and obscenely high military spending. The same fate has overcome quietist judging. Conservative judges and their Republican ideological backers have not hesitated to reverse long-standing precedent, for example, when legislating morality or ensuring the Bush presidency in a disputed election. The judiciary is now as activist as it has been at any time since the Warren Court. Federalism and states' rights have suffered a similar fate. Abandoned when they conflict with a value the New Right wants to advance, such as the right to life, criminalization of marijuana use for medical purposes, or medical euthanasia, federalism and states' rights have been reduced to the status of tired platitudes, trotted out when convenient and ignored when they cut against something the conservative constituency really wants.

Deregulation has fared little better. Reducing the role of such agencies as the Environmental Protection Agency (EPA), the Occupational Safety and Health Administration (OSHA), the Federal Drug Administration (FDA), and the Federal Emergency Management Agency (FEMA) has accelerated global warming, increased the number of workplace injuries, freed drug manufacturers to sell dangerous and poorly tested pharmaceuticals, and slowed the national response to disasters such as Hurricane Katrina.[6]

Other New Right measures, such as privatization, which might have worked had the Republicans pursued them consistently and honestly, have instead been invoked to justify an orgy of self-dealing and enrichment of friends and favored industries. Republicans, who professed mock horror at Clinton's sexual adventuring, have been guilty of tolerating one of the most corrupt regimes in recent U.S. history. Even when privatization is not wielded corruptly, it simply does not work. A more interdependent, densely populated world needs (as Hurricane Katrina showed) more social coordination, not less. A system of dikes and levees works, for example, only if the government operates and maintains it. A city where each home had its own dike (with the richer homes higher than the rest) would be an absurdity.[7]

In looking at a few of the main conservative ideas, as well as some of the reasons—primarily anti-intellectualism and greed—for their failure, we show how these ideas are in many cases shams, cases of bait and switch: The Republicans promise one thing—a bracing, attractive program, such as deregulation or merit-based competition—and deliver another. We identify the main underlying values that shape the conservative agenda: (1) greed and personal enrichment for their wealthy friends and (2) the politics of fear for the rest of us. Our concern is that the patterns we identify are likely to become long-term trends. New Right politicians do not learn from their mistakes, so that if the public does not replace them, they will go on as they have been doing. They will merely learn how to fleece the public, embroil us in foreign wars of aggression, and siphon wealth to their rich backers more and more effectively, so that, over time, their power and influence will become, for all intents and purposes, unassailable.

The Best Ideas? Anti-Intellectualism and the New Right

Some conservative ideas are simply anti-intellectual and dogmatically held. Writing in 1964, on the eve of the rise of the New Right, E. Digby Baltzell, the late sociologist, observed that a general perception had taken root of Republicans as anti-intellectual.[8] Spiro Agnew did nothing to dispel this popular view in the next few years with his attacks on the "effete corps of impudent snobs who characterize themselves as intellectuals."[9] Despite the flood of ostensibly scholarly tracts emerging from right-wing think tanks and the emphasis conservatives have placed on ideas, the New Conservatism has been meager in intellectual content.[10] As Michael Lind put it: "What is the result of the conservative intellectual renaissance of late twentieth-century America? A few position papers from think tanks subsidized by the aerospace and tobacco industries; a few public-policy potboilers slapped together by second-rate social scientists or former student journalists subsidized by pro-business foundations; a few collections of op-eds by right-wing syndicated columnists."[11] Even George Nash, the sympathetic historian of U.S. conservatism, concedes that at the close of the seventies, ideas were distinctly subservient to the exigencies of practical politics.[12] Many conservatives attack the university because their ideas are unable to gain a foothold there in competition with others; others urge that it stop serving as a laboratory for new ideas and go back to a former role of character development (i.e., indoctrination in traditional values).[13]

Certainly Ronald Reagan displayed scant interest in exploring the world of ideas (not surprisingly, all four of his children were college dropouts). Reagan, however, looks like a heavyweight compared to George W. Bush, who practically revels in anti-intellectualism, as do his leading Christian supporters.[14] Their disdain for logic, facts, and scholarship has allowed members of the New Right to range freely over a broad expanse of territory, justifying one cause or action at any time, only to jettison it for something else later. This also weighs against their claim to have come to power on the strength of their ideas.

Greed Masquerading as Competition

Despite its professed reliance on the ideas of such thinkers as Edmund Burke, Leo Strauss, Friedrich von Hayek, Ludwig von Mises, Ayn Rand, and other seminal thinkers, modern-day conservatism ultimately boils down to naked self-interest—or, to put it less politely, greed. Unlike John Stuart Mill and William Gladstone—predecessors who were deeply concerned with the general welfare—today's conservative policymakers ask but one question: "What's in it for me and my crowd?"

It is extraordinary to recall how capitalism, which conservatives profess to adore, was at one time characterized by self-denial.[15] The capitalism of John Winthrop and the Puritan forefathers, for example, was steeped in asceticism. But this spiritual impulse has all but disappeared, even among members of the Christian Right. Although "America is one of the most religiously observant countries in the contemporary world,"[16] its citizens are among that world's most materialistic.[17] As the historian Morris Berman observes in his 2000 *The Twilight of American Culture,* U.S. consumerism has become a full-blown religion.[18] "It is not unfair to say," adds the political scientist Andrew Hacker, who has studied American attitudes toward money, "that the freedom to shop—to select, from an array of options, whatever appeals to you—is the choice Americans cherish most."[19] Though they see themselves "as morally upright, God-fearing people," one critic, echoing Alexis de Tocqueville, marvels, "Americans chase wealth with a single-minded obsessiveness that strikes foreigners as coarse."[20]

This is especially true of today's conservatives, who deny themselves very little. *Sacrifice* and *responsibility* are not part of their vocabulary. The word *greed* itself leaves them perplexed since it implies too much of something, and they cannot fathom the idea that a person can accumulate too much money. This confusion is obvious to Robert Wuthnow, sociology professor at Princeton University, another scholar who has carried out extensive studies on American attitudes toward wealth and ethics: "Greed is a baffling concept to most Americans.... While most people ... believed greed was immoral and something they wouldn't abide, they also couldn't define it and said no one had ever taught them what it meant. They'd say 'greed is wrong,' then minutes later tell you, 'I would really like to have a whole lot more money and buy a whole lot more things.'"[21]

Expensive cars, cell phones, personalized license plates—there is never enough. And yet, despite this excess, most U.S. capitalists do not hesitate to call themselves Christians or ask what a Kenneth Lay—or a Jerry Falwell, for that matter—has in common with the Man from Galilee. Apologists for capitalism may give lip service to Jesus' words, but the last thing they want to do is emulate his example.

One conservative who makes no apologies for his economic views is Leonard Peikoff, who founded the Ayn Rand Institute, a libertarian think tank. Displaying refreshing candor, Peikoff wonders why Americans celebrate Christmas as a religious holiday, as a spiritual event: "Life requires reason, selfishness, capitalism; that is what Christmas should celebrate—and really, underneath all the pretense, that is what it does celebrate. It is time to take the Christ out of Christmas, and turn the holiday into a guiltlessly egoistic, pro-reason, this-worldly, commercial celebration."[22]

Under Republican economics, the rich greatly increased their wealth and share of the nation's assets. The share of income going to the richest Americans—the top 0.1 percent—grew significantly in a recent year, while the share going to the other 99 percent fell. The effective income tax rates paid by the top 0.1 percent dropped sharply, declining at more than ten times the rate for everyone else.[23]

Bogus Merit

As glaring as the avarice reflected in wanton moneymaking is the hypocrisy that accompanies it. Capitalists and their boosters constantly extol the virtues of a meritocracy. One particularly exuberant fan is Harvard economist Robert J. Samuelson, who shares his Panglossian perspectives regularly in *Newsweek*. As evidence of this meritocracy, the optimistic columnist points out that even Bill Gates, the biggest success of all, was a college dropout, conveniently neglecting to inform his readers that the college was Harvard.[24]

For all their talk about meritocracy, members of the corporate elite, like most other affluent Americans, are heirs of inherited wealth: "In reality, of course," Michael Lind reminds us, "most wealthy Americans have made their money the old-fashioned way: mom or dad died. But you would never know this from conservative propaganda, which treats entrepreneurs and inventors, rather than the hereditary rich or corporate executives, as though they were typical of the rich in America."[25]

Inherited wealth is particularly common among the Right's leading ideological boosters. Consider William Buckley Jr., "blithely using dad's money to champion rugged individualism."[26] The best example, of course, is President George W. Bush himself. During the Supreme Court battle over affirmative action in 2003—precipitated by the admissions policies of the University of Michigan Law School—the president, unsolicited, jumped into the fray on the side of meritocracy, seemingly unaware that he is the poster child for inherited privilege. As Molly Ivins, who has known him since high school, indicates in an unflattering biographical sketch appropriately titled "The Uncompassionate Conservative," Bush Jr. has led a charmed life:

> The reason there is no noblesse oblige about Dubya is because he doesn't admit to himself or anyone else that he owes his entire life to being named George W. Bush. He didn't just get a head start by being his father's son—it remained the single most salient fact about him for most of his life. He got into Andover as a legacy. He got into Yale as a legacy. He got into Harvard Business School as a courtesy.... He got into the Texas Air National Guard—and sat out Vietnam—through Daddy's influence.... Bush was set up in the oil business by friends of his father. He went broke and was bailed out by friends of his father. He went broke again and was bailed out again by friends of his father; he went broke yet again and was bailed out by some fellow Yalies.[27]

"George W. Bush, in fact, may be the most spectacular affirmative-action success story of all time," columnist Michael Kinsley writes.[28] (The names Buckley and Bush suggest another little-known fact about modern right-wing luminaries: Dig into their lives and, more often than not, you hit ... oil.)

Until Americans are willing to diminish the role that family wealth and connections play, all calls for advancement based solely on merit ring hollow. Critics who expose these inconsistencies or point out the massive poverty that festers in the midst of plenty are mercilessly assailed from all sides for fomenting "class war."[29] Among these outraged critics is the president himself.[30] Of course, "cutting social welfare spending, expanding high-end tax breaks, firing workers by the thousands—somehow these attacks against America's nonaffluent majority are never described as 'class warfare.'"[31] As the liberal economist Robert Kuttner put it: "The real class warfare in America today is top-down as it has been ever since Ronald Reagan."[32] By the mid-1990s, the U.S. government was providing the rich three and a half times more welfare than the poor.[33] The discrepancy is even wider today.

In fact, even the middle class, those staunch defenders of sobriety and self-reliance, receive considerably more perks than the lower class. Recall, for example, the tax deduction for owning a home (one would think that it would be those without property who would get the tax break).[34] And though corporations were the major beneficiaries of California's tax revolt measure Proposition 13, middle-class homeowners also shared in the bonanza. Moreover, according to the Queens College political scientist Andrew Hacker, "Social Security pensions subsidize the middle class and, in fact, the very rich. Even workers with minimum-wage earnings are made to support senior citizens with benefits well above the amortized worth of the recipients' own contributions. A middle-class family that sends its children to its state university, vacations in national parks, and commutes on interstate highways gets more value from public amenities than it paid in taxes."[35]

Welfare for the Rich

Welfare for the wealthy takes a variety of forms. None, however, is as lucrative as military spending. "The United States," it has been argued, "spends more on arms than all the other industrial nations combined."[36] Huge profits are made in the defense industry. A B-52 bomber costs $2.2 billion; a Seawolf submarine, $2.4 billion; a nuclear-powered aircraft carrier, $3.5 billion.[37] Raytheon's Tomahawk cruise missiles are a bargain—only $750,000.[38] Given these astronomical figures, who can blame Lockheed for charging the Pentagon $640 for a toilet seat?[39] And, of course, the same U.S. firms that equip the American military have also captured lucrative arms contracts across the globe. Hence the unintentional irony of the 2003 U.S. attack on Iraq: "The United States, the world's leading arms supplier, is taking the world to war to stop arms proliferation in the very country to which it shipped chemicals, biological seed stock and weapons for more than ten years."[40]

Fueled by mythical "gaps" between U.S. military capacity and that of our enemies, the defense budget has become even more bloated since the collapse of the Soviet Union. In 2000, for example, the Pentagon asked Congress to replace the F-15, "the world's most advanced aircraft," with the F-22, "the world's most advanced aircraft." The latter, according to

East Asian expert Chalmers Johnson, would cost three times more than the plane it was replacing.[41] And, of course, Star Wars is only the latest example of a useless military expense (the 2005 federal budget includes $10 billion for this boondoggle).[42] While neocon strategists and military contractors, such as Raytheon, wax eloquent when advocating this missile defense, they and the flag-waving media forget to divulge that it doesn't work and probably never will.[43]

As mentioned previously, the constant shuffle of powerful individuals among the Pentagon, the federal bureaucracy, and the governing boards of major defense contractors and allied industries is not a coincidence. The sociologist Jerome Himmelstein gives examples from recent history:

> Alexander Haig, Reagan's first secretary of state, was president of United Technologies, a director of several other corporations, and a member of the Council on Foreign Relations. George Schultz, his successor, was president of the Bechtel Corporation and a director of the Council on Foreign Relations. Caspar Weinberger, Reagan's first defense secretary, was a vice president of Bechtel and a member of the Trilateral Commission. Finally, Donald Regan, first Reagan's treasury secretary and later his chief of staff, was head of Merrill Lynch, a trustee of the Committee for Economic Development, and a member of the Council on Foreign Relations.[44]

Not surprisingly, given the Schultz and Weinberger ties to the Bechtel Group, the Bay Area engineering and construction giant received a $680 million contract, after a limited, invitation-only bidding, to spearhead the rebuilding effort in Iraq in the aftermath of the 2003 war. Dick Cheney's old company, Halliburton, the Dallas-based global oil field services firm, was the other major sweepstakes winner; the Texas firm (and its subsidiaries) is the leading contractor for the U.S. military in the war-ravaged country.[45] The Republicans prefer to worship at the altar of competition and free-market economics. But once in power, it's get what you can for yourself and your crowd.

Spreading Democracy—While Helping Your Friends at the Same Time

Consider another example of a well-connected policymaker: current secretary of defense Donald Rumsfeld, an enthusiastic Bechtel booster in the eighties, when the company tried to build a major oil pipeline from Iraq to the Jordanian port of Aqaba.[46] That same Rumsfeld made at least $4.7 million in investment earnings in 2001, so it's not as if he needs the job.[47]

The Pentagon connection can be quite lucrative. Admiral Leon Edney, Admiral David Jeremiah, and Lieutenant General Charles May, all retired, have served Northrop Grumman or its subsidiaries as either consultants or board members; and May, along with retired Lieutenant General Paul Cerjan and retired Admiral Carlisle Trost, have also been on the payroll of Lockheed Martin, the nation's largest military contractor.[48] Ex–army secretary Thomas White retired from the military as a brigadier general in 1990. He immediately joined Enron as vice chairman of Energy Services before President Bush nominated him to the army post, where he served from April 2001 to April 2003. General Wesley Clark, who retired from the military in 1999 to join the nation's biggest investment banking firm off Wall Street, now manages his own consulting firm. As chairman of the board at WaveCrest Laboratories, he collected $195,000 in 2002 "for consulting on the design and distribution of the company's motorized bicycle, which is being marketed to the U.S. military."[49] American taxpayers pay a heavy price for subsidizing the political-military-industrial complex; huge profits in the private sector are sustained by massive corruption in Congress and endless waste in the Pentagon.

Given the constant shuffle of individuals between the public and private sectors, is it any wonder that cronyism runs rampant? (In mid-2004, rather than disclose the details of his considerable business interests in the Middle East, Henry Kissinger resigned as chair of the National Commission on Terrorist Attacks upon the United States, the panel that was convened, despite Bush opposition, to investigate the government response to September 11.)[50] One of the most striking examples—recently under congressional investigation—was a $23.5 billion contract the U.S. Air Force awarded Boeing in 2003. Not only was the Chicago-based aerospace giant awarded the coveted contract after the Pentagon allowed it to rewrite the official government specifications to suit itself, but it prevailed despite having been underbade by its competitor, Airbus, to the tune of $10 billion. Criticized by the White House Office of Management and Budget (OMB) and several independent agencies as unnecessary and exorbitant in cost, the controversial deal received the go-ahead only after intervention by the Bush White House.[51]

Tax Relief for the Rich

Another instrument that the rich have employed for financial benefit, courtesy of the government, has been the tax system. Since 1977, an unending series of "tax reforms" have preserved the extraordinary profits reaped by the fortunate few, ostensibly to jump-start the economy. "Despite obfuscations," the Princeton economist Paul Krugman, the most consistent and respected critic of the president's tax policies, concludes, "it remains true that more than half of the Bush tax cut will eventually go to the top 1 percent of families."[52] Individuals who make $1 million or more a year are slated to receive an average annual cut of $90,000.[53] The long conservative campaign against the IRS seemed to have ended with a resounding victory.

The appetites of the wealthy, however, are insatiable. Not content to win a radical decrease in the inheritance tax—which is supposed to be gradually phased out in increments through 2010, then reestablished the following year at the 2001 level—George W. Bush and his advisers insist that it be abolished altogether.[54] This is, of course, a tax that only the wealthiest 2 percent would ever have to pay, a tax on today's super-rich and their heirs. Indeed, it has been estimated that the beneficiaries of repeal would be less than 0.5 percent of all estates.[55] Already in dire financial straits, the federal government would see its total debt climb to $7.7 trillion by 2005, more than $25,000 per person.[56] Nonetheless, labeling the levy "the death tax," critics have convinced the majority of Congress that repeal would be a good idea. (The measure for total abolition was defeated in June 2002 only because it failed to get the necessary sixty votes in the Senate.) Why the people and their representatives in a democracy, ostensibly committed to the idea of merit, would wish to preserve the estates of a small number of individuals who already have far too much money at the cost of jeopardizing essential services such as Social Security and Medicare certainly gives pause.[57]

Trickle-Down Economics That Drips into the Cayman Islands, Not to Struggling U.S. Workers

The labyrinthine tax codes contain so many loopholes that lawyers representing both companies and wealthy individuals hardly need to break a sweat finding them. Not the least of these loopholes designed specifically for the economic elite is the use of offshore tax havens such as Bermuda and the Cayman Islands that cost the IRS billions of dollars a year.[58] More than one million U.S. corporations and individuals registered in a recent year as citizens in Bermuda alone, presumably to avoid paying federal taxes.[59] Among the tax haven users have been Harken Energy, which set up an offshore tax dodge while Bush was serving on its board, and Halliburton, which under Vice President Cheney's leadership went from nine to nearly five times that number of offshore tax dodges.[60] Thanks to these tax loopholes, the General Accounting Office (GAO) reported in 2004, more than 60 percent of American corporations failed to pay any federal taxes whatsoever during the boom period from 1996 through 2000.[61] Undoubtedly contributing to this state of affairs is that the IRS's capacity to enforce tax laws has been cut in half during the post-Reagan era.[62]

Starving the Beast (Read: Programs for the Poor)

By September 2003, about 2.7 million payroll jobs had been lost on Bush's watch.[63] While the middle class struggles, the plight of the working poor—the 20 percent of the working population with annual incomes ranging between $10,000 and $20,000 in 2001—has been especially precarious.[64] The Bush administration's prescription—cut taxes—is no different from what he prescribed when the economy seemed healthy, notes *Newsweek* economist Allan Sloan.[65] By 2004, federal tax receipts as a share of national income were at the lowest level since 1950.[66] Reviewing the Bush tax policies, it is hard to disagree with Paul Krugman, for whom the ultimate goal of the New Right is to create "a system in which only wages are taxed—a system ... in which earned income is taxed but unearned income is not."[67]

Many critics conclude that another major objective lies behind Bush's radical tax measures. According to Jay Bookman, deputy editorial page editor of the *Atlanta Journal-Constitution*:

> There is ... a deeper logic behind this [tax] policy, a logic never uttered by elected politicians but suggested often in the right-wing think tanks and magazines that set this administration's agenda. It goes like this: Putting the federal government deep into hock will eventually force it to abandon the social programs that conservatives abhor, but that most Americans support as legitimate government functions. In other words, this is a con game and we're the pigeons. If we fall for the scam, we will fall for the same reason that every mark ever fell for a con: Greed.[68]

When the hurricane-drenched Gulf Coast cities needed urgent relief in the wake of the 2005 hurricane Katrina, Republican administrators were nowhere to be found.[69] It is interesting to note that nationally the income of the poorest fifth of Americans fell 8.7 percent in inflation-adjusted dollars since 1999. In 2004, 1.1 million were added to the 76 million already living in poverty.[70]

Budgetary Responsibility

Conservatives are often perceived, especially by their liberal critics, as inflexible ideologues. Nothing could be further from the truth. In fact, right-wing policies have been unusually inconsistent. (Indeed one could argue that the single unifying thread boils down to this aspiration: the maximization of profits.) Consider the conservative stance on the federal budget. The GOP has traditionally been seen as a steadfast opponent of deficit spending. And yet under Ronald Reagan, who made balancing the budget one of his leading campaign promises ("When they insist we can't reduce taxes . . . and balance the budget too, one six-word answer will do: *Yes we can, and yes we will*"),[71] Republicans pushed the national debt from under $1 trillion to a record $3.5 trillion. When the elder Bush left office on January 20, 1993—to become a traveling investment bank promoter during the next decade for the Carlyle Group, a private global investment firm based in Washington, D.C., in China and Saudi Arabia—the debt had escalated to $4 trillion.

Eventually, profiting from the economic boom of the nineties—"The Roaring Nineties," as Joseph E. Stiglitz, chairman of President Clinton's Council of Economic Advisers, called that frenetic decade—Democrats not only balanced the budget, they created a healthy surplus. In the process, "the Clinton years brought the longest, strongest, broadest, fairest economic expansion in American history."[72]

This period of fiscal responsibility proved short-lived. George W. Bush won election in 2000 largely on his promise to give American taxpayers a huge tax break, and when elected, he immediately instituted a cut of $1.35 trillion spread out over a ten-year period. Republican analysts forecast that citizens had nothing to fear, that the national surplus would rise to $5.6 trillion during that period. Immediately *after* the tax cut they conveniently discovered a clerical error: They had overestimated by $4 trillion. In mid-2003, the White House OMB projected that the deficit for the fiscal year would reach $455 billion, $151 billion more than estimated earlier in the year; in fact, when Bush first entered office in 2001, the White House predicted a $334 billion *surplus* in 2003, a $789 billion swing.[73] In August 2003, the nonpartisan Congressional Budget Office (CBO) predicted that the federal government would go into debt in 2004 by a record $480 billion—$173 billion more than the 2001 Bush predictions—and accumulate almost $1.4 trillion in new debt over the next decade, assuming President Bush does not make his tax cuts permanent.[74] It seems likely that even this was an underestimate: A recent study showed that since the end of 2000, federal debt is up by $1.1 trillion.[75]

Given these massive tax cuts, which predictably benefited the wealthy at the expense of the impoverished, the current administration must now rely on deficit spending. Moreover, it has had to dip into Social Security funds, which it had promised, before the election, not to touch—shades of George Sr. ("read my lips"), who also made grandiose preelection pledges. "The president's approach," former Vermont governor Howard Dean charges, "is the equivalent of mortgaging your house to get spending money for the weekend."[76] His boosters must wonder how George Bush Jr. ever made it as a businessman.

Surprisingly, the Republican Party does not seem particularly disturbed at the prospect of deficit spending. (Nor, apparently, do most Americans: In October 2003, consumer debt—excluding mortgages—reached a record

$1.98 trillion, about $18,700 per household.)[77] Although it is hard to believe, given the current state of affairs, this was the same party that in the late seventies was actually proposing a constitutional amendment to mandate a balanced budget. Indeed, it became a centerpiece of Newt Gingrich's Contract with America in 1994, when Republicans regained control of the House of Representatives after more than forty years. In retrospect, this GOP initiative, like so many others, emerges as part of a well-coordinated strategy to discredit Democratic administrations. In fact, Republicans have a powerful interest in maintaining an *unbalanced* budget. Common sense dictates that owing money is an unwise policy—for debtors—but we often forget that debts are *owed to* someone, with interest. And in this case, the creditors are bondholders, mostly corporate interests at home and abroad.[78] "Interest payments on the debt ... represent a transfer of wealth from ordinary American taxpayers to rich Americans and foreigners without precedent in history."[79] "For a select few ... ," the historian Morris Berman observes, "national collapse is a good business opportunity."[80]

It is important to remember that the Reagan and Bush I deficits—plus massive tax cuts and military budgets—put incredible amounts of money into the pockets of a small group of investors. The annual interest tax-payers paid to bondholders on the Reagan-Bush $3 trillion debt increase (calculated at an average of 7 percent) was $210 billion by 1995.[81] Is it any wonder that the fortunate few are continually lobbying to see Ronald Reagan's face carved on Mount Rushmore, a favorite Grover Norquist project?

Free Trade

Republicans are paladins of free trade. But their record in office hardly bears this out. The GOP enthusiastically supported the North American Free Trade Agreement (NAFTA) during the Clinton administration, as one might expect, given their ideological position. But the Bush administration barred exports of tomatoes from Mexico to the United States in 2001 in violation of that agreement—at a cost of close to $1 billion to Mexican producers—because those tomatoes sold so well in this country. "In other words," MIT professor Noam Chomsky concludes, "the free market was working, but with the wrong consequences."[82] In the following year, President Bush again violated his own party's free-trade principles when he levied a stiff tariff on steel imports, essentially imposing a 30 percent surcharge on U.S. steel consumers. According to the editors of the *San Francisco Chronicle*, "It's hard to find a stranger contradiction: free-trade Republican George W. Bush slapping on tariffs to protect struggling U.S. steel mills and labor unions."[83] The president, a *Chronicle* reporter wryly noted, "apparently has been studying ... manuals on how to buy union votes in swing states."[84] Certainly the GOP's electoral prospects quickly brightened in the Rust Belt states of Pennsylvania, West Virginia, and Ohio (the state that would eventually deliver the presidency to the GOP in 2004).

Big Government

Republicans and other conservatives are opposed to "big government." But are they? And is shrinking government, when they do it, good for the country? The powers of the federal government increased dramatically between 1865 and the 1990s.[85] The Depression and World War II, in particular, required strong central authority. At least since the creation of the welfare state in the thirties, the GOP has consistently voiced opposition to the expansion of federal power. Before the 2000 election, for example, hardly a day went by that Republican politicians did not rail against the evils of Washington, D.C.—evils personified by "Slick Willie" and "The Bitch."

Despite what they say, Republicans find nothing wrong with big government—so long as they are in power. Indeed, in the aftermath of September 11, defense spending soared, while federal intrusion into the lives of the citizenry grew greatly. "By abandoning many of the checks and balances established in the Constitution to keep any branch of government from becoming too powerful," one critic argues, "Bush has already achieved the greatest expansion of executive power since Nixon."[86] Kevin Baker concurs: "For all of the rhetoric about limited government since the advent of Reagan and the current Republican hegemony the federal government has by almost all objective measures become larger, more intrusive, more coercive, less accountable, and more deeply indebted than ever before."[87]

Moreover, the USA PATRIOT Act, passed in October 2001, appears to be only the beginning of an assault on the rights of the individual by a variety of governmental agencies. The new Department of Homeland Security (DHS) was to implement a "Total Information Awareness" system that would feed into its massive surveillance apparatus constructed after September 11. This project was the brainchild of John Poindexter (b. 1936).[88] Fortunately, this onetime Reagan national security adviser, a key figure in the Iran-contra scandal, was forced to resign his office in August 2003 after proposing a harebrained scheme: a federal betting parlor, to alert U.S. citizens to the dangers of terrorism.[89] Conspicuous by their absence in defense of the Bill of Rights have been conservative organizations and legal foundations—though a few principled individuals, such as columnist William Safire, have raised occasional protests.[90]

Trading One Tyrant for Another: Corporate Power Resurges

In one area, small government has been enforced effectively and profitably by the new Republicans—and that area is enforcement of the antitrust laws and laws against nepotism, insider dealing, and other forms of corruption. Unlike the citizenry, major corporations have little to fear from Republican administrations. Now that labor has been reduced to a mere shadow of its pre–Reagan era self—union membership fell from 35 percent of the labor force in the seventies to 11 percent in the nineties[91]—the only source of effective opposition to corporate capitalism, barring a grassroots revolt, is big government. But under GOP administrations, corporations have enjoyed free rein.[92] And why not? After all, members of Congress, Democrats as well as Republicans, win election to office largely on the strength of campaign contributions from Fortune 500 companies. In Washington, they are wined and dined by corporate lobbyists. And after leaving public office, they join the payroll of the very corporate elites whose interests they served.

Government agencies charged with protecting the public from predatory businessmen have practically ceased to function because of budgetary restraints and the appointment of hostile critics to key positions. Television executives, for example, carpet-bomb children with sex and violence during prime-time viewing hours with impunity since the nation's chief public watchdog in this area, the Federal Communications Commission (FCC), has adopted a hands-off approach, according to author James P. Steyer, who explains why our elected officials, who are supposed to provide oversight, do so little: "With rare exceptions . . . politicians are deep in the pocket of the media industry."[93]

Corporate influence isn't always subtle. Shortly before being sworn in as Speaker of the House in 1994, Newt Gingrich accepted a two-book deal from HarperCollins, with a whopping $4.5 million advance. The unprecedented deal fell through, however, in the face of widespread public indignation. An unrepentant Gingrich—who earlier had attacked Democratic House Speaker Jim Wright for a similar book agreement—was forced to pass on the advance. HarperCollins, of course, is a subsidiary of News Corp., which is owned by Rupert Murdoch. During this period, the ambitious publisher was actively lobbying the FCC to ease regulations that would permit him to expand his enormous media empire, circumstances that made the lucrative offer highly suspect. Under contract to author four novels, Gingrich still got to write the other two books, under a more modest agreement. As for Murdoch, he might have lost the battle, but he won the war: In 1995, congressional Republicans passed legislation that enabled the publisher to turn a tidy profit.[94]

The chair of the FCC during Bush's first administration was Colin Powell's son, Michael K. Powell (b. 1963), a former media lawyer. And

Janet Rehnquist (b. 1957), daughter of the chief justice, served as inspector general of the Department of Health and Human Services (HHS), another agency that has a poor record of protecting the public interest against corporate fraud.[95] Nepotism seems to be a Bush family tradition. Under Bush I, Wendy Gramm (b. 1945), former senator Phil Gramm's wife, was head of the Commodity Futures Trading Commission, which gave Enron such a sweet deal; she then was awarded a lucrative seat on the Enron board of directors.[96]

And what was Bush's Security and Exchange Commission (SEC), our watchdog against fraud by Wall Street firms, doing while unscrupulous executives at Enron Corp., WorldCom, Xerox, Global Crossing, Tyco, Qwest, Arthur Andersen, and other giant companies, using "creative" accounting procedures, ripped off taxpayers and stockholders alike? Very little. The SEC was again asleep at the switch when major mutual fund firms, notably Putnam Investments, Strong Financial, and Morgan Stanley, initiated a pattern of widespread illegal trading, a scandal that only surfaced thanks to the efforts of New York attorney general Eliot Spitzer in September 2003 (the rules don't need to be altered, Spitzer avers; "They need to be enforced").[97]

One has every reason to believe that business scandals will multiply rather than abate so long as regulatory agencies themselves continue to be headed by ex-employees of large corporations and their subsidiaries. Could the SEC, for example, really address fraud and other financial abuses when—as Senator John McCain (R-Ariz.) complained at the time—the newly appointed chair, Harvey Pitt (b. 1945), had previously served as a top lobbyist for numerous Wall Street brokerage firms and the accounting industry?[98] Democrats were even more cynical. "Choosing Harvey Pitt to patrol financial crooks," Paul Begala, a Democratic Party strategist, quipped, "is like hiring John Gotti's lawyer to run the FBI."[99] Indeed, Pitt and his congressional allies made an unsuccessful effort to stymie the Spitzer investigations.[100] "How can Bush crack the whip on Big Business," asks *New York Times* columnist Maureen Dowd, "when he's a wholly owned subsidiary of it?"[101]

Contrary to popular perception, right-wing control of government aims not only to combat regulation—thus permitting the strong to take advantage of the weak—but to *actively* support the interests of big business, which include free trade and an aggressive foreign policy. Military contractors—Bechtel, Boeing, Dow Chemical, DuPont, General Dynamics, ITT, Lockheed Martin, and Halliburton—are generally among the most enthusiastic supporters of the GOP, as are their stockholders. Moreover, in spite of their fanatical support of a free market, Republican administrations have no problem bailing out businesses that can't compete in the marketplace. A prime example is the savings and loan industry in the eighties, which took advantage of deregulation under the Reagan administration to put fabulous profits into the pockets of a few individuals before it threatened to go belly up. Financed by floating thirty-year bonds, the Reagan bailout will cost U.S. taxpayers at least $157 billion, possibly as much as $1.4 trillion, before it is all over.[102] Time and again, the U.S. business community is able to capitalize on the old strategy of socializing risk while privatizing gains.

Corporate welfare is fine; it is only welfare for the needy that seems to bother the wealthy. Best-selling author Michael Parenti sums it up as well as anyone in his book, *Democracy for the Few*:

> Conservatives are for strong or weak government depending on what interests are being served. They denounce as government "meddling" those policies that appear to move toward an equalization of life chances, income, and class, or that attempt to make business more accountable to public authority. But they usually advocate a strong government that will enforce "law and order," restrict dissent, intervene militarily in other countries, and regulate our private lives and personal morals.... Conservatives say they are for cutting government spending and bureaucracy, but the cuts they propose are selective, focusing on domestic services to the needy, while ever greater sums are given to the largest bureaucracy within the federal government—the Department of Defense.... Conservatives decry all government handouts except defense contracts, corporate subsidies, and tax breaks for business and the well-to-do.[103]

Privatization

Another conservative standby is privatization of governmental functions, an especially popular cause among free marketeers. "Free-market capitalists," as the perceptive Parenti notes, "are hostile toward any sector of the economy that performs important social services on a nonprofit basis."[104] They oppose anything public—whether a park, a school, a library, a radio station, a rescue operation for thousands of stranded poor blacks after a devastating flood, or any other operation catering to the general welfare. Anything from which they cannot extract a profit is practically taken as a personal affront.

An excellent example is Social Security. Conservatives, as we have seen, yearn to privatize the system, which would generate massive profits for the financial sector. Even though the program produced a $68 billion annual surplus in 2003,[105] right-wing Republicans, especially those with strong ties to Wall Street, have gone to great lengths to convince the American people that the system is on the verge of collapse. These fears are greatly exaggerated, according to the economist Robert Kuttner, who adds: "If the

Bush tax cuts are pared back by less than half, the money can be used to replenish Social Security, and the vaunted 'crisis' disappears. Whether to cut Social Security benefits for 96% of Americans in the system or reduce tax cuts for the top 2% is, of course, a political choice."[106]

Right-wingers have also targeted Medicare, once again relying on scare tactics. Insisting that the program is too expensive and will become unmanageable once baby boomers begin tapping into benefits, they have proposed a number of solutions, all centering on privatization. Here, too, the fear is unwarranted; the system can be fixed easily enough. Once again, it is simply a matter of priorities. Moreover, as *Newsweek* economist Jane Byrant Quinn explains, "The irony [of the right-wing campaign] is that private plans are more expensive and less efficient than traditional Medicare, which remains America's most popular program."[107]

The mania for privatization is so pronounced that even national defense has become a target.[108] During the past decade, but especially under the current Bush administration, prodded by Dick Cheney, many of the functions traditionally carried out by the Pentagon have been contracted out to private firms—opening up myriad opportunities for crony capitalism. The degree to which private citizens now perform military functions, particularly special operations, only came to the attention of the American public during the pacification of Iraq. By mid-2004, about 10 percent (some twenty thousand soldiers) of the U.S. occupation force consisted of contractors working for private companies.[109] Despite administration efforts to stonewall investigators, it came out that some of the worse abuses at Abu Ghraib prison occurred at the hands of these adjuncts, some of them former Green Berets and Navy SEALS. Apparently the Bush administration used contractors extensively because they were subject to fewer legal restrictions in combating the enemy than was the regular military, and their status under American criminal law was ill defined.

The idea that government should turn as many services as possible over to the private sector permeates the GOP. Republican politicians, however, are not shy about feeding at the public trough themselves—any more than are their political rivals. Consider Texas Republican Phil Gramm (b. 1942), at one time the biggest recipient of oil and gas money in the Senate. Although he recently retired, "Gramm, the great crusader against government spending," fellow Texan Molly Ivins charges, "has spent his entire life on the government tit. He was born at a military hospital, raised on his father's Army pay, went to private school at Georgia Military Academy on military insurance after his father died, paid for his college tuition with same, got a National Defense Fellowship to graduate school, taught at a state-supported school, and made generous use of his Senate expense account."[110] Ivins would be glad to know that Gramm is no longer on the public payroll. His new job? Working for UBS Warburg, the company that purchased Enron's trading operation.

Republican hypocrisy lives on at the very highest levels of government even while GOP leaders rail at the decline of traditional values. Consider that champion of personal responsibility William Bennett, author of the best-selling *The Book of Virtues,* who reputedly lost $8 million in casino gambling during the past decade.[111] Or consider the current occupant of the White House, a recovering alcoholic who has been arrested on three occasions (that we know of), whose wife killed a friend at the age of seventeen when she ran a stop sign, and whose underage twin daughters were busted in the summer of 2001 for trying to purchase liquor in Austin with falsified drivers' licenses. (Not to mention a sister-in-law, Jeb's wife, who tried to smuggle $19,000 worth of jewelry into the country; or a brother, Neil, who, as divorce proceedings divulged, regularly made use of prostitutes on business trips.)[112] "It would be possible—although grim and morally exhausting—to write an entire book about nothing but ethically dingy Bush business deals," claims veteran journalist Joe Conason.[113] Indeed, the president's history of shady deals as a businessman has been amply documented, though, as usual, the public remains largely oblivious.[114]

Character Counts

When Bill Clinton occupied the White House, conservative pundits continually reminded the American people that character counts. Among his most vociferous critics were Bennett, the gambler; Limbaugh, the drug abuser; and Gingrich, the adulterer. Critics were right—character counted then, and it counts now. It is doubtful anyone would confuse GOP standard-bearers George W. and Laura Bush with Ozzie and Harriet. And yet this is the God-fearing couple who provide inspiration for the Party of Family Values. A born-again Christian, the president—who declared that Jesus was his favorite political philosopher during his pursuit of the 2000 Republican presidential nomination[115]—receives the enthusiastic support of the Christian Right.

Clearly, contradictions abound in both Republican theory and practice; what drives the GOP agenda is opportunism rather than principle. Their few ideas do not work and are readily sacrificed when another opportunity looms. Still, Republican success at the polls is undeniable. Either voters do not see the inconsistencies or care little about them. How, then, have conservatives dominated at the ballot box? Lacking a consistent set of ideas, Republican political strategists have increasingly relied on an emotional appeal rather than an intellectual one. They have tapped a wide array of emotions, both positive and negative. The latter, however, have yielded the greatest political benefits. Most Americans truly believe in those principles that conservatives have packaged and marketed under the label "family values," but it is not love of family, country, or God that GOP strategists emphasize. As we shall see, it is the *threat* to those values that serves Rove and company so well. Human beings are moved more readily by fear, Machiavelli accurately perceived centuries ago, than by altruistic motives. Recognizing this reality, conservatives have tapped into these anxieties and reaped massive political advantages. Republican success has been built on a foundation of insecurity and fear.

CHAPTER SIX

CONSERVATISM AND THE POLITICS OF FEAR

The dawn of the twenty-first century found conservatives firmly in control of the major instruments of power, at both the state and the federal levels. Given the current fragmentation of the Democratic Party and the failure of liberals to offer a credible alternative—Joe Lieberman, Evan Bayh, and other party leaders are practically indistinguishable from their counterparts on the other side of the aisle—all indications are that right-wing dominance will only intensify in the immediate future.[1] How has this state of affairs come to pass? How has such a markedly antidemocratic agenda that benefits business elites at the expense of everyone else achieved such resounding success? It is not as if the right-wing agenda has been imposed by a dictatorship. In fact, election after election has been won by conservative Republicans; the elites could not have prevailed without the active collaboration of the masses. How this can be so, according to journalist Thomas Frank, is "the preeminent question of our times."[2] "In any other democracy, the majority would have coalesced by now in a populist rebellion," marvels another critic.[3]

A Typical Operation

Part of the answer is that the Republican Party has both articulated a set of coherent, integrated, and well-thought-out strategies and disseminated its views widely and effectively. As we saw previously, its dense network of think tanks and policy institutes has played an indispensable role, as has dominance of the national media. Right-wing policies were generally conceived, refined, and ultimately drafted in think tanks by well-paid merchants masquerading as scholars. Godfrey Hodgson cogently explains the process by which these pro-establishment ideas are marketed:

> A typical ... operation would begin with an article by a reputable social scientist in a journal such as *The Public Interest*. ... These "new" ideas

73

would then be discovered, commended, circulated in a host of other publications, all ultimately supported by the same ring of half a dozen foundations committed to conservative ideology. Conferences would be organized. Speakers would be carefully and selectively invited. The right (and right) journalists would be invited to attend. The favored ideas would duly circulate through media more and more closely approaching the objective mainstream until they had received the widest possible exposure and, it was hoped, acceptance. Thus the trail from the avowedly partisan conservative fringe to the op-ed columns of major newspapers could be blazed by patient, dedicated conservative scouts. If necessary, an incipient counterattack could be beaten off, sometimes with surprising *ad hominem* acerbity. Throughout, it would have been made unambiguously clear that the glittering prizes of career advancement, research posts, research assistance, publication, and promotion awaited those, and only those, who hewed close to the ideological line. Such skillful use of the carrot and the stick has succeeded in creating, in the Washington think tanks, in some newspapers and magazines, and in some university departments, a sort of conservative *nomenclature*; and this careful process has enabled the conservatives, to a remarkable degree, to drown out discordant voices.[4]

University of California linguistics professor George Lakoff points out—as do scholars Jean Stefancic and Richard Delgado—that right-wing think tanks are funded through massive unrestricted grants and are virtually guaranteed long-term funding. As a result, their fellows can develop long-term, high-level strategies that cover a wide range of issues.[5] Liberal think tanks, vastly underfunded compared with their adversaries, cannot provide their scholars this luxury.

Celebrity Sells

Using Madison Avenue techniques, conservative strategists have marketed their product, a right-wing agenda, with consummate skill. With close links to the corporate world, Republicans know what a consumer-oriented society wants—entertainment. And employing market research and public relations firms, they have proven adept at delivering the product. Television, as communications theorist Neil Postman convincingly argues in an insightful study, *Amusing Ourselves to Death,* has radically transformed political discourse, as it has virtually every other aspect of modern life.[6] Because corporate conglomerates monopolize the electronic media, they are in a position to control this discourse.

Second only to profits, television is about entertainment. When it presents information, it does so "in a form that renders it simplistic, nonsubstantive, nonhistorical and noncontextual."[7] Even the news is distorted, and not just on television. The news media in general, according to media critic Norman Solomon, "with their addiction to ratings have evolved into infotainment."[8] The process by which conglomerates have encouraged this trend, and thus destroyed the credibility of broadcast journalism, is traced by Bonnie Anderson, an ex-CNN vice president, in her revealing exposé, *News Flash.*

Serious news analysis, like investigative reporting, has been replaced, critics like Anderson lament, with a steady diet of celebrity stories. The coverage of Ronald Reagan's death provides a dramatic example (the week of his death, *Newsweek* ran a twenty-three-page feature on the popular ex-president, followed the next week by an eighteen-page lead article and several related features). The lives of "the rich and famous," safe stories that rarely offend the power elite, are less expensive to cover than hard news.[9] More important, however, as the renowned historian Haynes Johnson notes, celebrity sells.[10] And the cult of celebrity is not confined to mass culture. In 1997, the regents of the University of Wisconsin–Superior awarded an honorary doctorate to Arnold Schwarzenegger![11] Exposed to mindless programming and endless commercials, is it any wonder that the public has suffered a gradual erosion of its capacity for critical thinking? Unable to distinguish fact from fiction, the citizenry is ill equipped to handle the political responsibilities that a true democracy requires.

Moreover, because image is everything, the field of entertainment has also opened up new vistas to celebrities wishing to enter the political arena. Americans are so fascinated by celebrities that entire industries inform the public about the lives of famous personages. Autobiographies not just of the stars themselves—Bill Clinton's memoir was one of the greatest publishing successes of 2004[12]—but of the relatively inconsequential individuals who interview them, serve as their bodyguards, or even sleep with them are overnight best sellers. The GOP, drawing on its business acumen, has been quick to seize the opportunity to tap into the popularity of media stars. The corporate world has provided the model. The use of celebrities, such as Bob Hope and Ronald Reagan, to market merchandise on television was commonplace from the fifties to the seventies. (Celebrities still hawk products on television, often without acknowledging that they are being handsomely subsidized by corporate sponsors.)[13]

It was only a small step to use these popular personalities, despite the mistrust of Hollywood types by born-again Christians, to market political agendas. Then, in the eighties, the celebrities themselves were marketed as politicians. Postman notes that during this decade came a deluge of politicians who "put themselves forward, intentionally, as sources of entertainment."[14] Politicians, like everyone else on television, were required to elicit warm feelings and avoid controversy. Consequently voters are asked to vote not in their own interests but on a candidate's likeability. "We are not permitted to know who is best at being President or Governor or Senator," Postman writes, "but whose image is best in touching and soothing the deep reaches of our discontent."[15] The apotheosis of Ronald Reagan leaps to mind.

An excellent recent example is the election of Arnold Schwarzenegger to the California governorship in October 2003, after the successful recall of Democrat Gray Davis over a budgetary catastrophe largely brought on by former GOP governor Pete Wilson's deregulation of the utilities industry. "How is it possible," asked an incredulous but bemused journalist, Lewis Lapham, "to elect Arnold Schwarzenegger governor of California except in the belief that he will bring to Sacramento the secret stone of power that Conan the Barbarian rescued from the sorceress in the castle of Shain?"[16] How extraordinary that a candidate with few credentials for the job, a bodybuilder and Hollywood actor who made his name by starring in a series of violent action films, should defeat an incumbent who served as an officer and won a Bronze Star in Vietnam, graduated from an elite university (Stanford), and had many years of experience in the political arena—one, moreover, who had recently been elected fair and square by the voters of the state to be their chief executive.

Clearly, what won the Austrian-born box office star the election was his celebrity status—and that of his wife, Maria Shriver, a member of the famed Kennedy clan and a popular news reporter on national television. During the period leading up to the election, Schwarzenegger films aired endlessly on television; and the Terminator himself, though he refused to participate in debates and answer questions from legitimate journalists, was only too glad to appear as a guest on shows hosted by Oprah Winfrey, Howard Stern, Jay Leno, and Larry King.[17] He was featured simultaneously on the covers of *Time* and *Newsweek.*

Beyond name recognition, "Arnie," as a fawning media quickly dubbed the actor, also enjoyed one other awesome advantage, the trump card GOP candidates seem to always have—lots of money. His campaign raised $27 million, about a third of it coming from thirty-seven donors who provided six-figure checks, even though the "populist candidate" initially promised not to take donations from special interests.[18] Moreover, even his backers admitted that the single most important factor in getting the recall drive off the ground in the first place was the $1.7 million of his own money that conservative politician and millionaire businessman Darrell Issa shelled out to initiate and sustain the effort during its first weeks.[19] Mike Davis, an astute social commentator, observed that the new "populist" revolution that resulted in the triumph of Schwarzenegger—and the stealth return of Pete Wilson, his chief political adviser—won its most enthusiastic support not among the down-and-out but among the state's wealthiest residents, such as Mike Davis's own friends and neighbors in San Diego's most affluent suburbs.[20]

Hardball for Our Enemies

Although the Schwarzenegger camp was relatively free of mudslinging during the hard-fought battle (even though the actor himself was accused by his political opponents of chronic sexual harassment, an accusation he acknowledged), this is not always the case in GOP campaigns. The tactical ruthlessness that the young Republicans of the Nixon and Reagan years displayed in running negative political campaigns still plays well to audiences accustomed to being entertained. Consequently, the take-no-prisoner maneuvers associated with Lee Atwater and Karl Rove are continually employed today not only in political campaigns but in the media as well, especially on right-wing "shout" radio and cable television. "Democracy," E. J. Dionne Jr. observed in 1991 in his popular *Why Americans Hate Politics,* "takes on all the dignity of mud-wrestling."[21] If the situation was bad then, serious political discourse has become a rare commodity in the electronic media, where most people get their news. Not that the masses seem to mind—Fox News does much better than C-SPAN.

Big Lies

As both comedian–political analyst Al Franken and investigative journalist Joe Conason have amply documented in their 2003 best sellers, *Lies and the Lying Liars Who Tell Them* and *Big Lies,* conservative ideologues, often employing Orwellian newspeak, have consistently relied on deceit and manipulation to deliver their message to a gullible public. From the president on down, bait-and-switch techniques have been elevated to an art. "Bush's lies now fill volumes," charges columnist Molly Ivins. "He lied us into two hideously unfair tax cuts; he lied us into an unnecessary war with disastrous consequences; he lied us into the Patriot Act, eviscerating our freedoms."[22] "So constant is his fibbing," another critic of George W. Bush charges, "that a history of his lies offers a close approximation of the history of his presidential tenure."[23] The most damning personal criticism of all, however, comes from highly regarded political analyst Kevin Phillips in his recent book, *American Dynasty: Aristocracy, Fortune, and the Politics of Deceit in the House of Bush,* a searing indictment not just of the current president but of four generations of his family.

Taking their cue from the intemperate politicos, right-wing pundits have followed suit. Perhaps the most extreme has been Ann Coulter, author of three outrageous best-selling hits.[24] The mercurial pundit also has her own blog (AnnCoulter.com), one of the most popular on the conservative side. An appeal that extends even beyond her hard-core right-wing base leaves serious media scholars perplexed. Many would share the view of Susan Raskey, a senior lecturer at UC Berkeley's Graduate School of Journalism: "I would argue that Ann Coulter is provocative for the sake of being provocative. She's not attempting to make any sort of journalistic argument. I don't know what you'd call her—'pundit' seems too distinguished."[25] Unleashing the Limbaughs, the Hannitys, and the Coulters with their omissions, half-truths, and outright lies may have coarsened political discourse, but this steamroller approach has paid the GOP huge dividends.

Just Plain Folks

Another effective tactic of the populist New Right is to convince voters that the Democrats are effete intellectuals who have lost touch with their constituencies while the Republicans are the party of the people. The latter, particularly, would seem to be a hard sell considering the traditional association of the GOP with the rich since the time of FDR. Nevertheless, right-wing luminaries have proven remarkably successful in convincing the middle class that its interests are identical to those of the GOP. Indeed, conservative ideologues such as Coulter and Limbaugh are relentless in pushing the idea that they themselves are just "plain folks," not ivory tower intellectuals like their ideological opponents.

Apparently this antielitist message gets an enthusiastic welcome since even George W. Bush cannot resist the temptation, at every opportunity, to remind his audiences that he's just "like y'all," which is true—if you attended Phillips Andover, Yale, and Harvard; if your grandfather was a senator from Connecticut; and if your father was president of the United States.[26] The ruse, though, seems to work every time. "It amazes me," Morris Berman writes, "that Americans are quick to call intellectuals—who have no power at all—'elitist,' yet remain oblivious to the real oligarchic elites, which are corporate."[27] While it is hard to believe that ordinary people actually buy into this transparent egalitarian claptrap—after all, Limbaugh lives in a $30 million mansion—election results indicate otherwise.

It is clear, then, that conservatives have been much more successful than liberals in taking their message to the public. Nevertheless, the simple volume of information disseminated via the media fails to fully account for their success at the polls. The question remains: Why have voters consistently supported candidates and policies that are apparently inimical to their own self-interest?

What, Me Vote?

Part of the answer to this complex question is that many Americans have simply opted out of the system. Only about half of the electorate bothers to cast a vote in even the most important national elections (51 percent voted in the 2000 presidential election). "Politically," journalist Mark Hertsgaard remarks, "we live in a democracy that barely deserves the name. Our government lectures others on how to run elections, yet most of our own citizens don't vote. Abdication of this basic civic responsibility may be rooted partly in the complacency that affluence can breed, but surely another cause is the alienation many Americans feel from a political system they correctly perceive as captive to the rich and the powerful."[28]

Political lethargy is most pronounced among the youth, who are distracted by a multitude of other priorities, the media for one. Sitting before a television set four hours a day, a national average, leaves little time for anything else, nor does it do much to hone critical thinking skills.[29] Youth are also understandably distracted by the demands of school, late adolescence, family, and dating.

Political apathy also runs rampant among the impoverished, who are preoccupied with immediate concerns, including putting food on the table. The working poor, moreover, are conditioned to act passively on their jobs. Social researcher Barbara Ehrenreich explains:

> If low-wage workers do not always behave in an economically rational way, that is, as free agents within a capitalist democracy, it is because they dwell in a place that is neither free nor in any way democratic. When you enter the low-wage workplace—and many of the medium-wage workplaces as well—you check in your civil liberties at the door, leave America and all it supposedly stands for behind, and learn to zip your lips for the duration of the shift. The consequences of this routine surrender go beyond the issues of wages and poverty. We can hardly pride ourselves on being the world's preeminent democracy, after all, if large numbers of citizens spend half their waking hours in what amounts, in plain terms, to a dictatorship.[30]

Although difficult to quantify, another cause of the pronounced apathy of Americans in general, not just the youth and the impoverished, is the high incidence of drug use. "Although marijuana remains illegal," claims journalist Ruth Rosen, "mind-altering drugs are as common as a double latte or a Big Mac."[31] How can we expect people to meet their civic responsibilities when we live in a medicated society? This point is made forcefully by the historian Morris Berman, who adds that a vital democracy requires a citizenry that actually wants to get out of bed every morning.[32]

Given the lethargy of large segments of the population, huge numbers of Americans have paid scant attention to the workings of government. Unquestioningly obedient to authority, many citizens have lost sight of their own true interests. For example, ample evidence suggests, according to Princeton political scientist Larry Bartels, that most middle- and lower-income Americans who support the Bush tax policies "have failed to connect the tax cuts to rising inequality, their future tax burden or the availability of government services"; not realizing that they themselves will be the victims, they are in fact motivated by what Bartels calls "unenlightened self-interest."[33]

In the past few years, then, large segments of the American population simply haven't been paying attention. Writer Robert D. Kaplan foresees a time when the problem will grow worse. "Increasingly," he muses, ". . . one can be an expatriate without living abroad. One can have Oriental rugs, foreign cuisines, eclectic tastes, exposure to foreign languages, friends overseas with whom one's life increasingly intertwines, and special schools for the kids—all at home. Resident expatriatism, or something resembling it, could become the new secular religion of the upper-middle and upper classes, fostered by communications technology."[34] At the moment, however, it is not clear why the affluent would forsake a political system that has served them so well for so long.

Indeed, the people who *do* count in political calculations and actually exercise their vote today come predominantly from the well-to-do. A significant number of these voters—perhaps a third of the middle class—back the Republican Party for perfectly rational reasons: They benefit directly and immediately from conservative policies. These boosters include owners, managers, and major shareholders in large corporations and the lawyers of the top legal firms who represent these powerful organizations. Writing in 1959, Columbia University professor C. Wright Mills commented that "every one of the very rich families [in America] has been and is closely connected—always legally and frequently managerially as well—with one of the multi-million dollar corporations."[35] This nexus is even more evident today. Sometimes labeled the superrich, their incomes are in the top 1 percent, which means they made at least $293,000 in 2001.[36]

Identification with the Aggressor

Beyond these elites, however, self-interest also dictates that corporate employees, from executives to janitors, will support probusiness policies. It is not difficult, for example, to convince an aircraft worker in Seattle or St. Louis that what's good for Boeing is good for America. Thus, the privileged set extends well beyond the superrich, or even the upper class, and incorporates the upper-middle class. (Already by the late 1980s, Ehrenreich estimated, more than 60 percent of this class—made up predominantly of managers and professionals—"earns its living in the direct service of corporate power.")[37] Their numbers are most evident in the suburbs of the nation's major metropolitan areas, especially in the newer, upscale outer suburbs, where every third vehicle is an SUV and gourmet restaurants are packed even at midweek. Political economist Robert Reich refers to these privileged elites, who dominate the upper ranks of the political as well as the corporate hierarchies, as "the fortunate fifth" since he estimates that collectively they represent the upper quintile of the nation's wage earners.[38] (*Harper's Magazine* editor Lewis Lapham prefers the term "the equestrian classes.")[39]

However, most voters are not directly tied to corporations, at least not yet. Indeed, their interests mostly tend to run counter to those of the elites. Mostly members of the middle class, they expect to enjoy hard-earned entitlements such as Medicare and Social Security. Yet during the past thirty or thirty-five years, huge numbers of these same voters have regularly sustained the Republican Party with its regressive tax policies and escalating assault on the welfare state. This was not always the case. From the thirties through the sixties, the middle class tended to vote solidly in favor of Democratic candidates in national elections. Defections to the GOP began under Nixon; they became an avalanche under Reagan ("Reagan Democrats"); and, after flirting with Clinton, they seem to have returned to the Republican fold under George W. Bush. How has the GOP been able to win this battle for the hearts and minds of Americans so completely?

"Moral Values"

According to George Lakoff, the GOP has constructed a kind of popular appeal. Specifically, he posits that Republicans, in contrast to their Democratic rivals, have displayed a much greater appreciation of human psychology. They have understood and employed a key concept discovered by Freud in the late nineteenth century: People are moved less by rational arguments than by emotional appeals. The emphasis on moral messages, religious and otherwise, has paid rich dividends to GOP strategists such as Paul Weyrich and Ralph Reed. Dominated by the secular humanistic tradition emanating from the eighteenth-century Enlightenment, liberal Democrats have been slow to grasp this truth. "As long as liberals ignore moral, mythic and emotional dimensions," Lakoff, himself a staunch liberal, cautions, "they will have no hope."[40]

Undoubtedly, the conservative emphasis on moral values has resonated with significant segments of the American public, especially those who take their religion seriously. However, even hard-core traditionalists must feel, from time to time, a lingering suspicion that the champions of the Republican Party and particularly its chief beneficiaries, "the rich and the famous," hardly enjoy a monopoly on family values. Republican success at the polls exhibits, rather, a different dimension: the appeal to baser instincts.

Fear

To understand the conservative ascendancy, both politically and intellectually, one has to appreciate the widespread *fear* that haunts American society, as filmmaker Michael Moore illustrates in his popular 2002 documentary *Bowling for Columbine.* This at the very moment, ironically, when our nation has emerged as the only superpower on the globe, when we appear to be so self-confident, even arrogant in our dealings with other nations.

The roots of this insecurity—which some observers date from the Kennedy assassination in 1963—are complex. As mentioned previously, the rise of formerly disenfranchised populations—notably women and racial minorities—on the one hand, and the emergence of secular humanism, on the other, are important factors. The loss of the Vietnam War, too, created a crisis of conscience. It is almost impossible for young people today to appreciate how divisive the conflict in Southeast Asia was and how much soul-searching America went through in the aftermath. Massive immigration into the country, mostly from underdeveloped areas, has altered the American cultural landscape dramatically, calling into question the whole notion of what it means to be an American.[41] Immigration, however, was but one cause of xenophobia.

International terrorism became more than simply a nuisance after September 11, 2001, when American complacency shattered irrevocably. Though shock waves reached every corner of life, politics experienced the greatest impact. The Bush administration was quick to seize on the pervasive fears generated by the jihadists for its own ends, easily winning popular support for the enactment of a host of programs, notably the USA PATRIOT Act, which gave the chief executive virtually unprecedented powers.[42] Moreover, in the presidential elections following that singular act of terrorism, his handlers deftly portrayed George W. Bush, a Vietnam War draft dodger, as a resolute wartime leader—while his opponent, John Kerry, a decorated war veteran, was accused of being wavering and indecisive—thus paving the way for Bush's 2004 reelection.

This fraudulently whipped-up fear has powerful social and political consequences. Social scientists have long known that in times of crisis, citizens rally around a strong leader and are impatient with critics. The perception of threat solidifies followers, boosts patriotism, and strengthens support for military action. Conservatives trade on all these fears. [43] Leo Strauss taught that intellectuals should spread an ideology of good versus evil, to mobilize the ordinary people against the enemies of freedom. The neoconservatives learned his lesson all too well.

This is not, of course, to deny that terrorism is real or that fear and vigilance are not rational responses to foreign threats. The world is a dangerous place. But neoconservatives have gone far beyond what is warranted to safeguard our security. They have eroded civil liberties more than is necessary or desirable and may have made the nation less, not more, secure by alienating our allies and inflaming the Arab world.

Job Insecurity

Second to terror as a profound cause of insecurity has been the series of economic dislocations wrought by globalization—defined by Nobel Prize–winning economist Joseph Stiglitz as "the closer integration of the countries of the world as a result of lowering of transportation and communication costs." [44] The historian William C. Berman, professor emeritus at the University of Toronto, points out that America's rightward turn was hardly unique; much of western Europe—notably England under Margaret Thatcher and Italy under its wealthiest citizen, Silvio Berlusconi—followed the same path. [45] The common denominator, he argues, is the changing global economy, particularly the expansion of international markets and labor pools. These extraordinary changes, observes Kevin Phillips, have been as momentous as those that accompanied the Industrial Revolution of the eighteenth century. [46]

Globalization, as many scholars have noted, naturally privileges the GOP. [47] After all, as Morris Berman explains, greater investments in complexity are always "accompanied by a greater share of the pie for the elite." [48] Among the many destabilizing consequences has been the virtual destruction of trade unions under the impact of massive immigration from abroad and the ability of multinational corporations to find cheap labor in underdeveloped regions of the globe.

Job security among U.S. wage earners is rapidly fading. More and more workers are being forced into part-time employment, a trend that has increased threefold since 1968. [49] Two-thirds of Kmart's workforce and almost all of Starbucks' employees are part-timers. [50] (This same trend is evident in institutions of higher learning.) Corporations are also increasing profits by outsourcing jobs and by hiring workers on long-term temporary contracts. The use of "temp" labor in the United States, according to award-winning investigative journalist Naomi Klein, increased 400 percent from 1982 to 2000. [51] By the mid-1990s, Manpower Temporary

Services, an international temporary employment agency, had replaced General Motors as America's largest private employer.[52] Needless to say, these kinds of low-wage jobs, called "McJobs" by critics, bring few fringe benefits or none at all. While Clinton's welfare reforms managed to get some people off the welfare rolls and into the workforce, many of them still remained impoverished—despite the rosy predictions made by conservatives—given the meager wages provided by businesses such as McDonald's and Wal-Mart.[53]

The fear of modernization that some scholars see as the essence of the fascist revolution of the twenties and thirties seems to be very much in evidence today. In some quarters, the fear accompanying the breakdown in traditional society has become almost pathological. How else can one explain the huge upsurge in interest in the Apocalypse among evangelical Christians, reflected in the extraordinary success of the "Left Behind" novels coauthored by New Right activists Reverend Tim LaHaye and Jerry Jenkins (over sixty-two million copies sold)?[54]

Alienated? Pick a Scapegoat

The Republican Party has been masterful in tapping into this discontent. It has done so by creating a series of scapegoats and playing on popular fears, time-tested tactics since the days of Senator Joseph McCarthy.[55] Captured by the New Right in the seventies, the GOP, though thoroughly modern itself, according to journalist William Greider, was now prepared to pose "as the bulwark against unsettling modernity."[56] Greider, one of America's most astute political commentators, observes in this regard:

> In this period of history, it is perhaps not an accident that so many of the effective political managers are southerners. The South understands alienation better than the rest of the nation. Feelings that were once peculiar to a single section of America—the defeated region within the nation—have now taken over the national mood. The winning strategies of modern Republicans owe more to George Wallace than to Barry Goldwater.[57]

Indeed, the politics of fear so characteristic of the South at one time are pervasive throughout the country today and largely define the modern conservative movement. At the outset, in the seventies and eighties, Communists were the scapegoat of choice for the New Right, red-baiting the best tactic in the Republican repertoire for mobilizing mass support. (The only place where red-baiting still works today as effectively as it did thirty years ago is Dade County, Florida.) Ronald Reagan got a lot of mileage out of his crusade against "the evil empire" (a term coined by Reagan speechwriter

Tony Dolan). As Joe Conason, author of *Big Lies,* illustrates, with the end of the Cold War in 1989–1990, the GOP discovered that liberals were even worse than Communists.[58] The permissiveness rampant in society in the aftermath of the eighties, the "Me Decade," was conveniently blamed not on Reagan or even consumer capitalism, where it belonged, but on liberal intellectuals, the group that the New Right had contemptuously labeled the New Class in the seventies.[59] The antiliberal crusade, under the leadership of Newt Gingrich, preached a continuing struggle between good and evil. One of Gingrich's young admirers at the time later recalled the tremendous appeal of the Georgia firebrand's message: "The apocalyptic 'us versus them' paradigm was gratifying, for it held out the promise of assuaging my insecurities and giving me a sense of finally belonging."[60]

Weird Oriental Terrorists with Curved Swords and Shoe Bombs

More recently, especially after September 11, the fear of Islamic terrorists has served the Republican agenda, especially the bellicose pro-Israel neoconservatives, nearly as well as the fear of political radicals. Iraqis fighting against an illegal occupation of their own country are routinely labeled "insurgents" or "terrorists."[61] These labels have been used to discredit virtually anyone the Bush administration opposes. Recall how, angered by opposition to GOP educational policies, Bush's first education secretary, Rod Paige, went so far as to charge that the largest teachers' union in the United States, the National Education Association, was a terrorist society! Terrorist warnings by the Department of Homeland Security have been commonplace in the past three years, keeping the American people on the edge of panic. "The Bush administration is deliberately fostering fear," warns philanthropist George Soros, a staunch critic of George W. Bush and his policies, "because it helps to keep the nation lined up behind the president."[62] Even administration sympathizers see the danger. "Every other word out of this administration's mouth is 'terror' or 'terrorism,'" laments syndicated columnist Thomas L. Friedman, a three-time Pulitzer Prize winner who lent his support to the recent Iraq war. "We have stopped exporting hope, the most important commodity America has."[63] (Ironically, the United States government has not hesitated to use terrorism itself or sponsor state terrorism in other lands when this policy suited its purposes, as Noam Chomsky has amply documented.)[64]

The Party of the White Man

Ultimately the paranoia that has benefited the GOP the longest and the most successfully has been racism: "Race," according to Greider, "is only one of the bridges [used by conservatives to link their divergent constituencies] though surely the most powerful."[65] As sociologists Michael Omi and Howard Winant have shown, most students of the rise of the New Right have understated "the crucial importance of *race* as a defining issue."[66] Perhaps the writer who has done the most to make the linkage between racism and recent Republican victories is *Washington Post* journalist Thomas Byrne Edsall, particularly in his landmark 1992 best seller, *Chain Reaction,* written with his wife, Mary Edsall.[67]

With the adoption of the southern strategy by Richard Nixon in 1968, the Edsalls and other students of the New Right illustrate, the Republicans decided to play the race card. It was a calculated gamble that has paid huge dividends for the party, as GOP strategist Kevin Phillips foresaw at the time (the same Kevin Phillips who today makes a living by writing excellent studies critical of his old party).[68] In fact, this momentous decision is as important in the history of the Republicans as was the abandonment of southern blacks during Reconstruction in the interests of northern industrialists, thus initiating the transformation of the party of Lincoln into the party of big business that it remains today.[69] The appeal to racial prejudice, coded and overt, explains to a large extent why voters have often been willing to support conservative causes that seem to fly in the face of their own self-interest (and, Ehrenreich makes abundantly clear, this is true not only of the much-maligned working class—"Charley Six-Pack"—but also of the middle classes). Such inconsistency is especially the case in the South, the citadel of GOP strength. As Alabama native Diane McWhorter puts it:

> What the racist Southern gentlemen of old and the modern-day Republicans have both cannily appreciated is that poor people do not like to consider themselves poor. Low-income whites would rather identify with rich folks than with their own class, especially if their partners in poverty happen to be black. That helps to explain why, in clinging to its nostalgia for the underdog ("special interests" to the uberdogs), the pre-Clinton Democratic Party lost much of its base—the Reagan Democrats—to the rival party. The now Solid Republican South is a tribute to the cleverness of the haves at getting the have-nots to work against their own interests. The main attraction the Republicans hold for the "regular people" who make up the bulk of their Southern constituency is that they are the party of the white man.[70]

In other words, poor southern whites today pursue the same objective that led them to fight to preserve the Peculiar Institution during the Civil War, even though they received minimal benefits from the status quo ante bellum—white supremacy.[71]

Yet this race-based GOP strategy has proven nearly as successful in Boston and Chicago as in Selma and Little Rock, resulting in what the historian Godfrey Hodgson has labeled the "Southernization" of national politics.[72] In the North and other parts of the country, reacting in part to the mass exodus of southern blacks into their cities, whites had been migrating to the suburbs since the fifties, isolating themselves from the urban poor (71 percent of the white population would reside in suburbs by the end of the century).[73] Left behind in the inner city were impoverished whites and people of color, particularly blacks.

More recently, as author Mike Davis points out, minorities, too, have become suburbanites, but the basic problems remain as the white population moves from old suburbs, increasingly brown in complexion, farther out from the city centers, into so-called edge cities, suburbs that provide jobs as well as exclusive residential tracts, new and old suburbs now competing for diminishing resources.[74] Typical is the greater Los Angeles metropolitan area, where old white suburbs, fashionable residential areas in the fifties, in places such as the San Fernando Valley, have become densely populated by people of color, and white residents have relocated to rapidly growing, affluent communities on the periphery such as Simi Valley, Palmdale, and Palm Desert.

Sociologist Andrew Barlow elaborates on the relationship between race and suburban communities: "Explicit racial discrimination by developers, realtors, banks, government agencies, and individual home buyers revealed the widespread awareness of the importance of race in the suburbs: These new communities were seen from the beginning as privileged places whose residents were going to do whatever they could to improve the quality of their personal lives at the expense of urban America—that is, people of color."[75] Living in lily-white settings, these new suburbanites were especially vulnerable to conservative arguments that essentially justified the continuing assertion of white privileges. These white suburbs today represent the citadel of Republican strength in many parts of the country.

Black gains in the aftermath of the landmark 1954 Supreme Court decision *Brown v. Board of Education* precipitated a revolution in the American political landscape. In the South, anxieties born of the civil rights movement, "which sought not to survive racial oppression, but to overthrow it," reached a fever pitch after the passage of the Civil Rights Act of 1964 and the Voting Rights Act of 1965.[76] These fears, also fanned by the race riots of the mid-1960s, found expression in the surprisingly strong showing by George Wallace in his 1964 and 1968 bids for the presidency. Nor was his electoral support confined to the South; the Alabama governor managed to make inroads into some traditional Democratic strongholds in the Northwest and Midwest. Wallace made race the central issue of his campaign—apparently the source of his appeal to large segments of the electorate. After losing his bid for the Alabama governorship in 1958 to a fanatic antiblack bigot, Wallace had sworn that "no other son-of-a-bitch will ever out-nigger me again."[77]

Wallace's influence on Republicans proved incalculable, though it is probably a legacy that few movement conservatives would willingly acknowledge, at least in public. Seeing the racial hysteria engendered by the prospect of a black resurgence—the one thing whites dread most, says political scientist Andrew Hacker, is that blacks will treat *them* as contemptibly as they have treated blacks historically[78]—Paul Weyrich and other GOP strategists, many of them Barry Goldwater supporters in 1964, sensed that the time was ripe to woo southern Democrats. It was no mean task, given traditional ties to a vehicle that had served the South for so long and so well. But in the end, the tacit endorsement of the doctrine of racial supremacy by GOP conservatives proved irresistible. (Tellingly, during the mid-1970s, Weyrich, Richard Viguerie, and Howard Phillips abandoned the Republican Party, temporarily, in an unsuccessful attempt to gain control of Wallace's Klan-ridden American Independent Party.)[79] By the mid-1970s, the ex-Dixiecrats had abandoned the Democrats and were being welcomed into the GOP. Appropriately, this shift came to completion under Nixon, who saw blacks as genetically inferior, according to loyal lieutenant John Ehrlichman.[80]

If Nixon displayed little concern for the welfare of black communities, Ronald Reagan exhibited even less—the former, after all, did pass *some* civil rights legislation. Insisting alternately that racism was no longer relevant, that America was now "color-blind"—"in a world where racial privilege is structured into everyday life," Andrew Barlow reasons, "the best defense of racial privilege is to deny that it exists"[81]—and then turning around and assuring whites that it was *they* who were the victims of reverse discrimination, the ex-actor cynically appealed to white privilege. He proved immensely successful: In 1980, 22 percent of the Democrats—virtually all of them white—defected to vote for the GOP candidate.[82]

"On issues of race," historian Dan Carter states, "Reagan compiled an abysmal record in his sixteen years as governor of California and president of the United States."[83] As both governor and president, the ex-Democrat consistently opposed civil rights legislation. In California, he attempted to repeal the Rumford Act, which outlawed housing discrimination based on religion or race, and even criticized the Civil Rights Act of 1964 and the Voting Rights Act of 1965. "That his policies are not only unfair," Roger Wilkins charged in 1984, "but also demonstrably racist is crystal clear."[84] Time after time, the Great White Hope sponsored legislation that sacrificed the interests of blacks and other minorities for those of the wealthy elites that he knew and loved.

"His friends," a Reagan biographer noted, "were people like himself, successful self-made men who enjoyed the good California life.... Like

Reagan, many of them had left behind humble origins to come west to find their destiny. They, too, had invented themselves. Their proudly displayed trappings of success, Mercedeses and Jaguars, their oceanfront and desert vacation hideaways, were emblems of worth."[85] These friends included multimillionaires, notably oil geologist Henry Salvatori, brewer Joseph Coors, and publisher Walter Annenberg.

In fact, the president seemed to have little compassion for the less fortunate members of society generally, the main victims of his supply-side economic policies. Yale University scholar Harold Bloom later gave a candid assessment of this aspect of Mr. Reagan's inheritance: "I think that the United States has been almost destroyed by Ronald Reagan and his legacy. He came into office that charming, smiling fellow, and he assured us we could all emancipate our selfishness, and that is what we have proceeded to do on a national level. And I think we have done terrible things to the poorer people in this country."[86]

Not only poor Americans suffered under his watch. During his administrations, Reagan launched wars against a series of lightweight nations—Lebanon, Libya, Grenada, Nicaragua, and El Salvador—all of them inhabited by people of color. Reagan may have been "remarkably popular" among white Americans, but minorities were considerably less sanguine in their judgment; by a three-to-one majority, blacks agreed that the ex–Hollywood actor was a racist.[87]

Of course, this charge is considered blasphemous today by conservatives, who can brook no criticism of their favorite president—witness their successful 2003 campaign to have CBS pull its television miniseries on the Great Communicator (it was not celebratory enough).[88] During the past decade, right-wingers have waged a concerted crusade to raise the status of the Alzheimer's-afflicted former president (whose approval rating was a modest 40 percent in 1987), and with considerable success.[89] Shortly before his death, they attempted to elevate Reagan to secular sainthood by promoting a campaign to have his visage replace that of Franklin D. Roosevelt on the dime. Only Nancy Reagan's intervention put an end to this initiative; her husband, after all, had voted for FDR on four occasions.[90]

A New England patrician, George H. W. Bush could afford to take the high road on racial issues, but even he was perfectly willing to use the race card as an electoral tactic. Trailing Michael Dukakis in the 1988 presidential campaign, a desperate Bush agreed to let Lee Atwater and advertising man Roger Ailes air the notorious Willie Horton ad, an inflammatory piece of racial propaganda. Released from prison on a furlough program instituted in Massachusetts by then-governor Dukakis, Horton, a black man convicted of homicide, escaped and committed a brutal rape before he was recaptured. The controversial ad linking Horton with the Democratic candidate played on widespread racial fears among voters and saved the day for Bush.[91]

When the going got tough, George Bush Jr., too, turned to what had by now become the most reliable vote getter in the Republican arsenal—race baiting. Trailing John McCain in the polls during the Republican primaries in 2000, Bush had his operatives in South Carolina use racial innuendo to discredit his foe, win the state election, and practically assure himself the party nomination. No one ever discovered the identity of the person who put into circulation the vicious fabrication that the Arizona senator had had a love child by a black prostitute, but Karl Rove's fingerprints were everywhere.[92]

Fear of Immigrants

Fueling racist fears in the beginning of the twenty-first century has been the huge influx of immigrants, mainly Latinos, both legal and illegal, due to the liberalization of U.S. immigration laws in the mid-1960s. Unlike the great waves of immigrants one hundred years before, predominantly European in origin, the overwhelming numbers today are people of color. Groups such as the Federation for American Immigration Reform (FAIR), founded in 1979 by John H. Tanton, and U.S. English, the oldest and largest English-only organization, cofounded in 1983 by Tanton and S. I. Hayakawa, fan anti-immigrant resentment. A retired ophthalmologist, Tanton (b. 1935) has founded or cofounded thirteen anti-immigrant organizations, including three considered hate groups by the Southern Poverty Law Center.[93] Opportunistic politicians quickly climbed on the bandwagon as well. The most strident jingoists in the public arena in recent years have been Ross Perot, Pat Buchanan, and Representative Tom Tancredo. As social historian David Montejano has observed, "The 'crowded lifeboat' has become the metaphor of choice for anti-immigrant pundits."[94] "By the mid-1990s," he asserts, "the anti-immigrant campaign had become generalized into a sweeping anti-minority one."[95] Not surprisingly, the anti-immigration campaign has been heavily subsidized by the Pioneer Fund, a right-wing foundation that makes no apologies for its extreme views.[96]

Racial hysteria has been most pronounced in California, the destination of about one-third of these newcomers entering the country. "The political backlash resulting from recent demographic transformations has been perhaps more extreme in California than elsewhere," the urban sociologist Janet L. Abu-Lughod concurs, "a backlash that, because of the 'over-representation' of remaining Anglos on the voter rolls, has up to now been relatively unrestrained by counterforces."[97] Colorado has not been far behind.[98]

Mexicans, the largest single national group entering the country since 1960, are dramatically changing the ethnic landscape of the Golden State, particularly the southland.[99] Predominantly Indian, most Mexicans see themselves, and are seen by others, as nonwhite. These hardworking immigrants (how often do you see a Latino panhandler?) are the most convenient scapegoats when the economy suffers a downturn, something that California experienced in the late eighties and early nineties.[100] Anti-immigrant sentiment during the severe recession gave rise to a number of popular state measures. These included Proposition 63 in 1986, making English the official language; Proposition 187 in 1994, denying state services to illegal immigrants (subsequently declared unconstitutional); Proposition 209 in 1996, banning government affirmative action programs; and Proposition 227 in 1998, repealing bilingual education.

The enthusiastic support for these ballot initiatives among voters, particularly in the southern part of the state, reflects the growing fear of people of color, both native and foreign born. "Hispanics in America today," claims English First president Larry Pratt, "represent a very dangerous, subversive force that is bent on taking over our nation's political institutions for the purpose of imposing Spanish as the official language of the United States."[101]

This view is popular among some members of the intellectual elite. Samuel P. Huntington, the respected Harvard political scientist, is the most prominent of these critics. Given their massive numbers and non-European origins, Huntington sees the new immigrants, particularly Mexicans, as a major threat to the American way of life, which he defines as Anglo and Protestant.[102] While he met with almost universal acclaim in right-wing circles, so outspoken was the Ivy League scholar in expressing nativist (by his own admission) views that he evoked a storm of protest among laypeople and academics alike.[103]

Abu-Lughod, who spent almost a year living and working in Los Angeles, recalls a graphic illustration of this paranoia: Along the half mile of upscale residences between her apartment and the UCLA campus, she once counted 176 signs threatening trespassers with "armed response" from private protection agencies.[104] Out in the more modest suburbs of Los Angeles, ethnic tensions often result in hate crimes and other manifestations of a "low-intensity race war."[105]

This anxiety caused by a rapidly changing demography is not confined to California and the Southwest, where Mexican barrios have been in place for over two hundred years. The 2000 U.S. census shows that Mexican-origin people have become a national, not simply a regional, minority, and some 40 percent of them are immigrants.[106] Numbering 38.8 million in 2003, *mexicanos* and other Latinos—a category that has now surpassed blacks as the country's largest minority—constitute 14 percent of the U.S. population, and their numbers will only escalate in the future, given high birthrates and current levels of immigration.[107] Already in 1997, 80 percent of the children enrolled in the Los Angeles Unified School District, the second largest in the nation, were of Spanish-speaking background.[108] Because many businesspeople see immigrants as a cheap source of labor as well as a means of breaking unions, the Republican Party is split on the question of immigration, as the campaigns surrounding the California propositions have illustrated.[109] Nevertheless, party strategists have not hesitated to manipulate nativist sentiments for their own ends.

Exploiting Racial Fears

The terrorist attacks of September 11, 2001, only heightened American fears of both immigrants and people of color. The Bush administration's manipulation of anti-Islamic and anti-Arab prejudices to gain moral and financial support for the war on terrorism both at home and abroad—as well as partisan advantage—did not escape Islamic community leaders in the United States, whose support of Bush was lukewarm in the 2004 election.

Adept at manipulating racial fears to advance the conservative agenda, Republican politicians and political pundits reserve out-and-out racist remarks for the friendly confines of their country clubs—with notable exceptions such as legendary race warriors Jesse Helms and Pat Buchanan. In public forums, the racism generally emerges in coded language, such as diatribes on welfare queens, busing, terror, immigration, affirmative action, and ghetto crime.[110]

Consider New York mayor Rudolph Giuliani's actions during his 1999 quest for a U.S. Senate seat (ill health later forced his withdrawal). During the hotly contested campaign, the fifty-five-year-old Catholic Italian American candidate launched a blistering attack against the depiction of a black Virgin Mary by black artist Chris Ofili. He did so without mentioning color, a calculated strategy that gained him, despite his marital infidelities, not only Catholic votes but white votes generally. The historian David R. Roediger comments on the significance: "Without mentioning race—indeed precisely by not mentioning race when it was patently obvious—Giuliani placed himself in a growing line of politicians who mobilize white votes with ostensibly raceless words."[111] While politicians excel at the game, media pundits, including Sean Hannity, Michael Savage, David Horowitz, Bill O'Reilly, and Ann Coulter, have elevated it to high art. "In fact," a Wallace biographer concludes, "George Wallace would probably come across as a mealymouthed moderate when juxtaposed with today's right-wing-radical talk-show hosts."[112] And books by these pundits, who pretend to be color-blind, are always best sellers—so much so that mainstream book publishers are joining right-wing stalwarts such as publishing house Alfred A. Regnery in aggressively pursuing conservative authors.[113]

All These Beautiful White People

What explains the phenomenal success of 1994's *The Bell Curve: Intelligence and Class Structure in American Life,* an eight-hundred-page bestseller written by Charles Murray and the late Richard J. Herrnstein, which argues that whites are genetically superior to blacks? The book, labeled "a manifesto of conservative ideology" by the late Stephen Jay Gould, received wide coverage in the media.[114] As Andrew Barlow notes, "One can gauge the extent to which racism is becoming intensified by the emergence of genetic racism."[115] Given the changing intellectual climate, even mainstream conservatives now feel almost as comfortable as the Far Right in reviving the discredited idea of biological racism.

Racism is today much more than an electoral ploy; it pervades the American Right. Everyone recognizes that this is so with the ultraright conspiracy-obsessed radicals in the Ku Klux Klan, the Aryan Brotherhood, the LaRouche network, the Church of the Creator, the Christian Identity movement, and literally hundreds of other fringe groups that cannot make up their mind who they detest more—Jews or racial minorities. The bigotry of these ultras—manifested in the scapegoating of a variety of historically disenfranchised groups in addition to the ethnics—is well documented by Chip Berlet and Matthew N. Lyons in their 2000 study, *Right-Wing Populism in America.* But, as the authors also illustrate, racism and the manipulation of racism for partisan advantage, though less pronounced, typify the more respectable Right.

Since most mainstream conservatives continue to disavow biological racism, their true sentiments are much harder to gauge. Occasionally, in unguarded moments, slips of the tongue reveal deeper prejudices by mainstream conservatives, as in 1980 when Nancy Reagan gushed to a group of admirers in New Hampshire that she wished her husband could be there to "see all these beautiful white people," a faux pas she immediately regretted.[116] Two well-publicized incidents in 2003 illustrate the point. The first occurred when Republican senator Trent Lott from Mississippi wistfully evoked segregationist policies at a celebration of Strom Thurmond's hundredth birthday, a gaffe that forced him to step down as majority leader in the Senate. Later, fellow right-wing champion—and famous drug addict—Rush Limbaugh, who for some odd reason was hired as a football commentator by ESPN for its *NFL Sunday Countdown,* felt obliged to suggest on the air that the National Football League had given star treatment to Philadelphia Eagles black quarterback Donovan McNabb because of his race rather than his ability, an inflammatory remark that led to his resignation.[117] In both cases, right-wing media pundits displayed uncharacteristic compassion, coming to the defense of the two "victims" against their "politically correct" critics.

Establishment Blacks

Playing the race game can be tricky. While conservatives unceasingly appeal to their base, well-to-do whites, they also desire to recruit greater numbers of minority voters into their ranks. This campaign has enjoyed little success. Only 10 percent of the black vote went to Bush in the 2000 election.[118] The GOP has enjoyed only slightly better luck in pursuing an allied strategy—one suggested by none other than Karl Marx himself—co-opting leaders of the oppressed community.[119] Party strategists have been able to entice a small cadre of minority intellectuals and pundits into their ranks, people worth their weight in gold. Typical is Linda Chavez, whose *Out of the Barrio,* an attack on entitlements for Hispanics, received funding by the John M. Olin Foundation, the Angeles T. Arredondo Foundation, the Lynde and Harry Bradley Foundation, and the Strake Foundation. Her latest book, continuing in the neoconservative tradition of beating up on lightweights, is an attack on labor unions.[120] Other Hispanic heroes of the Right include the late Richard Estrada, Roger Hernandez, and Ruben Navarrette Jr.[121] Among blacks, the best-known conservative voices are Shelby Steele, Thomas Sowell, Walter Williams, Larry Elder, Ward Connerly, Armstrong Williams, and Ken Hamblin.[122]

The strength of antiminority sentiment is so pronounced among conservatives, however, that even these subsidized fellow travelers—most of whom enjoy close ties to right-wing think tanks—have often found themselves alienated from the GOP mainstream. In 1988, for example, a private memo by John Tanton, cofounder of U.S. English, was leaked to the press. The communication was so vitriolic in its condemnation of the alleged sexual debauchery of Latinos that an irate Chavez, then chair of the English-only organization, resigned her post in protest.[123] A few years later, when the American Enterprise Institute (AEI) helped to finance the publication of Dinesh D'Souza's *The End of Racism,* essentially endorsing racism, two prominent black conservatives affiliated with the AEI, Robert L. Woodson Sr., founder of the National Center for Neighborhood Enterprise, a Washington, D.C.-based research and development agency, and Glenn Loury, a professor of economics at Boston University, left the think tank, charging racial bigotry.[124]

Finally, many political opponents suspect that it was his party's failure to seriously address black issues and to take him seriously that led J. C. Watts, ex–University of Oklahoma football star and the only black GOP representative in the House, to quit Congress in 2002.[125] (Though declining to run for reelection, the Southern Baptist preacher, who sits on the board of directors of Clear Channel, continues to be politically active, serving as chair of GOPAC, an organization that develops GOP candidates for state office.)[126] In light of this poor track record, one wonders how comfortable Colin Powell and Condoleezza Rice could have felt on the

2000 Bush team, especially the latter, whose function as national security adviser was essentially usurped by Dick Cheney.[127]

Voting for Colonel Sanders

After reviewing "conservatism's awful racial record," Conason concludes, "To anyone familiar with this shabby history, the inescapable question is not why more minorities don't flock to conservatism and vote Republican. The wonder is why any would at all."[128] Among the perplexed is Watts's own father, Buddy, who once quipped that "a Black man voting for the Republicans is like a chicken voting for Colonel Sanders."[129] But the GOP cannot be too disappointed. On balance, the subtle racism it promotes gains it more support among mainstream voters than it loses among minorities. Herein is found the key to much of its success in recent decades.

"The dominant politics of this era," according to scholar Andrew Barlow, "has been to galvanize and appeal to white middle-class voters' fear of falling. From anti-immigrant policies to attacks on civil rights policies such as affirmative action, to a high-profile war on drugs, to the expansion of prisons and the use of the death penalty, to the war on terrorism, politicians have become highly skilled at creating dangerous foes to attack and contain."[130]

Right-Wing Catholics

Fear, too, is the key to understanding another aspect of modern conservatism: the pivotal, though little-appreciated, role played by Catholics among both the GOP rank and file and, more especially, among the leadership. As one surveys the roster of right-wing operatives during the past half-century, one is struck by the unusually high numbers of adherents to the Catholic faith: Joe McCarthy, William Buckley Jr., Brent Bozell III, Paul Weyrich, Richard Viguerie, Patrick Buchanan, R. Emmett Tyrrell Jr., William Simon Sr., William Bennett, Phyllis Schlafly, Antonin Scalia, Clarence Thomas, Michael Novak, Robert Novak, Bill O'Reilly, Sean Hannity, John McLaughlin, Dinesh D'Souza, Alexander Haig, and many others. While Protestants, particularly born-again Christians such as George Bush and Tom DeLay (and John Ashcroft is gone but not forgotten), seem to have a firm grip on the levers of power in the three branches of government, Catholics play a disproportionately large role as both policymakers and boosters of the Conservative Revolution.

This phenomenon, paralleling the rise of the New Right, has roots that go back several decades. After World War II, many American Catholics supported the anticommunist scare tactics of Jesuit-trained Joseph McCarthy, just as years before they had embraced the fascist and anti-Semitic cause of Father Charles Coughlin. The presidential candidacy of John F. Kennedy in 1960 did not receive universal support from his co-religionists. It is estimated that more than a quarter of YAFers were Catholics during the sixties.[131] Robert Welch, its founder, guessed that about half of the early members of the John Birch Society embraced Catholicism.[132]

In 1972, for the first time a Republican presidential candidate, Richard Nixon, garnered a majority of the nation's Catholic votes.[133] Ronald Reagan and the first George Bush, too, won Catholic majorities. (Among Reagan's Catholic supporters in 1980 was onetime liberal antiwar champion and former Democratic senator Eugene McCarthy.)[134] The rightward drift of American Catholicism has continued into the present.[135] Although Pope John Paul II condemned the illegal U.S. 2003 attack on Iraq as an unjust war, the great majority of American Catholics, over 60 percent, remained loyal to the younger Bush and backed the war effort. Arguably, the most popular single Catholic politician in recent years has been right-wing zealot Pat Buchanan.

During the Clinton years, many Republican strategists, among them Ralph Reed and Paul Weyrich, noting the growing conservatism among socially mobile Catholics, argued that an alliance between Catholics—who currently constitute one-third of the national electorate—and Protestant evangelists made perfect sense. Both religious groups see eye to eye on a variety of social issues, especially abortion, "the catalyst which has galvanized the trans-denominational right," according to Professor William Dinges of the Catholic University of America.[136] Consequently, since the mid-1990s, efforts to construct this alliance, orchestrated by GOP operatives, have been under way.

The results, however, have been mixed.[137] Anti-Catholic views die hard, especially among southern Protestants (Bob Jones University, a conservative Baptist college in South Carolina, for example, remains a notorious hotbed of anti-Catholicism).[138] Possibly the biggest stumbling block, however, has been a deep division between the two sides on the question of welfare. While GOP conservatives lose little sleep over the lack of responsibility of rich people, notably corporate executives and Republican presidents, they are constantly preaching to the poor about meeting *their* obligations. The conservative attitude toward welfare—which in their view diminishes personal responsibility—and more generally toward the poor, is somewhat hypocritical, yet a view that Christian fundamentalists share. (Despite George Bush's desire to see welfare administered by churches, when federal money does not fall into their laps, these Christian conservatives are not that compassionate.) Catholics see it differently. "Ironically," writes a South African journalist surveying life in the United States at the turn of the century, "the Catholic Church has deepened its commitment to social justice at a time in history when their congregants are typically no longer have-nots, but have instead become highly educated members of the middle and upper middle classes. As Catholics are swept into the mainstream, they have, it seems, neither forgotten their roots nor lost their social consciousness."[139] Though the Catholic hierarchy, more than the rank and file, does have some strong conservative senti-ments—illustrated recently by the efforts of some Catholic prelates to deny the sacraments to liberal Catholic politicians (e.g., John Kerry) who support abortion (right-wing prochoice Catholic politicians such as Arnold Schwarzenegger and Tom Ridge, intriguingly, rarely come up in these discussions)[140]—it is well to remember that Catholic bishops in the United States have consistently supported nuclear disarmament. Following the pope's lead, these bishops also condemned the U.S.-led war against Saddam in 2003. Traditional Catholic conservatism, then, among both the church hierarchy and the congregations, is tempered by a concern for the general welfare.

Certain other aspects of Catholicism, on the other hand, lend them-selves toward a typical conservative agenda. According to George Lakoff, conservative and liberal moral systems are based on different models of the family; more specifically, they are products of two different ways of raising children.[141] Liberals are brought up in nurturing environments ("nurturant parent model") and develop altruistic attitudes. Conservatives are products of a strict upbringing ("strict father model") that encourages discipline and respect for authority. Lakoff is on to something. Certainly the Irish-dominated Catholic Church in the United States, austere and puritanical, has been characterized by a pronounced authoritarian bent, not only in its organization but also in its teachings. Neither one of us remembers his Catholic training as an experience that would encourage open discussion of issues, theological or otherwise. In our generation, religious instruction pretty much boiled down to memorizing the *Balti-more Catechism.*

More important, however, than psychological links are sociological ones. White Catholic descendants of late nineteenth- and early twenti-eth-century immigrants from Ireland, Italy, and other western European nations are predominantly middle-class. The majority, having abandoned the cities, inhabited more and more by people of color, now live in white suburbs. With their increasing affluence came a significant shift in politi-cal attitudes.[142] "As many Catholics climbed the socioeconomic ladder," a religious scholar notes, "tax cuts became more attractive than minimum wage hikes, and property values more important than union member-ship."[143] More specifically, these ethnics tend to be lower-middle-class, the very sector that Weyrich claims as his base of support.[144] Many historians have seen this social group as the backbone of the fascist movements that arose throughout Europe in the aftermath of World War I. No one was more critical than social psychologist Erich Fromm, who described the "social character" of the German lower middle class in this way:

> As a matter of fact, certain features were characteristic for this part of the middle class throughout its history: their love of the strong, hatred of the weak, their pettiness, hostility, thriftiness with feelings as well as with money, and essentially their asceticism. Their outlook on life was narrow, they suspected and hated the stranger, and they were curious and envious of their acquaintances, rationalizing their envy as moral indignation; their whole life was based on the principle of scarcity—economically as well as psychologically.[145]

While scarcity is hardly a distinguishing characteristic of the American lower middle class, Fromm sees the defining characteristic of this group, in *any* capitalistic society, as insecurity. They work hard to achieve upward mobility, but their economic situation is always precarious, hence their frustration. As Ehrenreich argues in her provocative 1989 book *Fear of Falling,* even those elements of the middle class who are relatively secure financially, the professional-managerial elites, are beset by the fear of losing it all, an anxiety that has distanced them from the social sectors beneath them and encouraged the abandonment of a liberal political perspective.[146]

When threatened, the bourgeoisie are quick to look for scapegoats. In Europe, they find them in the Jew (the roots of the Holocaust are to be found in the Middle Ages, and even beyond). In the United States, the counterpart of anti-Semitism is racism. During their Great Migration from the South to the northern industrial centers from the twenties to the sixties, the largest internal migration in U.S. history, it was blacks who represented the main threat to the well-being of white ethnics. Subsequently, the influx of Latino immigrants into this country has only added to their anxiety, one that the New Right has deliberately fomented.[147]

The manipulation of a large part of the working and middle class to vote against their own interests by stoking their fears of people different from themselves is a major accomplishment of the conservative propaganda machine that Weyrich and other New Right strategists developed in the sixties and seventies. Fervent believers in the Machiavellian dictum that the end justifies the means, these youthful radicals were prepared to do whatever it took to defeat their ideological opponents. Their win-at-any-cost attitude permeates every aspect of modern-day conservatism and is undoubtedly one of their most enduring legacies. In their zeal to propagate the conservative gospel by creating a mass movement, as we have seen, they felt few scruples about mobilizing resentment and fanning fear as organizing principles.[148]

CHAPTER SEVEN

DEMOCRACY FOR THE FEW

The Government, Inc.

The modern corporation arose in the late nineteenth century, during the Gilded Age. By the mid-1990s, according to scholar Andrew Hacker, some 3.9 million corporations were registered and operating in the United States alone.[1] Of course, most of these bodies are tiny, little more than shells to confer economic benefits to individuals of relatively modest means. Moreover, many of the great business establishments are owned by individuals and families rather than by shareholders; technically they are not corporations at all. Nevertheless, it is the corporate structure that defines the giant business firms, the Fortune 500, which are linked to one another through strategic alliances, contracting networks, and interlocking board directorates (at one point, Clinton adviser Vernon Jordan sat on one dozen boards, including those of American Express, Daimler Chrysler, Dow Jones, Revlon, Sara Lee, Xerox, and Callaway Golf).[2] Collectively they constitute what scholars call Corporate America, also known as "big business."

Originally set up to accumulate large amounts of capital exceeding the means of families and individuals, the corporation has proven an extraordinary success. "Two hundred corporations, led by giants such as GE, Time Warner, and Philip Morris," writes Boston College sociology professor Charles Derber, "dominate America's economy—and much of the rest of the world."[3] As markets have expanded, so has the size of the corporation. Today, with the globalization of economic production, the largest of these bodies control more wealth than many countries. Multinational corporations such as Exxon Mobil and Daimler Chrysler report annual revenues that exceed those of Norway and Singapore.[4] During the past generation, particularly, corporate wealth has soared, the product of new technologies, mergers, and cheap immigrant labor. Subcontracting, outsourcing, and downsizing have made for greater "efficiency" (profits) as well, as has the mushrooming use of part-time workers.

As indicated before, corporations have also benefited from the largesse of taxpayers. Indeed, corporate bodies have gained mightily from public subsidies, now as in the past, proving the truth of Ambrose Bierce's definition of a corporation: "An ingenious device for obtaining profit without individual responsibility."[5] In 1999, led by future vice president Dick Cheney, not only did Halliburton, with forty-four registered offshore tax havens, pay no federal taxes; it received an $85 million rebate.[6] Firms like Halliburton have been able to take advantage of government handouts by virtue of their successful claim to be entitled to the same rights that the Constitution provides for citizens, a claim that the Supreme Court recognized in 1886. As journalist William Greider notes, corporations may even enjoy *more* rights than individuals do:

> A corporation, because it is an "artificial legal person," has inherent capacities that mortal citizens do not possess. For one thing, it can live forever. For another, a corporation, unlike people, can exist in many places at once. Or it can alter its identity—chop off its arms or legs and transform itself into an utterly different "person." Or it can sell itself to new owners, including owners who are not themselves Americans. Are these foreigners now empowered as U.S. "citizens" by virtue of owning an "American corporation"?[7]

Under the terms of the NAFTA agreement, corporations can sue foreign governments, while private citizens cannot.[8] This and other forms of corporate welfare—public subsidies and tax breaks—reflect the great power wielded by corporate bodies in Washington, D.C.

Perhaps no corporations are more influential in the nation's economic life than financial institutions. Wall Street bankers represent the pinnacle of American capitalism. The powerful Federal Reserve System, established in 1913 to adjust interest rates and encourage employment, according to author Robert Sherrill, "is literally owned by the largest national banks, and the Fed's board, which meets in secret, has never had a member who came from the labor movement or at least momentarily entertained a populist thought."[9] The 2005 bankruptcy law, which essentially condemns citizens in over their heads in credit card debt to years of debt bondage, is a testimony to the power financial institutions exert on lawmakers.[10]

Corporate political power finds expression daily in a variety of ways: think tanks, foundations, K Street lobbying groups, political action committees (PACs), and, of course, the infamous revolving door that links government and business. Greider makes an apt analogy:

> Washington now is more aptly visualized as a grand bazaar—a steamy marketplace of tents, stalls and noisy peddlers. The din of buying and

selling drowns out patriotic music. The high art of governing—making laws for the nation and upholding them—has been reduced to a busy commerce in deal making. Thousands and thousands of deals are transacted every day in diffuse corners of the city. The rare skills required for politics at the highest level are trivialized as petty haggling, done with the style and swagger of rug merchants.[11]

As longtime Beltway critic Elizabeth Drew puts it: "Private interests have tried to influence legislative and administrative outcomes through the use of money for a long time.... But never before in the modern age has political money played the pervasive role that it does now. By comparison, the Watergate period seems almost quaint."[12]

Buy a Senator—It's Your Constitutional Right

"Campaign financing is by far the most important mechanism for overclass influence in government," states a prominent political observer.[13] The era of large-scale political contributions, what amounts to legalized graft, began in the aftermath of the landmark 1976 U.S. Supreme Court case *Buckley v. Valeo,* in which a Republican-appointed majority ruled that spending money on elections was a form of political expression and a First Amendment right.[14] Certainly the increasingly large-scale funding of elections is today the most obvious and effective form of influence peddling. Financial guru and sometime political consultant Warren Buffett puts it bluntly: "Corporations think they are getting their money's worth or they wouldn't be writing checks."[15] Corporate investments in political elections rose dramatically in the seventies, when corporate PACs mushroomed and the cash flow to candidates for both houses of Congress increased from $8 million to $39 million.[16] Political fund-raisers have become the most important players in the nation's capital—at the time we write, House Majority Leader Tom DeLay ("The Exterminator") had no equals in eliciting donations.[17] It should be noted, however, that this pecuniary influence is limited to a relatively small number of people. Only about 0.25 percent of U.S. citizens make a contribution of $200 or more, a group that is "disproportionately white, wealthy, male and conservative."[18]

The greatest beneficiaries of corporate campaign financing have been Republican presidential candidates. During the 2000 presidential campaign, individuals who "bundled" (collected) and contributed $100,000 to the George W. Bush campaign were designated "Pioneers." The most recognizable of these big-time contributors was Bush's good friend Ken Lay of Enron, a corporation that has been the president's largest single benefactor throughout his political career. During the campaign, the presidential candidate claimed 212 individuals as Pioneers, but three years later, campaign documents put the number at more than 550.[19] That some of these Pioneers subsequently received ambassadorships to Austria, Belgium, Belize, France, Ireland, Norway, and Portugal should come as no great surprise.[20]

The corporate dollar is a special favorite of the political crowd; the overwhelming majority of Bush's "Rangers," a new category of individuals who raised at least $200,000 for his 2004 reelection campaign, have corporate ties.[21] Finance, insurance, real estate, and pharmaceutical firms are always among the top political contributors. The defense industry is not far behind: During the 2000 presidential campaign, arms manufacturers gave Bush $190,000, four times as much as they contributed to his Democratic rival.[22] And defense contractors have reaped the greatest returns on their investment, especially "the big three": Lockheed Martin, Boeing, and Northrop Grumman. (Of course, it also helps that thirty-two major appointees in Bush's first administration had "direct or indirect links to the arms industry.")[23] Defense contractors are eagerly cultivated not only because of the lavish campaign contributions and the potential for future employment that they provide to politicians, but also because of the plethora of defense industry jobs they can create in their constituencies. While corporate money finds its way into the coffers of both major parties, the Republicans receive the lion's share—one reason why the GOP has led the opposition to campaign finance reform.[24]

Influence Peddling—An Even Better Investment

Corporations and other special interest groups also make their influence felt through massive lobbying. Indeed, as Ken Silverstein, coeditor of *CounterPunch*, an investigative newsletter on Washington politics, illustrates in his 1998 book, *Washington on $10 Million a Day: How Lobbyists Plunder the Nation*, "Dollar for dollar, lobbying is a better investment than campaign contributions, one reason business spends far more on the former than the latter."[25] By 1998, we know—thanks to the Lobbying Disclosure Act of 1995—at least 11,500 lobbyists were registered in Washington.[26] The largest lobbies were generally those representing the leading campaign donors, especially defense and pharmaceutical industries. In 1998, for example, one defense contractor, Boeing, had an "army of roughly 70 lobbyists" on its payroll.[27] Four years later, lobbyists employed by pharmaceutical companies outnumbered members of Congress by 623 to 535.[28]

The most potent lobby of all, however, according to Senator John McCain, is that of the broadcast industry.[29] This is not surprising given the heavy reliance by members of Congress on favorable media coverage. "The media's power," notes political insider Joseph Stiglitz, "comes not from their campaign contributions, but from their coverage of the candidates and the issues. Politicians offend them at their peril."[30] Moreover, the heavy reliance on political advertisements creates a symbiotic relationship between politicians and the media. By 2002, political ads accounted for about 10 percent of commercial television revenue (up from 3.8 percent ten years before).[31] The most sought-after lobbyists by corporations and other special interests are ex-Pentagon bigwigs and ex-politicians, especially the latter. From 1995 to 2004, 272 former members of Congress registered as lobbyists.[32]

Other ex–government policymakers are almost as attractive to the business community. An outstanding example is Thomas A. Scully, the Health and Human Resources (HHR) administrator in charge of Medicare who proved vital in getting Congress to pass President Bush's massive pharmaceutical industry–friendly Medicare drug bill in November 2003. A reluctant Congress only approved the legislation after the president verified the cost to be $395 billion. The true tab, however, as the president's budget office conceded after Bush signed the bill into law in December, would turn out to be more than $500 billion, a figure that Medicare's top actuary, Richard S. Foster, had calculated prior to the congressional vote but had been ordered not to divulge by his boss, Scully, who resigned once the legislation went into effect.[33] Soon afterward, the former HHR head had the good fortune to be hired as a lobbyist by several clients who benefited from the legislation, including drug firms Abbott Laboratories and Aventis, pharmacy benefit manager Caremark Rx, and the American Chiropractic Association.[34] In February 2005, the White House again revised its cost estimate of the Medicare bill to $1.2 trillion.[35]

Individuals who maintain close ties to key government employees are also in high demand. When Newt Gingrich served as the powerful House Speaker in the mid-1990s, Microsoft retained his friend Grover Norquist as a lobbyist for $10,000 a month.[36] Before his fall from grace, few lobbyists were as well connected as longtime GOP insider Jack Abramoff, "once considered the most powerful lobbyist on Capitol Hill."[37] His intimates include Norquist and Ralph Reed, whom he first met in College Republicans. Tom DeLay has acknowledged him as "one of my closest and dearest friends."[38]

As Elizabeth Drew has illustrated, raising money has become a mania in Washington during the past thirty years. From the president on down, politicians seem to spend most of their time on this relentless quest, to the detriment of effective government. Certainly the quality of leadership has declined dramatically during this period. More serious still is the massive corruption that dominates American politics at the highest levels ("Wherever one looks—at the gerrymandered districts, the balloting methods, the fundraising—corruption steams like vapors from a putrid swamp").[39] Matters have worsened during the years of George W. Bush's crony capitalism, when, critics charge, our Medicare laws are drafted by major pharmaceutical companies ("Big Pharma") and our energy bills by oil executives.[40]

Write Your Congressman? Why Bother?

As the voice of big business has grown, it has practically drowned out that of common citizens. If you're planning to write your representative in Washington, don't. At least that's the advice of a young intern, a mail sorter, employed by Speaker of the House J. Dennis Hastert (R-Ill.), who claims that letters to members of Congress typically end up in the trash can—unopened. His boss, he writes, is typical: "He spends his jam-packed days meeting with leaders from the most powerful organizations and corporations in the country. He can't afford to take an interest in your opinion, though his staff is hard at work to provide you with the illusion of precisely the opposite."[41]

The corrupting influence of money is not confined to a single party, though Republicans have proven much more successful in tapping big business dollars than have Democrats.[42] Undoubtedly, one of the reasons the New Right has done so well in the public arena since the seventies is the weak resistance the New Democrats put up. For the most part, the liberal response to Reagan's reactionary program was "a shameful silence."[43] This failure has continued under the George W. Bush administration. Beginning with their steadfast refusal to contest the results of the 2000 presidential election, Democrats have displayed a remarkable lack of spine. More and more, their leaders have abandoned their traditional party principles—what Garrison Keillor fondly recalls as "the politics of kindness."[44]

Everybody Does It

Many reasons explain why liberals have failed to provide a real alternative to the Republican vision. The most important, by far, is that Democratic policymakers, beneficiaries of massive funding, have grown comfortable with the political status quo in Washington. "By 1988, House Democratic incumbents had become, for the first time, more dependent on PACs for financial support than on individual donors."[45] Increasingly dependent on funding by wealthy donors, the party began to move away from its popular base. As a result, Democrats have become almost as reliable as

Republicans in their support for corporate capitalism, a support that goes far beyond Bill Clinton. "The Democrats," Kevin Phillips reminds us, "are also a capitalist, middle-class party, if somewhat less enthusiastic and market-bewitched than the Republicans."[46]

It is important, too, to understand that class considerations tend to unite the leaders of both parties in Washington. Whether Republican or Democrat—"Republocrat" or "Demican," pundit Michael Parenti would say—the denizens of Capitol Hill are extremely wealthy, especially members of the Upper House. It has been estimated that 40 to 50 percent of the senators are millionaires (we would guess a higher figure).[47] These legislators often feel more comfortable with each other, regardless of party affiliation, than they do with their own constituents—they reside in the same affluent suburbs, send their children to the same tony private schools, dine in the same upscale restaurants, and generally move in the same lofty social circles.

Time and again, especially in recent years, Democrats have passed on the opportunity to take the moral high ground. For example, virtually every Republican initiative on regressive taxation going back to the Reagan years, and beyond, was sustained by Democrats on Capitol Hill. As author Michael Lind reminds us: "The shifting of the tax burden from wealthy rentiers, investors, corporate executives, and elite professionals to working Americans was not the work of backroom plotting by southern Dixiecrats and Republicans; it was done in broad daylight by Congresses dominated by a largely northern, socially liberal party, grown addicted since the seventies to cash flows from business PACs and wealthy individual contributors."[48]

Democratic support for Republican policies has not been confined solely to domestic policies. Rather than opposing the construction of an American military empire, Democrats have developed a hawkish posture that rivals that of Bush II and the GOP. Only one Democrat in Congress, Barbara Lee of California, voted against the U.S. invasion of Afghanistan. ("Now if that doesn't suggest ... a blurring between the parties," comments Matthew Rothschild, editor of *The Progressive,* "I don't know what will.")[49] Democrats were equally enthusiastic in their support for the illegal and unnecessary war against Iraq.

Republicans Lite

Why have these neoliberals demonstrated so little spine? As Lind indicates, money talks. As with their opponents, though not to quite the same extent, Democrats increasingly receive their campaign funding from large corporations. Beginning in 1984, corporate contributions to the party exceeded those from labor unions.[50] Ex-Republican Arianna Huffington reports that all but two Democratic senators accepted campaign contributions from WorldCom, Enron, and Arthur Andersen.[51] Indeed, many of the party's functionaries on the Hill have close corporate connections. The leading congressional champion of the powerful Asian lobby is Senator Dianne Feinstein from California, who maintains intimate personal and political ties with the military-industrial complex (her multimillionaire husband, Richard Blum, the chairman of a merchant banking firm, was a major beneficiary of taxpayer dollars that went into the recent reconstruction effort in the Middle East).[52] Likewise for Senator Tom Daschle, from the sparsely populated state of South Dakota, who before his defeat in the 2004 elections was heavily dependent on contributions from wealthy out-of-state contributors and who did his best to guard their interests.[53] A shameless lackey for the moneyed interest, Joseph Lieberman may be the worst of the lot: "Between 1997 and 2002, he received $371,867 from bankers, brokers, and accountants."[54] The Connecticut senator has to be the most probusiness advocate in Washington within the ranks of his party. With conservative positions more typical of Republicans than Democrats,[55] he and his like-minded cronies are indeed "Republicans lite."[56]

Swimming in corporate money, Democrat leaders have gradually lost touch with their traditional base, the lower two-thirds of the income spectrum. While their opponents play hardball, Democrats continue to play by the old rules of engagement (a contrast best illustrated by Gingrich, who went for the jugular every time, and by Clinton, who never did take off the gloves). Winning elections and returning to the halls of Congress has become the primary, often the only, concern. Now champions of the status quo, Democrats can hardly provide an alternative to the optimistic but vacuous GOP vision.

In spite of this dreary state of affairs in the nation's capital, big government is not the real culprit. The true obstacle to effective and democratic governance is unfettered corporate capitalism. Free-market capitalism is an economic system without a conscience.

Mao the Free Marketeer

Free-market advocates will appeal to high-minded principles—patriotism, religion, motherhood, whatever will get them or their proxies into office and keep them there—but all of these noble concepts go by the board if they stand in the way of profits. When, for example, Communist China complained to Rupert Murdoch, who benefits from a lucrative television satellite contract in that country, about a BBC broadcast he was carrying that cast Mao in a negative light, the right-wing mogul, ideological differences notwithstanding, terminated the BBC channel without hesitation.[57] And, of course, free-market capitalists have been pouring into China from all over the Free World during the past fifteen years, lured by cheap labor and expanding markets. This is not unusual in a consumer-oriented economy. Profits trump everything else. True capitalists would sell us the very air that we breathe—they are already retailing the water—if they could find a way of doing it. Nor are they concerned in the least that they have created a society where you have, on the one hand, a CEO who paid himself $1.4 billion a year, as computer maker Michael Dell did in 1998, and, on the other hand, more than forty million people who have no medical insurance whatsoever.[58] As Michael Parenti, a relentless critic of the establishment, has observed:

> Capitalism is a system without a soul, without humanity. It tries to reduce every human activity to market profitability. It has no loyalty to democracy, family values, culture, Judeo-Christian ethics, ordinary folks, or any other shibboleths mouthed by its public relations representatives on special occasions. It has no loyalty to any nation; its only loyalty is to its own system of capital accumulation. It is not dedicated to "serving the community"; it serves only itself, extracting all it can from the many so that it might give all it can to the few.[59]

This point is made, too, by award-winning journalist Eric Schlosser, who recently investigated the miserable working conditions of strawberry pickers in California, many of them Mixteca Indians from Mexico who have increasingly come to dominate the state's lowest-paid agricultural jobs. Left unchecked, he observes, the free market will always drive wages down. "All those who now consider themselves devotees of the market," he warns, "should take a good look at what is happening in California. Left to its own devices, the free market always seeks a work force that is hungry, desperate, and cheap—a work force that is anything but free."[60]

Shopping Mall Universities

As Karl Marx warned, capitalism threatens to overwhelm everything else. Like a cancer, its appetite is insatiable. "The market notoriously tends to universalize itself," the late Christopher Lasch noted.

> It does not easily coexist with institutions that operate according to principles antithetical to itself: schools and universities, newspapers and magazines, charities, families. Sooner or later the market tends to absorb them all. It puts an almost irresistible pressure on every activity to justify itself in the only terms it recognizes: to become a business

proposition, to pay its own way, to show black ink on the bottom line.…
Inexorably it models every institution in its own image.[61]

Truly, free-market capitalism has penetrated into every corner of American
life: sports, art, music, even those institutions like schools and churches
that would seem to be guided by principles antithetical to crass moneymaking. "Today," one pundit marvels, "the college campus looks like a shopping
mall."[62] Religion, another social commentator notes, is now organized as
a business and employs many of its techniques, including "advertising,
marketing, and the ethos and organizational discipline of sales."[63]

Spin Doctors for Capitalism

With notable exceptions, the media are unlikely to be too critical of the
juggernaut.[64] After all, their main job is to increase consumption.[65] Media
expert Robert McChesney reports that radio advertising has gradually
increased until it now stands at seventeen or eighteen minutes per hour.[66]
And ads take up about one in every three minutes of television, according
to longtime communications observer Mark Hertsgaard.[67] And it is not
just the electronic media; more pages of *Newsweek, Time,* and *U.S. News
& World Report* are devoted to ads than to hard news, a reflection of the
"hyper-commercialism" that permeates U.S. society today.[68] Ken Auletta,
media columnist for *The New Yorker,* argues convincingly in *Backstory,*
a collection of articles on modern journalism, that because of pressures
to achieve higher profit margins, the wall separating editorial opinion
and advertising in the news media has been steadily eroding since the
eighties.[69]

Media political pundits such as Bill O'Reilly, a "populist" who makes
$20 million a year, do not see a problem. Indeed, members of the media
establishment, one communications expert charges, "have so bought into
the conservative formulation that they now devote entire cable channels
and newspapers to business and finance but have not a single reporter
covering labor issues full-time."[70] Not surprisingly, as labor scholar Gregory
Mantsios charges, both the broadcast and the print news media generally
ignore poor people and poverty. Moreover, he adds, "The coverage … is
often distorted and misleading."[71]

But these talking heads and media executives, in spite of their high
salaries, are themselves tools of the owners and managers of corporations
who have so much money that they can hire dozens of spin doctors like
O'Reilly. And these corporate leaders want the public to believe that
what is good for the wealthy is also good for everyone else, even though
it is not—indeed, the gap between the rich and poor more than doubled
between 1979 and 2000.[72]

The Wealth Gap

Conservatives such as economist Robert J. Samuelson love to cite consumer indices to show that everyone benefits from the free-market system, but these statistics conveniently mask the tremendous differences in *wealth* among the classes, not to mention the enormous *debt* amassed by nonelites.[73] "Although America has higher per capita income than other advanced countries," economist Paul Krugman cautions, "it turns out that that's mainly because our rich are much richer."[74] Bill Gates, the ultimate example, owned as much wealth in 1999 as the bottom 40 percent of his fellow Americans.[75] Professor of political economy Gar Alperovitz agrees: "Wealth is far, far more concentrated than income. A mere 1 percent of Americans owns just under 50 percent of financial wealth; a mere 5 percent owns almost 70 percent of financial wealth."[76] Another economist, Edward Wolff of New York University, using 1998 census statistics, reports that while the wealth of the top 1 percent of households averaged $12.5 million, the bottom 20 percent "basically have zero wealth."[77]

The racial gap is particularly striking. According to Wolff's reading of the 1998 census returns, "The average African-American family has only 18 percent of the wealth of the average white family."[78] Other scholars draw similar conclusions. "The boom of the Clinton years," notes David R. Roediger, "left the net worth of 'Nonwhite or Hispanic' families at 17.28 percent of the net worth of 'White non-Hispanic' families."[79]

The widening wealth disparity has led to a massive increase in homelessness. In San Francisco alone, more than 12,500 people found themselves in this condition in 2003.[80] The Bay Area is not unique; "the streets of nearly all our major cities are blighted by homeless people, a sight that largely disappears when one travels to continental Europe or Japan."[81]

Capitalism = Democracy

Employing an army of public relations experts and political consultants, the wealthy are able to manipulate the public.[82] The GOP's protracted cultural war conveniently masks that the financial elites have been the main beneficiaries of the Republican ascendancy. It is this privileged minority, through its virtual monopoly of mass communication, which has come close to convincing the masses that capitalism and democracy are one and the same.[83] But the system we have is the antithesis of democracy, the product of a conservative movement built from the top down to preserve the interests of an oligarchy.[84] Political commentator Kevin Baker explains:

> The American right has, in fact, battened on nearly every antidemocratic development of the past four decades, from "white backlash" and the

illegal, undeclared war in Vietnam right through the sabotage of the 2000 presidential election by way of mob violence, racial manipulation of the voting rolls, and a partisan judiciary. Unable to sustain a mass base, the right has had to rely on all that limits mass participation, on everything that divides, alienates, and disqualifies voters—on the constant denigration of government itself as a somehow illegitimate entity, a malevolent intrusion into people's lives.[85]

Spreading Democracy

Historically, in fact, capitalists were only too happy to sustain authoritarian and even totalitarian regimes like those of Mussolini and Hitler, who in turn provided them with myriad benefits.[86] Advocates of the free market are not wedded to any particular political system.

American capitalists are no exception, though their star-spangled rhetoric often obscures this fact. Consider the realm of foreign policy. In the past, the United States has often justified imperial expansion into the third world as necessary to foster democracy, the most pivotal element—indeed, the essence of American exceptionalism. This concept, for example, became the rationale for the invasion of Iraq in 2003 once weapons of mass destruction—the initial (alleged) target for our preemptive strike—and the Saddam-terrorist ties both failed to materialize. But what the U.S. government fears in Iraq today is genuine popular elections because the wrong people (Shiite fundamentalists) might win them and ask Western forces to leave.[87]

Corporate power exhibits scant regard for democratic solutions. In fact, the last thing the economic and military elites who formulate U.S. foreign policy want in the underdeveloped world is representative governments. Authoritarian regimes, especially military dictatorships, are much better, if history is any guide. For all his talk of democracy, President Bush is perfectly willing to sustain those reactionary dictatorships that today dominate the oil-rich nations that emerged in the southern part of the old USSR.[88] Repressive governments, such as the ones we currently support in Pakistan and Saudi Arabia, represent the best guarantee of order and progress, providing American corporations a business climate where they can maximize profits. Moreover, since these oppressive governments must maintain themselves through armed might, they often rely on U.S. firms for weaponry and the Pentagon for military training. Their loyalty, especially during the Cold War, has been sealed by generous grants of U.S. foreign aid, ostensibly monies that will ultimately trickle down to humble villagers but that often wind up in Swiss bank accounts. (How else to explain how deposed Banana Republic tyrants retire to Europe to live out their days in the lap of luxury even though their origins were relatively humble?) Clearly, capitalism, at least in the United States, is not about democracy but profits. And so when President Bush and his fellow travelers make rousing speeches about the need to export democracy to developing nations, one suspects it is really free-market capitalism that they are promoting.

Better Than Other People

American exceptionalism, the idea that Americans are not only different but ultimately better than other peoples, also plays a role in maintaining democracy for the few. This peculiar notion, as journalist Katha Pollitt reminds us, is accepted only by citizens of the United States.[89] In this country, however, this chauvinist notion receives universal and enthusiastic endorsement by the Right—ironic, given conservatives' growing alarm over the permissiveness they see all around.[90] As Michael Lind puts it:

> The United States *is* exceptional, among industrial countries, in two respects, which have little to do with the liberal [i.e., free-market] democratic ideal of American universalists. Thanks to the unwillingness of affluent white Americans to pay the taxes necessary for police patrols and asylums, the cities of the United States resemble those of the Third World, with their swarms of homeless vagrants, often insane or addicted to drugs. And thanks to its lack of effective gun control laws, the United States has by far the highest rates of homicide and imprisonment, not only among English-speaking democracies but among all democratic countries. America is not significantly freer or more democratic than other industrial democracies today. It does, however, lead Europe and Japan in beggars, murders and prisons per capita.[91]

Low-Grade Criminality

William Greider, author of *The Soul of Capitalism,* has eloquently and persuasively argued that our free-market economic system is long overdue for a major overhaul.[92] Socialism is probably not a feasible solution, given the American tradition of rugged individualism, not to mention the constraints imposed by human nature. Based on self-interest, capitalism does have the advantage of being realistic. However, its fatal flaw is, and always has been, its amorality and affinity for a kind of low-grade criminality.[93] It also makes U.S. capitalists care little about justice and equity; tycoons of all ages have consistently fought against the right of workers to unions, medical benefits, environmental protections, Social Security, and all the other entitlements that have assured the American people a decent standard of living. Recall, for example, how many times in the last few years their representatives in Congress have beaten down attempts to raise the minimum wage.

Western European nations maintain capitalist economies that have proven better able than our own to distribute wealth throughout society. As economist Joseph Stiglitz puts it: "There are other countries which believe that their economic system is better, at least for them. They may have lower incomes, but they have more job and health security; they enjoy longer vacations, and lower stress may be reflected in longer lives. There is less inequality, less poverty, lower crime, a smaller fraction of their population spends a large part of their lives behind bars. There are choices, there are trade-offs."[94]

I Make Four Hundred Times What You Make, So Follow Orders

An average top executive in the United States makes more than four hundred times what the typical hourly employee earns in the same company, but this figure comes into bold relief compared with the ratios—in equivalent firms—of 25 to 1 in Britain, 19 to 1 in Italy, and 16 to 1 in France.[95] Significantly, for all their enthusiasm for outsourcing jobs, the one position corporate CEOs have not considered exporting, the one that clearly provides the least bang for the buck, is their own.

The major difference between the two systems is that European economies are heavily regulated. This fact was graphically illustrated in recent years by the staunch refusal by the European Commission, representing the European Union (EU), to permit American-based megacorporations General Electric (2001) and Microsoft (2004) to violate EU antitrust laws.[96] Americans were shocked by these rulings given their own tendency to accommodate these powerful companies. Only in the United States, after all, has the government put the interests of multinational corporations ahead of those of its citizenry.[97] The commission's chief antitrust enforcer, Mario Monti, represents a country, Italy, where the right to work (i.e., to support a family) is seen as a sacred right—not exactly an article of American faith.

The Microsoft ruling prompted one observer, a former U.S. Justice Department antitrust official, to comment, "There really is less stomach in Europe for the kind of Darwinian competition that we've embraced in the United States."[98] Europe, with its deep-seated corporate tradition in the Middle Ages (guilds, communes, religious fraternities, tower societies, etc.), retains a much stronger sense of the general welfare than does the United States, hence the emphasis there on regulation.

The Overworked American

Most Europeans realize that unbridled capitalism tends toward monopoly and exploitation of labor. Nor is it simply workers' wages that suffer. As Harvard economist Juliet Schor documented in her 1992 best seller, *The Overworked American,* capitalism, despite the claims of its boosters, creates longer working hours, not leisure.[99] The problem is most extreme in the United States, where work schedules have been expanding since the late sixties. Today these schedules far exceed those of their western European counterparts. For example, Germans work about five hundred hours less per year than Americans, which adds up to about three months of work time in the United States.[100] A study by the nonprofit Families and Work Institute released in early March 2005 found that one in three American employees reported being chronically overworked.[101]

In this country, in contrast to western Europe, government regulation is anathema, especially to probusiness Republicans, consequently "one firm alone, Merrill Lynch, has a bigger legal staff dealing with regulatory matters than the entire enforcement division of the SEC."[102] Individualism has truly assumed an extreme form in the United States.

Rugged Individualism and a Crop of Coconuts

As historian Garry Wills points out, capitalism and individualism are not identical; indeed, citing Adam Smith, he claims that capitalism calls for collaboration.[103] This is an aspect of the free-market system that its chief beneficiaries often overlook. For example, it is all too common to hear irate taxpayers whine about the government taking "my" money.[104] This lament—which President Bush encourages—ignores that moneymaking is a cooperative venture.

Let us assume that you could produce, and harvest, one million coconuts living on an island all by yourself. What have you gained besides a lot of coconuts? It's virtually impossible to make a million dollars without workers (labor) and clients (markets); wealth is a *social* product.[105] The myth of rugged individualism, however, in the economic realm, as in other aspects of American life, is virtually indestructible.

What, Me Pay Taxes?

In the absence of regulation, the gulf between rich and poor in the United States can only grow wider. Except for the Turks, Americans pay the lowest taxes of all peoples residing in industrialized nations. Moreover, total taxation in the United States, including local taxes, represents 30.6 percent of the nation's economy, the lowest rate among the twenty-seven nations that comprise the Organization for Economic Cooperation and Development (the highest taxes are paid by Sweden, 59.2 percent of the national economy).[106] These taxes, as we have seen, are increasingly regressive. Indeed, the superrich are often able to avoid taxes altogether. In four of the five years preceding its bankruptcy in 2001, Enron did not pay a single cent in taxes. And the Houston-based energy conglomerate—the leading financial donor to the Bush campaign in 2000—was not the only corporation that found itself in this enviable position.[107] As mentioned previously, more than half of American corporations failed to pay any federal taxes whatsoever between 1996 and 2000.[108] According to journalist Michael Scherer, "At least 82 companies in the Fortune 500 paid no income taxes whatsoever during at least one of the first three years of George W. Bush's administration."[109] Today, of the total amount of federal taxes paid, corporations pay less than 10 percent; in 1945, they paid 50 percent.[110] Who makes up the difference? Political gadfly Michael Moore has it right: you and your second job.[111]

Without a tradition of adequate controls, corporate malfeasance can only grow. Hardly a day goes by without the announcement of a new corporate scandal. We throw poor minorities into jail in wholesale lots: Minorities constitute about 70 percent of the more than two million men and women currently behind bars.[112] But, as sociologist Andrew Barlow observes, "The harmful acts committed by corporations—assaults on the environment, unsafe product designs, work conditions endangering workers' health and safety, and so on—are rarely covered by criminal statute and even more rarely lead to criminal prosecution of individuals."[113] Just as was the case one hundred years ago, when Teddy Roosevelt led a popular crusade against corporate power and privilege, so today, "malefactors of great wealth" need to be reined in. How can this be done?

Since the mid-1990s, as cultural critic Naomi Klein has chronicled in her well-researched book *No Logo,* a grassroots movement has appeared to protest the immense power of corporations. This is a start—consumer strikes have genuine potential—but it is not nearly enough, as law professor Lawrence E. Mitchell makes clear. "Only the government," he writes, "has the power, the resources, and the right to restrain corporate conduct and to demand corporate accountability. For far too long we've taken the attitude that business is business, as if that mantra exempted corporations from the normal moral and responsible conduct that we expect from individual citizens."[114]

People Who Hate America

But before government can protect society from corporate avarice, Washington itself must be purged of corporate influence. Columnist Molly Ivins is not exaggerating when she declares, "The government of this country has been bought by campaign contributions from corporate special interests."[115] Robert McChesney concurs: "Corrupt government available to the highest bidder is in some respects more prevalent today than at any time since the Gilded Age."[116] The wealthy use this system to reward their own. Almost 43 percent of the incoming members of Congress in 2002 were millionaires.[117] Robert D. Kaplan, foreign correspondent for the *Atlantic Monthly,* rightly observes, "The irony is that while we preach our version of democracy abroad, it slips away from us at home."[118] Many critics of the status quo argue that only an informed and active citizenry can accomplish a much-needed political transformation, thus paving the way for a just society—a commonwealth organized on the principle that the general welfare rather than vested interests should determine social policy.[119]

The best analysis of America's socioeconomic realities comes from academic gadflies like Noam Chomsky and Michael Parenti and journalists like Molly Ivins, Jim Hightower, and Michael Moore ("people who hate America," according to Bill O'Reilly and other right-wing ideologues). Ultimately, however, all progressives agree that the people have to assert themselves. William Greider succinctly states the case for populism: "People have it within their power to overcome all ... obstacles and restore a general sense of mutual respect to public life. That is the hard work of democracy, but it is not more daunting than what people faced and overcame at different times in America's past. The politics of restoration will start, not in Washington, but in many other places, separately and together, when people decide to close the gap between what they believe and what is."[120]

Unfortunately, this prescription—power to the people—is harder to achieve than its champions realize. Every major political thinker from antiquity to the late eighteenth century, and most since, saw democracy as the worst of all forms of government. Only with the Founding Fathers do we find partisans of the democratic principle, and even here, like James Madison, the overwhelming majority of the men who gathered in Philadelphia held strong reservations about the wisdom of the people. Others, fearing mob rule, were almost pathologically suspicious of the masses, notably Alexander Hamilton. The age-old fear of popular government reflects a profoundly cynical view of human nature. Machiavelli, Hobbes, Voltaire, Freud—indeed, most of the great thinkers—shared this prejudice, which in the United States finds its most eloquent expression in the writings of Mark Twain ("If you pick up a starving dog and make him prosperous, he will not bite you. This is the principal difference between a dog and a man").[121]

The Sheep Attack Lions

If American political institutions today are deeply flawed, the responsibility goes beyond a cabal of politicians and their patrons: "If Washington is a city infested by fools and knaves," Greider rightly asks, "where did they come from and who sent them?"[122] For all their mistrust of government, historically the American people have been easily manipulated. In 1846, the United States, already, according to Alexis de Tocqueville, a regional powerhouse, went to war claiming that it was attacked by Mexicans—along a disputed boundary. Subsequent wars were justified by alleged attacks by the Spanish "empire" (1898), with the sinking of the *Maine,* and by a "piss-ant" nation, North Vietnam, which fired on the *Maddox* (1964). In 2003, the Bush administration went one better. Claiming that someday it *might* be attacked by Iraq, a nation of some twenty-five million weakened by a twelve-year blockade, it waged an illegal war that killed at least ten thousand civilians.[123] In all these cases, U.S. citizens went to war blindly, buying into the odd notion that sheep actually attack lions.

Hope for Change

And yet the United States has not always been the errant country it is today. It has performed valiantly on occasion, at times even heroically. During most of its short history, it has served as an inspiration for people throughout the world. Surely, the massive immigration we see today in this country cannot be explained entirely by the search for material wealth. Moreover, in a nation established as a democratic republic, there are no other options but to rely on its citizenry. Americans have to initiate the process of restoring the national fabric, despite the massive obstacles. The place to begin is by exercising the vote, by throwing the current rascals out and then watching to see that others like them do not get in. Small steps lead to bigger ones.

Human beings, Machiavelli shrewdly observed in *The Prince,* will behave badly until they are constrained to do good. This is the key. In the past, Americans, despite their preoccupation with self-interest, were able to meet the challenge, time and again. Why? Vast changes, generally of an economic nature, created the conditions for renewal. It was the Great

Depression, for example, that forced Americans to think in terms of the general welfare after the mindless excesses of the flapper era.

The times now appear to be right for a new age of reform. The immense economic changes wrought by globalization have created shocking social and economic inequalities in the United States and elsewhere that cry out for solutions. Most Americans are slipping back, rather than moving forward. Many citizens are beginning to sense the escalating decline of the middle class. On the verge of personal bankruptcy, Americans are coming to recognize the moral bankruptcy of the conservative ascendancy. Of necessity the political pendulum must swing back toward a better balance.

→ CONCLUSION ←

A WELL-OILED MACHINE

Today, as in the past, it is the political and economic elites—the ruling class—who are the chief beneficiaries of conservatism. This hasn't changed. Rather, what distinguishes the New Conservatism that has come to dominate American political life in the past thirty-odd years from the Old Conservatism is a series of other factors. One of the most important of these is the new approach to gaining and maintaining power—the creation of a populist movement merging secular and religious conservatives. Equally significant, led by a well-funded and dedicated cadre, the New Right has adopted a more aggressive, take-no-prisoners style of political combat since the seventies.

Fascism with a Friendly Face

Beset by modernist tendencies they fear, conservatives have also embraced a radical and reactionary program that looks suspiciously like the "friendly fascism" political science professor Bertram Gross predicted more than a quarter century ago.[1] George W. Bush may have begun his presidency promising to be a "uniter, not a divider," but no sooner did his first term of office begin—even before September 11—than he set about implementing a series of controversial policies that would soon polarize the nation in a way that had not been done since the turbulent sixties.[2] Among the most divisive of recent decisions, as we have seen, was going out of his way to support the anti–affirmative action advocates in the University of Michigan case and, even more recently, a constitutional amendment forbidding gay marriage. Almost completely dominated by its right wing, the GOP seemed dead set on permanently altering the social contract that had sustained Americans since the Depression.

The economist Paul Krugman, Bush's most relentless and influential critic, makes the best and most compelling argument that the New Right

119

(mostly right-wing Republicans), rather than being a movement in the conservative mainstream, is in fact a radical revolutionary movement well outside that mainstream but intent on hijacking it.[3] This is a view that many scholars who have studied the Right accept, as indeed do some unhappy traditionalists, including Patrick Buchanan. If we are correct, contemporary conservatives have allowed themselves to become ideologues—"Radcons," as Brandeis professor Robert Reich calls them in his 2004 book, *Reason*—something that has not happened among their liberal opponents.

This explains why the two major parties appear to be playing the political game by entirely different rules. During the last few decades, Republicans, having purged their own moderates,[4] have been waging a war of attrition, something that most Democrats are only beginning to appreciate. "It is a war of ideology," says Paul Weyrich, whom the *New Republic* once dubbed the Robespierre of the Right, "a war of ideas, and it's a war about our way of life. And it has to be fought with the same intensity ... and dedication as you would fight a shooting war."[5] In waging this all-out assault, as the liberal historian Eric Foner puts it, "today's Republicans have abandoned the best parts of their heritage while retaining the worst."[6]

With many of the characteristics of a totalistic political movement—charismatic leadership, mass organizations, and a program of action—true-believer adherents of the New Right tend to see reality only in shades of black and white; their world is beset by a struggle between good and evil. Like other would-be revolutionaries who strive to create a heaven on earth, these "passionate simplifiers on the Right" also believe in the maxim "You're either with us or against us."[7]

Neutrality is not an option. Like their counterparts in other radical movements who believe in moral absolutes, many modern right-wingers adhere to a philosophy of all or nothing. Compromise is a sign of moral failing. Coming to near-absolute power after the 2004 elections has done little or nothing to moderate Republican views. The administration has proceeded methodically to demolish the system of government created by Franklin D. Roosevelt—unlike Ronald Reagan, Bush's leading role model, who threatened to dismantle the welfare state but ultimately made his peace with it. Indeed, many believe that the Republican leadership wishes to return America to the time not of President Hoover but rather of President McKinley (Karl Rove, a history buff, is an unabashed admirer of McKinley).[8]

In contrast to the Clinton administration, which continually tried to placate its political rivals—much to the chagrin of progressive Democrats who wondered when their beleaguered president would go on the offensive—the neoconservatives seem to have only contempt for their rivals. (Clinton himself was hated by his political adversaries—not disliked, not despised, but *hated*.) Compromise may well be the most essential feature of American politics (the three principles that have sustained the federal republic, according to the English expatriate, the late Alistair Cooke, a lifelong student and ardent admirer of the American system, are "compromise, compromise, compromise").[9] But GOP policymakers reject the notion outright—they despise weakness; they respect only strength—a quality that one associates with Far Right extremism, such as Christian Identity, Aryan Brotherhood, and the KKK, rather than the conservative mainstream.

However, adherents of the New Right are plainly more than a band of wild-eyed fanatics. After all, people who truly believe in all or nothing, and act consistently on that premise—French Jacobins and German Nazis, for example—inevitably wind up with nothing. Modern conservatism, in contrast, has been an unqualified success, dominating not only the political arena but also the intellectual climate. Despite the Clinton hiatus, conservative Republicans have steadily advanced their agenda since the seventies, demonstrating impressive flexibility as well as discipline. Disparate elements within the Republican Party have been willing to support candidates for public office that they do not particularly like in order to achieve long-term advantage. Actor Arnold Schwarzenegger, for example, garnered the support of most conservative Christians in his bid for the California governorship despite their sincere revulsion with Hollywood and the profligate lifestyle they associate with the entertainment capital. Right-wing Republicans have consistently kept their eyes on the prize: achieving political power and retaining it. In other words, ideological zeal has merged with Machiavellian pragmatism.

Consider, for example, the GOP cultivation of the Latino vote during the 2004 presidential elections. As previously mentioned, right-wing strategists have generally portrayed people of color, including Latinos, in a negative light, hoping to capitalize on widespread racial fears for their own political benefit—and consequently forcing Latinos to throw in their lot with the opposition. Under George W. Bush, however, the Republican strategy respecting this group has become more complex. Rather than serving as scapegoats, Latinos have increasingly come to be seen as potential allies. Cuban Americans, of course, were always reliably in the Republican fold given their vehement anticommunism—indeed, many political analysts attribute Bush's 2000 presidential victory to their support (Bush won 151,000 more Latino votes in Florida than Gore in 2000).[10] Equally important in forcing the GOP to reassess its Latino strategy, as journalist Thomas Edsall has indicated, were demographic trends.[11] Not only has the Latino population mushroomed in the past thirty years—permitting them to overtake blacks as America's leading racial minority—but the boom has centered on states with huge numbers of electoral votes: Florida, Texas, and California.[12]

Moreover, as a Texan, Bush is well acquainted with the *mexicano* population, their long history of political activism in his state, and their social conservatism.[13] Appealing to Latino family values and veneration of military service, Bush and Rove came to see, could be used to GOP political advantage. They recognized that cultivating the Latino vote was a gamble, given both the racial prejudice and the strong opposition to Mexican immigration within the GOP base: For example, "in Georgia, where nearly 1 million Hispanic immigrants have arrived since 1990, xenophobic hatred and violence are on the rise," the Southern Poverty Law Center reported in late 2004.[14] However, their political experience in Texas, where they gained 40 percent of the *tejano* vote in capturing the governorship, indicated that more stood to be gained than lost by adopting this strategy.[15] And apparently Republicans were justified in their calculations. Though the numbers are in dispute, President Bush seems to have captured about 42 percent of the Latino vote in the 2004 elections, compared to 35 percent four years before (Clinton had garnered 72 percent of that vote in 1996), which translated into a significant number of precious electoral votes.[16]

A sign of Bush's gratitude—and the importance his strategists placed on continuing efforts to encourage ethnic support—is the number of Latinos appointed to key government positions, including White House counsel Alberto Gonzales as United States attorney general and former Kellogg CEO Carlos Gutiérrez as head of the Commerce Department (another barometer of emerging Latino political clout was the election of two Latinos to the Senate: Mel Martínez [R-Fla.] and Ken Salazar [D-Colo.]).

The obvious question is why were *these* particular "chickens" (in the words of Buddy Watts's analogy) willing to support the Colonel? First, Republicans went after them, and they did so aggressively; as any Madison Avenue executive knows, this in itself guarantees some success, particularly if your key pitchman (Bush) speaks Spanish. Another reason is that the GOP tapped into the strong emphasis that most Hispanics place on the traditional family. But another quality, machismo, permeates Latino culture, where strength is respected and weakness despised. George Bush projects this image quite successfully. (GOP strategists did everything they could to depict John Kerry as a wimp.) Dubya's swagger and bravado may alienate more sensitive voters, but these very characteristics earn respect in Mexican *cantinas*—and, indeed, in working-class bars across the country. The reality is that Bush's "it's my way or the highway" approach plays well among many barrio dwellers.

The cultivation of brown votes does not mean that Republicans have forsaken the strategy of fanning and manipulating racial animosities, let alone other insecurities. What it does illustrate is that fear is a means to an end, not an end in itself. The objective of the conservative ascendancy, after all, is to gain and maintain power, and ultimately impose a probusiness agenda.

Duping the Worker Bees

The populist component of the New Conservatism, particularly Christian fundamentalism, has tended to obscure its true nature. Ultimately, the key to its success is less the zeal of the rank and file, or even the tactical and strategic genius of the young and not-so-young Republicans such as Roger Ailes, Ralph Reed, and Karl Rove, than the deep pockets of the superrich—more specifically, the corporate elite. GOP ascendancy is mainly about money. The business community sustained the New Right from the very beginning, when William Simon began his long and immensely successful 1978 campaign to solicit corporate funding for the conservative cause. This investment by the ex–Solomon Brothers executive paid off handsomely. Though little appreciated by the general public, the most consistent and far-reaching aspect of the movement has been the benefits it conferred on the economic elites, especially the so-called Wall Street Republicans.

Circuses and Culture Wars

This aspect has been deliberately obscured by its populist trappings—it can be argued that only a few New Right leaders such as Paul Weyrich ever took populism seriously—and by the emphasis party leaders have placed on the culture wars, a convenient distraction as well as a successful recruiting stratagem. Nevertheless, whenever the interests of these elites clashed with those of other factions within the GOP, the former prevailed. On the issue of immigration, for example, which so obviously pits corporate business interests against those of values-oriented colleagues, it has been no contest: Masses of worker bees, skilled and unskilled, have continued to pour into America during the long period of right-wing hegemony. Given Republican priorities, no wonder Christian evangelicals have continually been disappointed by GOP administrations, notably those of Reagan and the elder Bush. Republican strategists and politicians know where the power really resides.

Ultimately, ideologues such as Paul Weyrich, Richard Viguerie, and Grover Norquist, as important as they have been in mobilizing the troops, have been less crucial to the Republican ascendancy than the cold calculation and financial backing of the moneyed interests whose most visible representatives today are George W. Bush and Dick Cheney. ("His consistently right-wing ideology is the key to understanding Cheney, but eventually it all comes back to the money.")[17] As youths, Weyrich and other radical conservatives vowed to capture the GOP from "the country club set," but as we entered the new millennium, it was precisely Upper America—an alliance of entrepreneurial and old money elites—that has prevailed over conservative idealists, who have been largely co-opted.

It All Comes Back to the Money

If this is true, some dissenters might argue, how do we account for those other right-wingers who appear to be every bit as zealous as conservative Christians but are clearly more powerful in driving the GOP agenda—the neoconservatives? If anyone within the Republican Party deserves the label of zealot it would appear to be these individuals whose influence on policymaking is beyond dispute. Ex-insider Michael Lind argues that neoconservative stalwarts such as Paul Wolfowitz and Richard Perle are indeed inspired by ideological goals, first and foremost: "The neo-cons are ideologues, not opportunists."[18] Undoubtedly, any fair-minded observer would agree, neoconservatives do believe in the power of ideas, but Lind and like-minded analysts would do well to look beyond the surface. Was the neocon-inspired war against Iraq truly about democracy? Do neocons really lose sleep worrying about the fate of Iraqis living a hand-to-mouth existence in their war-torn homeland? Not likely. A self-proclaimed champion of democracy, Wolfowitz was mentored at the University of Chicago by Jewish intellectual Leo Strauss, who had no more use for democracy than did Friedrich Nietzsche.[19] As a Straussian, it is unlikely that Wolfowitz has any more faith in the masses than did his revered master.[20] The ex–Johns Hopkins professor, for all his patriotic bluster, is well connected with American business firms, especially defense industries. Before joining the Bush II team, he was a paid consultant for Northrop Grumman.[21] That Wolfowitz was named to head the World Bank, dominated by U.S. financial interests, is no accident.

In regard to financial ambitions, Richard Perle makes Wolfowitz look like a choir boy by comparison. Perle's multiple business dealings have often elicited charges of conflict of interest from his many critics. When serving on the Defense Policy Board, an advisory body to the secretary of defense, his good friend Donald Rumsfeld, Perle was caught, by investigative journalists, using his insider privileges to procure lucrative private contracts for his security-oriented investment group, Trireme, on three different occasions.[22] We're not talking small change. In one instance, Perle tried to convince Saudi business interests to invest $100 million in his firm. In addition, as a consultant for Boeing, Perle received $20 million for helping to solicit government contracts.[23] He sits on the board of directors of Turkish and British defense firms that do work for the Pentagon. "Perle's business ties," writes William Hartung, author of *How Much Are You Making on the War, Daddy?*, "are a work in progress, since he literally never seems to stop promoting himself for a fee."[24]

The most recent Perle financial scandal concerns charges that as a member of the board of directors, he rubber-stamped transactions initiated by media tycoon Conrad Black to plunder one of his own companies, Hollinger International, a global media giant whose holdings include the

Chicago Sun-Times. Though paid handsomely by Black for enabling the transactions, Perle claimed to federal investigators in late 2004 that he had no idea what he was signing.[25] The reconstruction of Iraq has proved to be extremely lucrative to well-connected corporations and individuals, and Perle, sometimes known as "The Prince of Darkness," not only helped to plan the unnecessary war but has been one of its financial beneficiaries. In fact, neocons such as Wolfowitz and Perle, both crony capitalists, are up to their eyeballs in corporate money. This is the very possibility that the journalist-historian Peter Steinfels feared most in the late seventies: "The great danger posed by and to neoconservatism is that it will become nothing more than the legitimating and lubricating ideology of an oligarchic America where essential decisions are made by corporate elites, where great inequalities are rationalized by straitened circumstances and a system of meritocratic hierarchy, and where democracy becomes an occasional, ritualistic gesture."[26]

It is tempting to attribute the triumph of conservatism to corporations, as many scholars have done, but this popular leftist interpretation is a little misleading. After all, the corporation does not live in a mansion, or drive a Mercedes, or take a vacation in Tahiti. Corporations are merely tools wealthy individuals[27] use to make and protect their fortunes. This has been the case since the nineteenth century. In the 1890s, virtually all the major railroad companies (corporations) in the country went bankrupt, but their real owners, the Vanderbilts, Huntingtons, Fricks, Goulds, and Harrimans, survived quite well, thank you.

Since the 1970s, U.S. productivity has witnessed a spectacular climb. From 1970 to 2000, the real GDP soared from slightly over $3.5 trillion to $9 trillion.[28] What happened to this massive wealth? Are U.S. workers earning that much more? Are their vacations that much longer? Are their fringe benefits that much better? No. Arnold Packer, a Johns Hopkins University economist, has calculated that employees' share of the nation's wealth has dropped to the lowest level since 1947.[29] Well, then, perhaps the huge profits have been used to enhance the general welfare. But are the nation's school systems significantly better? Have medical services improved markedly? Are social welfare programs better funded? No, again.

The truth of the matter is that the overwhelming portion of this wealth has gone into the pockets of a relatively small number of individuals. Collectively, these major beneficiaries constitute what Columbia University professor C. Wright Mills labeled the power elite, and, as journalist Michael Lind makes clear, virtually all of them belong to what he calls "the white overclass."[30] While this small group of oligarchs is extraordinarily homogeneous in ethnic and gender background, in other ways it is anything but monolithic. The oligarchy includes both capitalists (e.g., financiers, corporate executives, investors, and business owners) and noncapitalists (e.g., lawyers, politicians, and celebrities, including media celebrities). The power elite includes, too, heirs of long-established family dynasties such as the Mellons, the DuPonts, and the Rockefellers ("Old Money"), as well as newer dynasties such as those established by hugely successful entrepreneurs such as Sam Walton and Joseph Coors. While the majority of superrich Americans inherited most of their fortunes, many millionaires are self-made men (i.e., they inherited only part of their wealth): inventor-entrepreneurs such as Lawrence Ellison (Oracle), Michael Dell (Dell), and Bill Gates (Microsoft); media moguls such as Rupert Murdoch, Ted Turner, and John Kluge; Wall Street gurus such as Charles Schwab, George Soros, and Warren E. Buffett; and corporate managers such as Jack Welch (GE), Michael Eisner (Disney), and Carly Fiorina (Hewlett-Packard).

The last group, the chief executive officers, are perhaps the most visible symbol of American capitalism today, reflecting the extent to which the corporation dominates economic life. In the last generation, they have gained so much power and prestige that they are generally much better known than the owners of the corporations that employ them. Their compensation packages, at least those that represent Fortune 500 companies, have risen dramatically during the last generation, even while their firms have laid off thousands of employees and company profits have declined.

Indeed, if critic Arianna Huffington is to be believed, "rewarding CEOs for failure has become the norm rather than the exception."[31] How is this possible? These lucrative packages—consisting of salaries, stock options, bonuses, long-term compensation, low-interest loans, and other remunerations—are voted by the firm's board of directors. These individuals have a great incentive to ingratiate themselves to the CEO, who is usually also the chairman (very occasionally, chairwoman) of the board and to whom they likely owe their appointment, as well as their own compensation. Although many directors make more, the average salary for a director of a top 200 company board is about $137,000.[32] Moreover, many board members are themselves senior executives for other firms (disgraced CEOs Ken Lay of Enron and Dennis Kozlowski of Tyco sat on the boards of Eli Lilly and Raytheon, respectively). All of this makes for cozy in-house financial arrangements at the expense of stockholders. Though it would be impossible to generalize about their particular political affiliations, all members of the moneyed elites are deeply interested in politics.

An Interlocking Web

Clearly, it is this capitalist elite that has benefited the most from the so-called Conservative Revolution. Public policies originate in the boardrooms of their megacorporations. Like the corporation itself, the New Right is another instrument of the wealthy. It is these powerful businessmen who have funded the major right-wing think tanks such as the American Enterprise Institute and the Heritage Foundation; who dominate influential quasi-political associations such as the Business Roundtable and the secretive Council for National Policy; and who ultimately decide, mainly via hefty campaign contributions, who sits in public office.

Of course, the GOP, a coalition of several distinct groups with a variety of agendas, has other interests to protect besides those of the superrich. Some political analysts, in fact, see religious conservatives as sharing the driver's seat, particularly after their decisive role in securing George W. Bush's reelection in 2004. Certainly right-wing Christians carry more weight today than they did under either Reagan or Bush senior.[33] However, as noted, whenever the interests of this values-oriented wing—abortion, pornography, and so on—clash with those of the business-oriented wing, economic considerations always receive top priority. "You have the country-clubbers re-emerging," populist champion Paul Weyrich lamented at the end of George Bush the elder's presidency, "to take over the party and to produce candidates who don't relate to working-class conservatives. This is much more than a single issue like abortion. It's really a class issue."[34] What was true then is true today. The piper continues to call the tune.

A Cozy Cabinet

While the presidency of George W. Bush, with its many ties to the energy industry, clearly illustrates the symbiotic relationship between modern conservatism and the business community, the quintessential example is the administration of Ronald Reagan. The Hollywood actor became governor of California in the midsixties because he was chosen as the Republican candidate, not by the party but by his powerful friends, a small coterie of millionaires, including Henry Salvatori, Holmes Tuttle, Edward Mills, and A. C. Rubel.[35] His political career was carefully nurtured by these influential moneymen. In 1980, when Reagan was elected the fortieth president of the United States, they became the core of his Kitchen Cabinet, a body whose spectrum, according to the *Washington Post,* ranged "from millionaire to multimillionaire; from middle-aged to elderly, and all white male."[36] (Reagan's regular cabinet included such business stalwarts as George Schultz and William Simon.)

The most influential member of this group of advisers was Joseph Coors. The Reagan agenda, hammered out by the Heritage Foundation— which Coors and his associates funded and controlled (according to its president, Edwin Feulner, without Coors, "there would be no Heritage Foundation")[37]—was essentially *their* agenda. The president may have proved a disappointment to the Christian Right, but he gave his business associates everything they could want and more. The tax code changed to privilege the wealthy. The top personal tax income bracket dropped from 70 percent to 28 percent in just seven years.[38] Between 1980 and 1990, the after-tax profits of U.S. corporations skyrocketed from $82.3 billion to $229 billion.[39] The poor, on the other hand, suffered. Throughout Reagan's administrations, the minimum hourly wage was kept at $3.35, which meant that, given inflation, minimum-wage workers experienced an overall salary cut.[40] As Kevin Phillips demonstrates in *The Politics of Rich and Poor,* using a multitude of statistics, the Reagan era was a bonanza only for business elites, particularly for entrepreneurial capitalists—not a period of general prosperity, as Republican apologists claim. The legacy continues. For the superrich, the Republican Party is the gift that just keeps on giving.

Official Secrecy

Having considered the inner workings of the Republican ascendancy, let us end by briefly examining its outward style, one of the most controversial aspects of contemporary politics. In the midst of the bitter and ill-advised GOP campaign to depose President Bill Clinton, the First Lady, interviewed by *Today* show host Katie Couric, claimed that her much-maligned husband was a victim of a vast right-wing conspiracy, a charge she repeated in her best-selling autobiography.[41] More generally, some liberal critics see the advent of modern-day conservatism in this same way—as a product of a conspiratorial plot. How tenable is this view? If we accept Webster's definition of a *conspiracy* as "a planning and acting together secretly," the answer to this crucial question can be elusive.

Modern-day conservatives have a penchant for secrecy, one that begins at the very top. Robert Reich, formerly a member of the Clinton team, notes that the administration of George W. Bush has been the most secretive since the administration of Richard M. Nixon.[42] John Dean, President Nixon's White House counsel, goes one better in his 2004 book, *Worse Than Watergate,* charging, as the title suggests, that the Bush White House represents the most secretive presidency of the past fifty years, far worse than that of his ex-boss. All politicos make plans, of course, and they have advisers to help them, in both governmental and nongovernmental bodies. Most administrations have been relatively open about how they arrive at policies, at least most of the time. The Republicans prefer to divulge as little as possible, something that was true even before September 11. Both domestic and foreign policies are hammered out behind closed doors. The president is virtually paranoid about leaks. Loyalty is the attribute he demands and most admires in his subordinates, as Paul O'Neill discovered when, failing to fully support the president's tax cuts, he was unceremoniously dumped as secretary of the treasury.[43] President Bush dislikes talking to the press, and when he does, he is often evasive. If Bill O'Reilly is the master of spin, the chief executive gives him a run for his money: "President Bush," a longtime student of politics remarks, "has made a political career of transforming his weaknesses into strengths. A lack of eloquence? He's a straight talker. Not much for nuance? He has a clear vision. Disdain for detail? He's a big-picture leader."[44] The president's spokespeople follow his cue. Like their boss, they have become masters of newspeak.

Official Discipline

The secrecy of recent Republican administrations is understandable, for they have had much to hide. Recall how neoconservatives exaggerated threats of terrorism and weapons of mass destruction to justify war against Iraq, and when, again after careful preparation, the costs of the highly touted 2003 Medicare reform law—which, in fact, helped pharmaceutical firms far more than it helped the elderly—were understated by at least $100 billion to gain congressional approval.[45] When misrepresentations came to light, rather than apologize, Republicans have consistently shifted the blame: "Rarely has there been a president so loath to take responsibility for things he has done.... To George W. Bush, the buck stops anyplace but with him."[46]

Anyone challenging the team has been quickly discredited. The character assassinations of insider turncoats come to mind immediately: Paul O'Neill, who divulged the minute details of policymaking in the Bush cabinet, including the president's disengagement; ex-ambassador Joseph Wilson, who refused to back the administration's position on Iraq's alleged nuclear threat; Richard Clarke, the former White House antiterrorism czar who criticized Bush's September 11 response; and the nation's top Medicare actuary, Richard S. Foster, who divulged the bait-and-switch tactics used to gain passage of the controversial Medicare bill.[47] The attempt to demonize Democratic presidential contender John Kerry, a genuine war hero, becomes even more striking when one considers that most of his critics inside the Bush administration took a rain check on service in Vietnam and calls to mind the administration of Richard Nixon.

Contrary to one popular interpretation, the Bush agenda did not spring full-blown out of the fertile brain of one man; Bush is not that intelligent. Nor was it the brainchild of even Karl Rove or Dick Cheney, although these two individuals undoubtedly carry considerable weight with the chief executive. The policies of the current administration are, for the most part, products of ideas that have been simmering in conservative circles for the past thirty years.

Teamwork

The people who count in GOP policymaking are small in number. As one surveys the spectrum of conservative organizations, especially in the nation's capital, one is struck by the appearance of the same names over and over again among their leaders. They know one another, often intimately, and they meet frequently. Except for social gatherings, these meetings are largely closed to the public. Republican initiatives during the last thirty years reflect a high degree of coordination (what the Nazis called *Gleichschaltung*).[48] Republican discipline in Congress is unprecedented, a mirror of the kind of organization conservatives have achieved beyond Capitol Hill. The groups number in the hundreds and have worked together remarkably well. The genesis of the Republican national agenda is to be found here, at the local level. Sometimes these initiatives come out of think tanks, which by their nature are closed institutions. The public knows little about these elitist organizations, especially those that focus on military affairs, except what their representatives release for popular consumption via the media. In order to translate conservative ideas into public policy, through the executive or legislative branches of government, they need to gain the support of a wide variety of groups. Constant networking is required. Cooperation is essential. This mobilization is carried out in members-only meetings. Some are informal, others are formal.

An example of the former are the weekly Wednesday morning meetings that master GOP strategist Grover Norquist has been convening since 1993 in the nation's capital. Some one hundred of the city's most powerful right-wing power brokers—congressional and White House staffers, lobbyists, and think tank fellows—gather at the invitation-only meetings held in the conference room of the Americans for Tax Reform headquarters, where they brainstorm and swap intelligence. A rare outsider, a journalist, permitted to enter the inner sanctum, recalls, "There is no time for canned political rhetoric. The focus is on winning. Here, strategy is honed. Talking points are refined. Discipline is imposed." "Norquist's goal," the reporter concludes, "is nothing less than a well-oiled national, state, and local political machine that can roll over and crush the last few bastions of Democratic Party support."[49] Given the grim determination of Norquist and his high-energy colleagues, the conservative movement's prospects, in the short term, at least, appear to be excellent.

Drown It in the Bathtub

The highly secretive Council for National Policy (CNP) is an example of a highly institutionalized group that meets on a regular basis—three times a year. In this regard it resembles another conservative advocacy group, the Business Roundtable. Unlike this association of CEOs, however, the CNP keeps its membership directories confidential—as well it might: It sponsors an intensely ideological agenda. Founded in 1981 as a nonprofit educational organization by ultraright-wing millionaires and evangelical preachers, it has origins not in mainstream conservatism but rather in the nativist and reactionary circles of the Radical Right, including the John Birch Society.[50] Nevertheless, uniting religious and secular conservatives, the CNP is today considered a New Right organization. Paul Weyrich was a major player almost from the very beginning, and, although eclipsed in recent years, he remains influential today. (As mentioned previously, at the turn of the century, the executive secretary was a longtime Weyrich associate, Morton Blackwell.)

Both Richard Viguerie and Howard Phillips have been active members, as was Terry Dolan before his untimely death. However, neoconservatives are conspicuous by their absence—they have their own conclave, in Beaver Creek, Colorado, where they meet annually.[51] With this one exception, the membership list of some five hundred individuals, most of them leaders of smaller but prominent groups, reads like a who's who in modern American conservatism. Past and present members, according to researchers, include such prominent leaders as John Ashcroft, James Dobson, Larry Pratt, William Simon Sr., Gary Bauer, Jeffrey Coors, John Ankerberg, Pat Robertson, Rousas J. Rushdoony, Phyllis Schlafly, Oliver North, and Grover Norquist.[52] Right-wing luminaries George Gilder, Edward Teller, Jesse Helms, and William Rusher have also been members at one time or another.[53]

Initially established to formulate foreign policy initiatives, the CNP promotes the entire panoply of ideas dear to right-wingers. The organization's most important resource, though, is its moneymen. "There's no denying their influence: Money is transferred from benefactor to worthy cause. Aspirants meet benefactors."[54] The group sees itself as a counterweight to the alleged domination of the liberal establishment—which in fact has no exactly comparable body uniting its most high-profile leaders. So far the word *conspiracy* does not seem inappropriate to describe this interlocking network. Paul Krugman is representative of many scholars who share this view: "it's unrealistic to pretend that there *isn't* a sort of conspiracy here."[55] In spite of the shadowy reputation of the CNP and many other ultraconservative groups and the penchant for secrecy in the Bush administration, however, the Right can be disarmingly open about its political views, something that Krugman concedes.[56] Every four years, Republicans present their party platform very openly and clearly before the electorate. Moreover, the GOP agenda, as we have seen, is one that has been articulated throughout the years by party strategists representing the various factions that collectively make up the New Right, and these operatives have been unusually forthright in some of their public declarations about their common vision: "an America in which the rich will be taxed at the same rates as the poor, where capital is freed from government constraints, where government services are turned over to the free market, where the minimum wage is repealed, unions are made irrelevant, and law-abiding citizens can pack handguns in every state and town."[57] None of these spokesmen have been more blunt than Grover Norquist, who once famously explained how conservatives would shrink the federal government; he and his confederates fully intended, he announced, "to get it down to the size where we can drown it in the bathtub."[58] Conservative think tanks make no bones about their long-range objectives: Their programs are readily available on their Web sites.

Struck by this boldness, respected journalist Bill Moyers, an LBJ liberal, concludes, "You have to respect the conservatives for their successful strategy in gaining control of the national agenda. Their stated and open aim is to strip from government all its functions except those that reward their rich and privileged benefactors. They are quite candid about it, even acknowledging their mean spirit in accomplishing it."[59] If Norquist and his ideological soul mates are conspirators, they are extremely bold ones, and those who value democracy have much to fear.

→ APPENDIX A ←

MAJOR NEW RIGHT ORGANIZATIONS

The major New Right organizations listed here are divided into several somewhat arbitrary categories: foundations, think tanks and research institutes, advocacy groups, legal centers, and campus groups. (Not all conservative organizations can be classified as New Right. Obvious exceptions—such as the Ku Klux Klan, the John Birch Society, and the Posse Comitatus—have been omitted.) Furthermore, these New Right organizations can be divided into different categories in terms of their specific ideological orientation under the broad rubric of conservatism. As we have seen, there are a multitude of right-wing streams after World War II. However, because some organizations do not fit comfortably into one single designation and because it is sometimes difficult to distinguish the dominant trend—notably between neoconservative and traditional conservative—we have chosen to reduce the categories in this appendix to four: right, right center, Christian, and libertarian. An indication of one of the four ideological orientations follows the name of the organization, the date of its foundation, and the headquarters.

Foundations

Adolph Coors Foundation
Carthage Foundation
Charles G. Koch Foundation
Claude R. Lambe Foundation
David H. Koch Foundation
Earhart Foundation
Henry Salvatori Foundation
JM Foundation
John M. Olin Foundation
Lynde and Harry Bradley Foundation

Phillip M. McKenna Foundation
Pioneer Fund
Sarah Scaife Foundation
Smith Richardson Foundation

Think Tanks and Research Institutes

Admiral Jeremiah Denton Foundation (AJDF), 1983, Washington, D.C., right
Alexis de Tocqueville Institution, 1986, Arlington, Virginia, right
Allegheny Institute for Public Policy, 1995, Pittsburgh, right
American Enterprise Institute for Public Policy Research (AEI), 1943, Washington, D.C., right
American Legislative Exchange Council (ALEC), Washington, D.C., right
American Policy Center (APC), 1988, Warrenton, Virginia, right
Cato Institute, 1977, Washington, D.C., libertarian
Center for Immigration Studies (CIS), 1985, Washington, D.C., right
Center for Libertarian Studies, 1976, Burlingame, California, libertarian
Center for Public Justice (CP Justice), 1981, Annapolis, Maryland, Christian right
Center for Security Policy, 1988, Washington, D.C., right
Center for Strategic and International Studies (CSIS), 1962, Washington, D.C., right
Claremont Institute for the Study of Statesmanship and Political Philosophy, 1979, Claremont, California, right
Commonwealth Foundation for Public Policy Alternatives (The Commonwealth Foundation), 1988, Harrisburg, Pennsylvania, right
Competitive Enterprise Institute (CEI), 1984, Washington, D.C., right
Ethics and Public Policy Center (EPPC), 1976, Washington, D.C., right
Family Research Council (FRC), 1983, Washington, D.C., Christian right
Free Congress Research and Education Foundation (FCF), 1978, Washington, D.C., right
Free Enterprise Society, 1979, Fresno, California, right
George G. Stigler Center for the Study of the Economy and the State, 1993, University of Chicago, Chicago, right
Goldwater Institute, 1988, Phoenix, right
Heartland Institute, 1984, Chicago, right
Heritage Foundation, 1973, Washington, D.C., right
Hoover Institution on War, Revolution, and Peace, 1919, Stanford University, Palo Alto, California, right
Hudson Institute, 1961, Indianapolis, Indiana, right
Institute for Foreign Policy Analysis (IFPA), 1976, Cambridge, Massachusetts, and Washington, D.C., right

Institute for Policy Innovation (IPI), 1987, Lewisville, Texas, right
James Madison Institute (JMI), 1987, Tallahassee, Florida, right
Jewish Institute for National Security Affairs (JINSA), 1976, Washington, D.C., right
John M. Ashbrook Center for Public Affairs, 1983, Ashland, Ohio, right
Kuyper Institute, 1994, Washington, D.C., Christian right
Life Issues Institute, 1996?, Cincinnati, Ohio, right
Ludwig von Mises Institute, 1982, Auburn, Alabama, libertarian
Mackinac Center for Public Policy (MCPP), 1987, Midland, Michigan, right
Manhattan Institute for Policy Research, 1978, New York, right
Middle East Forum (MEF), 1990, Washington, D.C., right
Middle East Media Research Institute (MEMRI), 1998, Washington, D.C., right
National Center for Policy Analysis (NCPA), 1983, Dallas, right
National Center for Public Policy Research (NCPPR), 1982, Washington, D.C., right
National Strategy Information Center (NSIC), 1962, Washington, D.C., right
Pacific Research Institute for Public Policy (PRI), 1979, San Francisco, right
Pioneer Institution for Public Policy Research (PI), 1988, Boston, right
Political Economy Research Center (PERC), 1980, Bozeman, Montana, right
Progress and Freedom Foundation (PFF), 1993, Washington, D.C., right
Project for the New American Century (PNAC), 1997, Washington, D.C., right
RAND Corporation, 1948, Santa Monica, California, right center
Reason Public Policy Institute (RPPI), 1997, Los Angeles, libertarian
Rockford Institute, 1976, Rockford, Illinois, right
Washington Institute for Near East Policy (The Washington Institute), 1985, Washington, D.C., right center
Weidenbaum Center on the Economy, Government, and Public Policy, 1975, Washington University, St. Louis, Missouri, right

Advocacy Groups

Accuracy in Academia (AIA), 1985, Washington, D.C., right
Accuracy in Media (AIM), 1969, Washington, D.C., right
American Civil Rights Institute (ACRI), 1997, Sacramento, California, right
American Conservative Union (ACU), 1964, Alexandria, Virginia, right
American Family Association (AFA), 1977, Tupelo, Mississippi, Christian right

American Immigration Control Foundation (AIC Foundation), 1983, Monterey, Virginia, right
American Life League (ALL), 1979, Stafford, Virginia, Christian right
Americans for Tax Reform (ATR), 1986, Washington, D.C., right
Center for Equal Opportunity (CEO), 1995, Sterling, Virginia, right
Center for the Study of Popular Culture (CSPC), 1988, Los Angeles, right
Christian Coalition (CC), 1989, Chesapeake, Virginia, Christian right
Citizens for a Sound Economy (CSE), 1984, Washington, D.C., right
Coalition on Revival (COR), 1984, Murphys, California, Christian right
Committee for the Free World (CFW), 1981, New York, right
Committee on Media Integrity (COMINT), 1988, Los Angeles, right
Concerned Women for America (CWA), 1979, Washington, D.C., right
Conservative Caucus (TCC), 1974, Vienna, Virginia, right
Eagle Forum (EF), 1972, Alton, Illinois, right
Empower America, 1993, Washington, D.C., right
English First (EF), 1986, Springfield, Virginia, right
Federation for American Immigration Reform (FAIR), 1979, Washington, D.C., right
Focus on the Family (FOTF), 1977, Colorado Springs, Colorado, Christian right
FRC Action, 1992, Washington, D.C., right
Free Congress Research and Education Foundation (FCF), 1977, Washington, D.C., right
Independent Women's Forum (IWF), 1992, Washington, D.C., right
Leadership Institute (LI), 1979, Arlington, Virginia, right
Media Research Center (MRC), 1987, Alexandria, Virginia, right
National Journalism Center (NJC), 1977, Herndon, Virginia, right
National Right to Life Committee (NRLC), 1973, Washington, D.C., right
National Taxpayers Union (NTU), 1969, Alexandria, Virginia, right
Promise Keepers (PK), 1990, Denver, Christian right
State Policy Network (SPN), 1992, Richmond, California, right
Traditional Values Coalition (TVC), 1980, Anaheim, California, Christian right
U.S. English, 1983, Washington, D.C., right

Legal Centers

Alliance Defense Fund (ADF), 1994, Scottsdale, Arizona, Christian right
American Center for Law and Justice (ACLJ), 1991, Virginia Beach, Virginia, Christian right
Atlantic States Legal Foundation (ASLF), 1983, New York, right
Center for Individual Rights (CIR), 1989, Washington, D.C., right

Federalist Society for Law and Public Policy Studies (FS), 1982, Washington, D.C., right

Foundation for Research on Economics and the Environment (FREE), 1985, Bozeman, Montana, right

Home School Legal Defense Association (HSLDA), 1983, Purcellville, Virginia, Christian right

Institute for Justice (IJ), 1991, Washington, D.C., libertarian

Landmark Legal Foundation (LLF), 1976, Kansas City, Missouri, and Herndon, Virginia, right

Mountain States Legal Foundation (MSLF), 1976, Lakewood, Colorado, right

National Legal Foundation (NLF), 1985, Virginia Beach, Virginia, Christian right

New England Legal Foundation (NELF), 1977, Boston, right

Pacific Legal Foundation (PLF), 1973, Sacramento, California, right

Rutherford Institute, 1982, Charlottesville, Virginia, Christian right

Southeastern Legal Foundation (SLF), 1976, Atlanta, right

Washington Legal Foundation (WLF), 1977, Washington, D.C., right

Western Legal Foundation (WLF), 1982, Oakland, California, right

Campus Groups

Campus Crusade for Christ International, 1951, Orlando, Florida, Christian right

College Republican National Committee (CRNC), 1892, Washington, D.C., right

Institute for Educational Affairs (IEA), 1978, New York, right

Intercollegiate Studies Institute (ISI), 1958, Wilmington, Delaware, right

Madison Center for Educational Affairs (MCEA), 1991, Washington, D.C., right

National Association of Scholars (NAS), 1987, Rutgers, New Jersey, right

Students for Academic Freedom (SAF), 2003, Washington, D.C., right

Young Americans for Freedom (YAF), 1960, Wilmington, Delaware, right

MEDIA COMMENTATORS, 2004

Political Orientation

Radical/Progressive

Noam Chomsky
Alexander Cockburn
Kevin Danaher
Barbara Ehrenreich
Juan Gonzalez
Amy Goodman
Jim Hightower

Michael Moore
Ralph Nader
Christian Parenti
Michael Parenti
Arundhati Roy
Howard Zinn

Liberal

Gar Alperovitz
Jonathan Alter
Eric Alterman
Ben H. Bagdikian
David Barsamian
Paul Begala
Sidney Blumenthal
Eric Boehlert
Robert Borosage
David Brock
Ronald Brownstein
James Carville

Ira Chernus
Kate Clinton
Jeff Cohen
Richard Cohen
Joe Conason
Ruth Conniff
Marc Cooper
David Corn
Mike Davis
E. J. Dionne Jr.
Phil Donohue
Maureen Dowd

Elizabeth Drew
Daniel Ellsberg
Laura Flanders
Al Franken
Janeane Garofalo
Todd Gitlin
Richard Goldstein
Patrisia Gonzales
Ellen Goodman
William Greider
Charles Grodin
Terry Gross
Thom Hartmann
Nat Hentoff
Bob Herbert
Seymour Hersh
Hendrik Hertzberg
Arianna Huffington
Earl Ofari Hutchinson
Molly Ivins
Chalmers Johnson
John Judis
Michael Kinsley
Naomi Klein
Michael Krasny
Nicholas Kristof
Paul Krugman
Robert Kuttner
Lewis Lapham
Anthony Lewis
Ted Lyons
Rachel Maddox
Julianne Malveaux
Manning Marable
Colman McCarthy
Robert McChesney
Mary McGrory*
Mark Morford
Bill Moyers
Lars-Erik Nelson
Jack Newfield
John Nichols
Clarence Page

Gregory Palast
Rick Perlstein
Katha Pollitt
Bill Press
Anna Quindlen
Ted Rall
Robert Reich
Randi Rhodes
Frank Rich
Roberto Rodriguez
Richard Roeper
Ruth Rosen
Dave Ross
Matt Rothschild
Stephanie Salter
Bernie Sanders
Robert Scheer
Jonathan Schell
Orville Schell
Michael Scherer
Arthur Schlesinger Jr.
Daniel Schor
Ed Schultz
Sam Seder
Mark Shields
Ken Silverstein
Holly Sklar
Norman Solomon
George Stephanopoulos
Jon Stewart
Helen Thomas
Lester Thurow
Michael Tomasky
Laurence Tribe
Calvin Trillin
Cynthia Tucker
Brian Unger
Katrina vanden Heuvel
Bernie Ward
Tom Wicker
John Wiener
Garry Wills
Lizz Winstead

*Deceased

Moderate

Christiane Amanpour
Kevin Baker
Ashleigh Banfield
Jeff Birnbaum
Wolf Blitzer
David Broder
Tom Brokaw
Aaron Brown
Margaret Carlson
Connie Chung
Eleanor Clift
Alan Colmes
Katie Couric
Alan Dershowitz
Sam Donaldson
Howard Fineman
Tom Friedman
Jack Germond
Doris Kearns Goodwin
Meg Greenfield*
Christopher Hitchens
Al Hunt
Peter Jennings*
Haynes B. Johnson
Larry King
Joe Klein
Ted Koppel
Brian Lamb

Jim Lehrer
Mara Liasson
Chris Matthews
Al Neuharth
Leonard Pitts Jr.
Jane Bryant Quinn
Sally Quinn
Dan Rather
Richard Reeves
Geraldo Rivera
Cokie Roberts
Richard Rodriguez
Charlie Rose
Tim Russert
Joan Ryan
Morley Safer
Diane Sawyer
Hedrick Smith
Terence Smith
Ray Suarez
Nina Totenberg
Garrick Utley
Greta Van Susteren
Mike Wallace
Margaret Warner
Brian Williams
Juan Williams
Bob Woodward

Conservative

David Asman
Fred Barnes
Michael Barone
Robert Bartley*
Glenn Beck
William Bennett
Tony Blankley
Max Boot
Brent Bozell III

Warren Brookes
David Brooks
Tony Brown
Pat Buchanan
William F. Buckley Jr.
Eric Burns
Christopher Caldwell
Tucker Carlson
Neil Cavuto

*Deceased

Mona Charen
Linda Chavez
Lynne Cheney
Ward Connerly
Ann Coulter
Naomi Decter
Lou Dobbs
James Dobson
Robert Dornan
Morton Downey Jr.*
Matt Drudge
Dinesh D'Souza
Pete du Pont
Larry Elder
Rowland Evans*
Ambrose Evans-Pritchard
Jerry Falwell
Suzanne Fields
Samuel Francis
Francis Fukuyama
John Fund
Frank Gaffney
Maggie Gallagher
Trace Gallagher
David Gergen
Paul Gigot
Newt Gingrich
James Glassman
Jonah Goldberg
Lucianne Goldberg
Bob Grant
Paul Greenberg
Bob Greene
Alexander Haig Jr.
Ken Hamblin
Sean Hannity
Victor Davis Hanson
Jeffrey Hart
Roger Hedgecock
Daniel Henninger
David Horowitz
Brit Hume
Samuel Huntington

Don Imus
Laura Ingraham
Jeff Jacoby
Terry Jeffrey
Holman Jenkins Jr.
Robert Kagan
Michael Kelly*
Jack Kemp
Paul Kennedy
Alan Keyes
Brian Kilmeade
James Kirkpatrick
Jeanne Kirkpatrick
Larry Klayman
Mort Kondracke
Charles Krauthammer
Irving Kristol
William Kristol
Lawrence Kudlow
Howard Kurtz
Steve Largent
Michael Ledeen
Susan Lee
John Leo
G. Gordon Liddy
Carl Limbacher
David Limbaugh
Rush Limbaugh
Joseph Loconte
Rich Lowry
Frank Luntz
Michelle Malkin
Myriam Marquez
Mary Matalin
John McLaughlin
Michael McManus
John H. McWhorter
Michael Medved
Edwin Meese
Dennis Miller
Judy Miller
Dick Morris
Joel Mowbray

*Deceased

Ruben Navarrette
Lyn Nofziger
Peggy Noonan
Oliver North
Michael Novak
Robert Novak
Heather Nuart
Kate O'Beirne
Marvin Olasky
Bill O'Reilly
P. J. O'Rourke
Camille Paglia
Joseph Perkins
Richard Perle
John Podhoretz
Norman Podhoretz
Richard Posner
Dennis Prager
Dan Quayle
Dorothy Rabinowitz
Michael Reagan
Ralph Reed
Judith Regan
Pat Robertson
William Rusher
William Safire
Robert Samuelson
Debra Saunders

Michael Savage
Joe Scarborough
Phyllis Schlafly
Laura Schlessinger
William Schneider
Tony Snow
Thomas Sowell
Ben Stein
John Stossel
Kim Strassel
Andrew Sullivan
Tom Sullivan
John Sununu
Abigail Thernstrom
Stephan Thernstrom
Cal Thomas
John Tierney
R. Emmett Tyrrell
Ben Wattenberg
Paul Weyrich
George Will
Armstrong Williams
Walter Williams
Byron York
Cathy Young
Paula Zahn
Fareed Zakaria

NOTES

Introduction

1. We use the terms *New Right* and *New Conservatism* interchangeably. However, scholars differ on their definitions of both terms. Take, for example, the term *New Right*. Sara Diamond—*Not by Politics Alone: The Enduring Influence of the Christian Right* (New York: Guilford, 1998), 59—uses this term to refer exclusively to secular as distinguished from religious conservatives (members of what she calls the "Christian Right"). On the other hand, George H. Nash—*The Conservative Intellectual Movement in America, since 1945*, rev. ed. (Wilmington, Del.: Intercollegiate Studies Institute, 1998), 331—uses *New Right* (and *Religious Right*) to designate conservative Christians exclusively. For a history of modern conservatism, see Jerome L. Himmelstein, *To the Right: The Transformation of American Conservatism* (Berkeley: University of California Press, 1992); William C. Berman, *America's Right Turn: From Nixon to Clinton*, 2d ed. (Baltimore: Johns Hopkins University Press, 1998); and Lee Edwards, *The Conservative Revolution: The Movement That Remade America* (New York: Free Press, 1999). An unflattering view comes from New Right apostate Michael Lind, *Up from Conservatism: Why the Right Is Wrong for America* (New York: Free Press, 1996).

2. Godfrey Hodgson, *The World Turned Right Side Up: A History of the Conservative Ascendancy in America* (New York: Houghton Mifflin, 1996), 12.

3. The New Right displays almost all the traits that Eric Hoffer attributes to similar radical movements in his classic *The True Believer: Thoughts on the Nature of Mass Movements* (New York: Harper & Row, 1951). In our view, the movement consists primarily of three blocs: the probusiness mainstream, the Christian Right, and the neoconservatives. Of course, many other strands populate modern conservatism, both in and out of the Republican Party. The libertarians associated with the Cato Institute and the paleoconservatives who look to Patrick Buchanan continue to exert a significant influence within the Republican Party. The moderate-progressives (the tradition of Earl Warren, Nelson Rockefeller, and John Lindsay) have become increasingly marginalized within the GOP. The John Birch Society was prominent during the height of the Cold War but no longer plays a significant role. The eccentric faction associated with Lyndon LaRouche (b. 1922) is even more of a fringe element. A "lunatic Right"—the American Nazi Party, the Ku Klux Klan, the Liberty Lobby, the Posse Comitatus, and so on—have declining influence on the conservative movement today.

4. Al Franken, *Lies and the Lying Liars Who Tell Them: A Fair and Balanced Look at the Right* (New York: Dutton, 2003), 140; Elizabeth Drew, *The Corruption of American Politics: What Went Wrong and Why* (Woodstock, N.Y.: Overlook, 1999), 215. Clinton bashing has spawned an entire cottage industry among right-wing authors, whose hatred of the ex-president and his wife matches only their idolatry of Ronald Reagan. The hate campaign against Bill Clinton, however, was not entirely personal: "Fear and loathing of Clinton proved useful in uniting the diverse conservative coalition." Michael Schaller and George Rising, *The Republican Ascendancy: American Politics, 1968-2001* (Wheeling, Ill.: Harlan Davidson, 2002), 123.

5. Two British journalists for the *Economist* convincingly demonstrate that America today—not just the right-wing movement in the United States—is significantly more conservative (and religious) than any other part of the industrialized world. See John Micklethwait and Adrian Wooldridge, *The Right Nation: Conservative Power in America* (New York: Penguin Books, 2004), 11.

6. Lawrence Mishel and Ross Eisenbrey, "The Economy in a Nutshell: Wages & Incomes Down, Poverty & Debt Up," *Counterpunch*, December 23, 2005, http://www.counterpunch.org/mishel12232005.html. By way of comparison, Americans had a per capita gross domestic product of $33,900 in 1999, compared to the $27,800 of second-place Singapore, according to William D. Rohlfs Jr., *Introduction to Economic Reasoning*, 5th ed. (Boston: Addison-Wesley, 2002), 447.

7. Jennifer L. Hochschild, *Facing Up to the American Dream* (Princeton, N.J.: Princeton University Press, 1995), cited by Andrew L. Barlow, *Between Fear and Hope: Globalization and Race in the United States* (Lanham, Md.: Rowman & Littlefield, 2003), 49.

8. Barlow, *Between Fear and Hope,* 32.

9. While the gap is narrowing, in 2003, Democrats still outnumbered Republicans 32 percent to 30 percent. Adam Clymer, "Republicans Build Campaign Structure," *Contra Costa Times* (Walnut Creek, Calif.), May 25, 2003. For party affiliation, consult the U.S. Census Bureau Web site (www.census.gov), specifically figure 8.1 ("Political Party Identification of the Adult Population: 1960 to 1994") under "Elections." The statistics after 1994 are unavailable.

10. Many observers would contest this characterization of Americans' political orientation. "In fact," Joe Conason notes, "despite conservative political advances in recent decades, survey evidence gathered by pollsters of all persuasions suggests that Americans are still more liberal than conservative." *Big Lies: The Right-Wing Propaganda Machine and How It Distorts the Truth* (New York: Dunne, 2003), 7.

11. Tim Grieve, "Talking Hope, Selling Fear," *Salon.com*, February 3, 2005, http://www.salon.com/news/feature/2005/02/03/sotu_iraq/index_np.html.

Chapter 1

1. John A. Andrew III, *The Other Side of the Sixties: Young Americans for Freedom and the Rise of Conservative Politics* (New Brunswick, N.J.: Rutgers University Press, 1997), 3.

2. Thomas Byrne Edsall, with Mary D. Edsall, *Chain Reaction: The Impact of Race, Rights, and Taxes on American Politics* (New York: Norton, 1992), 48. For an overview of the Great Society, see Allen J. Matusow, *The Unraveling of America: A History of Liberalism in the 1960s* (New York: HarperCollins, 1986).

3. Paul Krugman, "For Richer: How the Permissive Capitalism of the Boom Destroyed American Equality," *New York Times Magazine,* October 20, 2002, 77.

4. David A. Horowitz and Peter N. Noble, *On the Edge: The U.S. since 1941,* 2d ed. (New York: West/Wadsworth, 1998), 227. New Right stalwarts Dick Cheney, Newt Gingrich, Richard Perle, George Will, and many other prominent hawks during the 2003 Iraq war apparently experienced no pangs of conscience opting out of military service in Vietnam. Antiwar activists have labeled these individuals "chickenhawks." The definition of a *chickenhawk,* according to the *New Hampshire Gazette*'s Chickenhawk database, is "a person enthusiastic about war, provided someone else fights it; particularly when that enthusiasm is undimmed by personal experience with war; most emphatically when that lack of experience came in spite of ample opportunity in that person's youth," http://www.nhgazette.com/cgi-bin/NHGstore.cgi?user_action=list&category=%20NEWS%.

5. Michael Lind, *The Next American Nation: The New Nationalism and the Fourth American Revolution* (New York: Free Press, 1995), 149.

6. A more charitable view of the New Right comes from Jonathan Martin Kolkey, who sees the movement as an attempt to solve the social and economic problems that a moribund liberalism had failed to do in the sixties. *The New Right, 1960-1968: With Epilogue, 1969-1980* (Washington, D.C.: University Press of America, 1983), 329.

7. Jim Danky and John Cherney, "The New Right," n.d., http://slisweb.lis.wisc.edu/~jcherney/newright.html.

8. Jerome L. Himmelstein, *To the Right: The Transformation of American Conservatism* (Berkeley: University of California Press, 1992), 85.

9. For important recent biographies of the coeditors, see Daniel Kelly, *James Burnham and the Struggle for the World: A Life* (Wilmington, Del.: Intercollegiate Studies Institute, 2002), and Kevin J. Smant, *Principles and Heresies: Frank S. Meyer and the Shaping of the American Conservative Movement* (Wilmington, Del.: Intercollegiate Studies Institute, 2002).

10. George H. Nash, *The Conservative Intellectual Movement in America, since 1945* (New York: Basic Books, 1976), 80. For a thorough discussion of Catholic conservatives during the fifties, see chap. 2 in Patrick Allitt, *Catholic Intellectuals and Conservative Politics in America, 1950-1985* (Ithaca, N.Y.: Cornell University Press, 1993).

11. Paul Gottfried and Thomas Fleming, *The Conservative Movement* (Boston: Twayne, 1988), 24-25.

12. Chris Weinkoff, "William F. Buckley Jr.," *Salon.com,* September 3, 1999, http://www.salon.com/people/feature/1999/09/03/wfb/print.html.

13. J. David Hoeveler Jr., *Watch on the Right: Conservative Intellectuals in the Reagan Era* (Madison: University of Wisconsin Press, 1991), 23.

14. Godfrey Hodgson, *The World Turned Right Side Up: A History of the Conservative Ascendancy in America* (New York: Houghton Mifflin, 1996), 71. See also Franklin Foer, "Once Again America First," *New York Times,* October 10, 2004.

15. On the conservative ascendancy within the Republican Party, see Mary C. Brennan, *Turning Right in the Sixties: The Conservative Capture of the GOP* (Chapel Hill: University of North Carolina Press, 1995).

16. For a concise and up-to-date overview of the counterculture during this period, see Van Gosse, *The Movements of the New Left, 1950-1975: A Brief History with Documents* (Boston: Bedford/St. Martin's, 2005).

17. Gottfried and Fleming, *Conservative Movement,* 78. After thirty years, Viguerie continues to pioneer innovative methods of raising money to benefit his political agenda and himself. His latest venture has been to set up three Virginia-based nonprofit lobbying groups—United Seniors Association, the 60 Plus Association, and the Seniors Coalition—which supposedly advocate for older Americans but in fact support the campaigns and causes of the Republican Party. The three groups also lobby extensively in Washington for legislation that will benefit drug companies, which is not surprising since, as one investigator concludes, "virtually all of their largest contributions in recent years have come from the same source—the nation's pharmaceutical industry." See Bill Hogan, "Pulling Strings from Afar," *AARP Bulletin,* February 2003, 3-5.

18. Himmelstein, *To the Right,* 80.

19. Arnold Forster and Benjamin R. Epstein, *Danger on the Right* (Westport, Conn.: Greenwood, 1964), 231-32.

20. The CSFC evolved into the Free Congress Foundation (FCF) in 1977.

21. See John Micklethwait and Adrian Wooldridge, "For Conservatives, Mission Accomplished," *New York Times,* May 16, 2004, for the origins of this organization.

22. Some observers trace the roots of the close collaboration of business-people and the resurgent conservative movement to the late sixties, when the captains of industry developed a fear of social revolution that was "palpable and genuine." Lewis H. Lapham, "Tentacles of Rage: The Republican Propaganda Mill: A Brief History," *Harper's Magazine,* September 2004, 33.

23. Kevin Phillips, *The Politics of Rich and Poor: Wealth and the American Electorate in the Reagan Aftermath* (New York: Random House, 1990), 115.

24. Himmelstein, *To the Right,* 145.

25. On the long Weyrich-Coors association, see Russ Bellant, *The Coors Connection: How Coors Family Philanthropy Undermines Democratic Pluralism* (Boston: South End, 1991). The portrait of Joseph Coors, as the title indicates, is anything but flattering.

26. Jonathan Mozzochi, Gillian Leichtling, and Steven Gardiner, "The New Right and the Christian Right," n.d., http://www.qrd.org/qrd/www/FTR/newright.html.

27. James L. Martin, "A Funding Father," *Washington Times,* September 20, 2003.

28. Andrew L. Barlow, *Between Fear and Hope: Globalization and Race in the United States* (Lanham, Md.: Rowman & Littlefield, 2003), 62.

29. David Friedman, "White Collar Blues," *Los Angeles Times,* August 3, 2003.

30. Tony Quinn, a GOP political analyst, suggests that what "really drove the South to the Republicans" was the immigration of Yankee immigrants who brought their Republican faith with them when they crossed the Mason-Dixon line, or, as he puts it, "far more important than race was air conditioning," a highly idiosyncratic view that few scholars would seriously entertain. "Cultural Conservatism Key to Recent Republican Success, Historian Says" (a review of *Grand Old Party: A History of the Republicans,* by Lewis L. Gould), *San Francisco Chronicle,* November 23, 2003.

31. Edsall, *Chain Reaction,* 41.

32. Eric Foner, *The Story of American Freedom* (New York: Norton, 1998), 314. After his death, it came out that the senator, once the nation's leading segregationist, had fathered a child by a black woman, a maid in the Thurmond family home. Michael Janofsky, "Thurmond Kin Accept Daughter," *Contra Costa Times* (Walnut Creek, Calif.), December 16, 2003.

33. Sanford D. Horwitt, "Democrats Have Shown Historical Cycles of Success and Retreat" (a review of *Party of the People: A History of the Democrats,* by Jules Witcover), *San Francisco Chronicle,* November 23, 2003.

34. Ronald Brownstein, "Lott's Record Shows No Sign of Modified Opinion," *Contra Costa Times,* December 22, 2002.

35. Foner, *Story of American Freedom,* 317. On the GOP-backed antifeminist campaign after the seventies, see Susan Faludi, *Backlash: The Undeclared War on American Women* (New York: Knopf, 1992). The Religious Right is the subject of several important volumes: Steve Bruce, *The Rise and Fall of the New Christian Right: Conservative Protestant Politics in America, 1978-1988* (New York: Oxford University Press, 1988); Sara Diamond, *The Politics of the Christian Right* (Boston: South End, 1989); Garry Wills, *Under God: Religion and American Politics* (New York: Simon & Schuster, 1990); William Clyde Wilcox, *God's Warriors: The Christian Right in Twentieth-Century America* (Baltimore: Johns Hopkins University Press, 1992); William Martin, *With God on Our Side: The Rise of the Religious Right in America* (New York: Broadway Books, 1996); and Esther Kaplan, *With God on Their Side: George W. Bush and the Christian Right* (New York: New Press, 2005).

36. Bryan F. Le Beau, "The Political Mobilization of the New Christian Right," n.d., http://are.as.wvu.ed/lebeau1.htm.

37. Le Beau, "The Political Mobilization of the New Christian Right."

38. Steven M. Gillon and Cathy D. Matson, *The American Experiment: A History of the United States* (New York: Houghton Mifflin, 2002), 1222. In 2004, 61 percent of the U.S. population believed that the biblical story of creation was "literally true," according to "Stats of the Union: Facts, Figures, and Uniquely American Absurdities," *Mother Jones,* May/June 2004, 62.

39. Sara Diamond, *Not by Politics Alone: The Enduring Influence of the Christian Right* (New York: Guilford, 1998), 7.

40. Lind, *Next American Nation,* 280. For the preeminence of the South as the nation's most religious region, based on regular church attendance, see Steven Thomma, "Poll: Religious Beliefs Sway Politics," *Contra Costa Times,* November 28, 2003.

41. Mark O'Keefe, "Frustration Gnaws at Religious Conservatives," *Contra Costa Times*, July 19, 2003; Sara Diamond, *Roads to Dominion* (New York: Guilford, 1995), 172.

42. Sara Diamond, *Facing the Wrath: Confronting the Right in Dangerous Times* (Monroe, Maine: Common Courage Press, 1996), 43.

43. Glenn H. Utter and John W. Storey, *The Religious Right*, 2d ed. (Santa Barbara, Calif.: ABC/CLIO, 2001), 8; John George and Laird Wilcox, *Nazis, Communists, Klansmen, and Others on the Fringe* (New York: Prometheus, 1992), 246–47. It is ironic that the Christian Coalition should support a politician whose campaign tactics were "destructive and downright racist," according to "Should He Be Missed? Jesse Helms," *Economist*, August 25, 2001. For an unauthorized biography of Helms, see Ernest B. Ferguson, *Hard Right: The Rise of Jesse Helms* (New York: Norton, 1986).

44. Ken Silverstein and Michael Scherer, "Born-Again Zionists: Christian Conservatives Are Teaming with Hard-Line Jewish Groups to Transform American Policy toward Israel," *Mother Jones*, September/October 2002, 56.

45. Diamond, *Not by Politics Alone*, 8, 11.

46. Greg Palast, *The Best Democracy Money Can Buy* (London: Pluto, 2002), 86.

47. On the neoconservative movement, see Peter Steinfels, *The Neoconservatives: The Men Who Are Changing America's Politics* (New York: Simon & Schuster, 1979); Sidney Blumenthal, *The Rise of the Counter-Establishment: From Conservative Ideology to Political Power* (New York: Times Books, 1986); and Irving Kristol and Arving Kristol, *Neo-Conservatism: The Autobiography of an Idea* (Chicago: Ivan R. Dee, 1999). For a critical view, see Gary Dorrien, *The Neoconservative Mind: Politics, Culture, and the War of Ideology* (Philadelphia: Temple University Press, 1993).

48. Hodgson, *World Turned Right Side Up*, 133. An Englishman who has resided in the United States on and off for the past fifteen years, Godfrey Hodgson does a masterful job of dismantling the myth of American exceptionalism in a recent work, *More Equal Than Others: America from Nixon to the New Century* (Princeton, N.J.: Princeton University Press, 2004), in which he concludes, "Great and growing inequality has been the most salient social fact about the America of the conservative ascendancy" (xvii).

49. John Ehrman, *The Rise of Neoconservatism* (New Haven, Conn.: Yale University Press, 1995), 37.

50. Barbara Ehrenreich, *Fear of Falling: The Inner Life of the Middle Class* (New York: HarperPerennial, 1990), 59.

51. David Rieff, "The End of Empire," *Mother Jones*, May/June 2004, 70.

52. Scott McConnell, "Among the Neocons," *American Conservative*, April 21, 2003, 7.

53. McConnell, "Among the Neocons," 7–11.

54. Justin Raimondo, "Norman's Narcissism: Podhoretz in Love," *Antiwar. com*, October 16, 2000, http://ww2.antiwar.com/justin/pf/p-j101600.html.

55. For clarification of the CIA connection, see Gregory Pavlik, "Neoconservatism: A CIA Front," *LewRockwell.com*, n.d., wysiwg://16/http://www.lewrockwell.com/orig/pavlik2.html. During the fifties, Kristol also belonged to an anticommunist organization that was secretly subsidized by the CIA, the

Congress for Cultural Freedom. Ellen Schrecker, *The Age of McCarthyism*, 2d ed. (Boston: Bedford/St. Martin's, 2002), 263. Godfrey Hodgson, who knew Kristol during this period, is convinced the future neocon leader was a CIA operative. See his *World Turned Right Side Up*, 329.

56. William E. Simon, *A Time for Truth* (New York: Reader's Digest Books, 1978); Brennan, *Turning Right in the Sixties*, 196.

57. Gregg Easterbrook, "'Ideas Move Nations': How Conservative Think Tanks Have Helped to Transform the Terms of Political Debate," *Atlantic Monthly*, January 1986.

58. Jacob Heilbrunn, "Washington Scene: Con Games," *New Republic*, October 20, 1997.

59. Eric Alterman, "What Liberal Media?" *The Nation*, February 24, 2003.

60. Gottfried and Fleming, *Conservative Movement*, 60, 63.

61. Earl Shorris castigates the Jewish neocons as careerists and betrayers of the Jewish liberal tradition; he sees neoconservatism as "a movement of self-interest, without mercy for the old or the poor." *Jews without Mercy: A Lament* (Garden City, N.Y.: Anchor/Doubleday, 1982), 36. For this controversy, see "Podhoretz in Retirement: A Report on the Morality of Friendship," a review essay by Albert S. Lindemann, September 27, 1999, http://www.english.upenn.edu/~afilreis/50s/podhoretz-review.html.

62. For an impressive list of neocon intellectuals, see Steinfels, *Neoconservatives*, 5.

63. Obituary of William Bright, *San Francisco Chronicle*, July 22, 2003.

64. For the Intercollegiate Studies Institute, see Forster and Epstein, *Danger on the Right*, 211–22. This work was commissioned by the Anti-Defamation League of B'nai B'rith.

65. David Brock, *Blinded by the Right: The Conscience of an Ex-Conservative* (New York: Three Rivers, 2002), 40–41.

66. Joe Conason and Gene Lyons, *The Hunting of the President: The Ten-Year Campaign to Destroy Bill and Hillary Clinton* (New York: Dunne, 2000), 4. Tactics typical of the College Republicans are illustrated in Michael Hirschorn's "Little Men on Campus," *New Republic*, August 5, 1985. Today these tactics continue to be popular, at all levels of political involvement. Consider the case of Kyle Vallone, a three-time GOP delegate, who has admitted to submitting scores of letters pushing right-wing agendas to Bay Area newspapers using fictitious identities. Sarah Krupp, "Letter Writer Fools Papers with Names," *Contra Costa Times*, April 24, 2005.

67. For an Atwater biography, see John Brady, *Bad Boy: The Life and Politics of Lee Atwater* (New York: Addison-Wesley, 1997).

68. The book to read on "dirty tricks" is *Blinded by the Right* by David Brock, who began his political career as a "right-wing hit man." The author begins his autobiography with this observation: "This is a terrible book. It is about what the conservative movement did, and what I did, as we plotted in the shadows, disregarded the law, and abused power to win even greater power. . . . The conservative culture I thrived in was characterized by corrosive partisanship, visceral hatreds, and unfathomable hypocrisy" (xvii).

69. Sidney Blumenthal, "Blues for Lee: Death of a 'Bad Boy,'" *New Republic*, April 22, 1991, 12.

70. The term *compassionate conservatism* comes from conservative Republican guru Marvin Olasky, an ex-Marxist but now a Christian fundamentalist and George W. Bush adviser. Utter and Storey, *Religious Right*, 26–27.

71. Mary Matalin and James Carville, *All's Fair: Love, War, and Running for President* (New York: Random House, 1994), 10. After George W. Bush's reelection in 2004, Matalin entered the publishing business, initiating a conservative book imprint for Simon & Schuster. *Newsweek,* April 11, 2005, 5.

72. Robert B. Reich, "The Rove Machine Rolls On," *American Prospect,* February 1, 2003, http://www.prospect.org/web/page.ww?section=root8name =ViewPrintsarticleID=6689.

73. Al Franken, *Lies and the Lying Liars Who Tell Them: A Fair and Balanced Look at the Right* (New York: Dutton, 2003), 146.

74. For Karl Rove's steady ascent to the halls of power, see Nicholas Lemann, "The Controller," *New Yorker,* May 12, 2003, 68.

75. David Frum, quoted in Richard Brookhiser, "The Mind of George W. Bush," *Atlantic Monthly,* April 2003, 60.

76. Ralph Reed, quoted in Martin, *With God on Our Side,* 318.

77. On Reed, see the biographical sketch in Utter and Storey, *Religious Right,* 107.

78. Charles Lewis, *The Buying of the President 2004* (New York: Perennial, 2004), 20.

79. Brock, *Blinded by the Right,* 70.

80. Brock, *Blinded by the Right,* 71.

81. For a detailed and informative account of the hardball tactics that Norquist and Reed employed and how they radically altered the "bloodthirsty" College Republicans, see chap. 6 in Nina J. Easton, *Gang of Five: Leaders at the Center of the Conservative Ascendancy* (New York: Touchstone, 2000). Aside from Reed and Norquist, this excellent book highlights the political careers of three other key conservative leaders: Bill Kristol, Clint Bolick, and David McIntosh. For an interesting biographical sketch of Norquist that focuses on his exceptional organizational skills, see Michael Scherer, "The Soul of the New Machine," *Mother Jones,* January/February 2004, 42–47.

82. Franken, *Lies,* 281.

83. Stephen Glass, "After the Fall: Why Ralph Reed Left the Christian Coalition," *New Republic,* May 26, 1997, 15.

84. According to Sara Diamond, the early conservative movement established a "tradition of blatant nativism, anti-Semitism, and racism." *Roads to Dominion,* 12.

85. Nash, *Conservative Intellectual Movement,* 338.

86. Chip Berlet, "Into the Mainstream," *Intelligence Report,* Summer 2003, 54.

87. McConnell, "Among the Neocons," 10.

88. Eric Alterman, "Perle, Interrupted," *The Nation,* April 7, 2003. The pivotal role of neoconservatives in launching the 2003 war against Iraq is clarified in James Mann, *Rise of the Vulcans: The History of Bush's War Cabinet* (New York: Viking Books, 2004).

89. See two columns by Jay Bookman: "Lure of the Siren Empire May Have Hold of Bush ... but May Not Be a Bad Idea," *Contra Costa Times,* October 6, 2002, and "The President's Real Goal in Iraq," *Atlanta Journal-Constitution,* October 29, 2002.

90. For the aggressive and highly successful public relations campaign by Bush and his advisers to deceive the American public, see Sheldon Rampton and John Stauber, *Weapons of Mass Deception: The Uses of Propaganda in Bush's War on Iraq* (New York: Tarcher/Penguin, 2003).

91. Quoted in David Wallis, "Ex-Weapons Inspector Berates War Plans," *San Francisco Chronicle,* September 14, 2002. Ritter's conclusion was essentially corroborated by the Carnegie Endowment. For its report, "Origins of Regime Change in Iraq," see the Endowment Web site: www.ceip.org.

92. Easton, *Gang of Five,* 11.

93. Phillips, *Politics of Rich and Poor,* xvii.

Chapter 2

1. Charles A. Beard, *An Economic Interpretation of the Constitution of the United States,* 2d ed. (New York: Macmillan, 1936).

2. Kevin Phillips, *Wealth and Democracy: A Political History of the American Rich* (New York: Broadway Books, 2002), 412-13.

3. Godfrey Hodgson, *The World Turned Right Side Up: A History of the Conservative Ascendancy in America* (New York: Houghton Mifflin, 1996), 303.

4. Ferdinand Lundberg, *The Rich and the Super-Rich: A Study in the Power of Money Today* (New York: Bantam, 1968), 202-4.

5. Quoted by David Lazarus, "Enron, a Political Courtesan," *San Francisco Chronicle,* February 22, 2002. Rubin had lots of company. According to a survey by the Center for Public Integrity, more than half of the top one hundred officials in the Clinton White House went on to work for companies they regulated while in office. M. Asif Ismail, "The Clinton Top 100: Where Are They Now?" Center for Public Integrity, 2001.

6. Center for Responsive Politics, "The Bush Administration: Corporate Connections," wysiwyg://29/http://www.opensecrets.org/bush/cabinet.asp. As of early 2005, Bush's second cabinet had only three individuals—Mike Leavitt (health and human services), Michael Chertoff (homeland security), and Jim Nicolson (veterans affairs)—without corporate connections, http://www.opensecrets.org/bush/cabinet.asp.

7. "U.S. Treasury Nominee Snow Vows to Divest," *Contra Costa Times* (Walnut Creek, Calif.), January 23, 2003.

8. Arianna Huffington, *Pigs at the Trough: How Corporate Greed and Political Corruption Are Undermining America* (New York: Crown, 2003), 58-59.

9. Derrick Wetherell, "The Bush 100: Center Releases Report on Bush's Top Appointees," Center for Public Integrity, 2001.

10. Jim Hightower, *If the Gods Had Meant Us to Vote They Would Have Given Us Candidates,* rev. ed. (New York: HarperCollins, 2001), 69.

11. Robert B. Reich, "Corporate Power in Overdrive," *New York Times,* March 18, 2001.

12. For the history and impact of these foundations, see Sally Covington, *Moving a Public Agenda: The Strategic Philanthropy of Conservative Foundations* (Washington, D.C.: People for the American Way, 1996). Ostensibly

philanthropic, foundations, of whatever ideological persuasion, are meant to preserve wealth. "Nearly all of the foundations," Ferdinand Lundberg argues, "have come into view since the enactment of the income tax and estate tax laws: The foundations are completely exempt not only with respect to income taxes but also to capital gains taxes." *The Rich and the Super-Rich,* 468.

13. G. William Domhoff, *Who Rules America? Power and Politics in the Year 2000,* 3d ed. (Mountain View, Calif.: Mayfield, 1998), 127. For up-to-date information on the grant making of conservative foundations, see the various reports and Web sites of the National Committee for Responsive Philanthropy.

14. Nicholas Lemann, "Citizen 501(c)(3): An Increasingly Powerful Agent in American Life Is Also One of the Least Noticed," *Atlantic Monthly,* February 1997, 18.

15. James A. Smith, *The Idea Brokers: Think Tanks and the Rise of the New Policy Elite* (New York: Free Press, 1991), 181.

16. See Jean Stefancic and Richard Delgado, *No Mercy: How Conservative Think Tanks and Foundations Changed America's Social Agenda* (Philadelphia: Temple University Press, 1996).

17. People for the American Way, *Buying a Movement: Right-Wing Foundations and American Politics* (Washington, D.C.: People for the American Way, 1996), 4.

18. See Web site: www.philanthropyroundtable.org.

19. Eric Alterman, *What Liberal Media? The Truth about Bias and the News* (New York: Basic Books, 2003), 245.

20. Karen Rothmyer, "The Man behind the Mask," *Salon.com,* April 7, 1998, http://www.salon.com/news/1998/04/07news.html; Robert G. Kaiser and Ira Chinoy, "Scaife: Funding Father of the Right," *Washington Post,* May 2, 1999.

21. By 1999, 111 conservative organizations had received grants from Scaife, according to Kaiser and Chinoy, "Scaife."

22. Nurith C. Aizenman, "The Man behind the Curtain: Richard Mellon Scaife—and $200 Million of His Money—Is the Man behind the Conservative Revolution," *Washington Monthly,* July–August 1997, 28.

23. Haynes Johnson, *The Best of Times: America in the Clinton Years* (New York: Harcourt, 2001), 262.

24. Carole Shields, "The Billion Dollar Imbalance in America's Great Debates," *NCJW Journal* (National Council of Jewish Women), Winter 2000, http://www.ncjw.org/news/winter99journal/shields1.htm.

25. This unsavory episode appears in Byron York, "The Life and Death of *The American Spectator,*" *Atlantic Monthly,* November 2001. Two writers describe the attempt to discredit Clinton this way: "It is . . . the story of the most successful and long-running 'dirty tricks' campaign in recent American history, fomented by a handful of professional Republican operatives and corporate lawyers, funded by a network of wealthy conservatives." Joe Conason and Gene Lyons, *The Hunting of the President: The Ten-Year Campaign to Destroy Bill and Hillary Clinton* (New York: Dunne, 2000), xiv.

26. Kaiser and Chinoy, "Scaife."

27. Tamar Lewin, "3 Conservative Foundations Are in the Throes of Change," *New York Times,* May 20, 2001.

28. Quoted by DeParle, "Next Generation of Conservatives (by the Dormful),"
New York Times, June 14, 2005.

29. David S. Bernstein, "Buying the Campus Mind," *Boston Phoenix,* October 4, 2005, http://www.peace.redding.org/Buying%20the%20campus%20 mind.htm.

30. John Nichols, "ALEC Meets His Match," *The Nation,* June 9, 2003, 15.

31. Karen Olsson, "Ghostwriting the Law," *Mother Jones,* September/October 2002, 17.

32. Stefancic and Delgado, *No Mercy,* 144–45.

33. Arnold Forster and Benjamin R. Epstein, *Danger on the Right* (Westport, Conn.: Greenwood, 1964), 239.

34. Stefancic and Delgado, *No Mercy,* 115.

35. "Jeff Gannon's Alma Mater: The Leadership Institute," *Media Matters for America,* February 11, 2005, http://mediamatters.org/items/200502120002.

36. Grover Norquist, quoted in William Martin, *With God on Our Side: The Rise of the Religious Right in America* (New York: Broadway Books, 1996), 362.

37. Blaine Harden, "In Virginia, Young Conservatives Learn How to Develop and Use Their Political Voices," *New York Times,* June 11, 2001.

38. For information on the Council for National Policy, see Marc J. Ambinder, "Vast Right-Wing Cabal? Meet the Most Powerful Conservative Group You've Never Heard Of," *ABCNews.com,* May 2, 2002.

39. "Jeff Gannon's Alma Mater."

40. Stefancic and Delgado, *No Mercy,* 4–5.

Chapter 3

1. G. William Domhoff, *Who Rules America? Power and Politics in the Year 2000,* 3d ed. (Mountain View, Calif.: Mayfield, 1998), 128.

2. James A. Smith, *The Idea Brokers: Think Tanks and the Rise of the New Policy Elite* (New York: Free Press, 1991), xiv.

3. For the ways these organizations exercise influence, see Jean Stefancic and Richard Delgado, *No Mercy: How Conservative Think Tanks and Foundations Changed America's Social Agenda* (Philadelphia: Temple University Press, 1996), and *$1 Billion for Ideas: Conservative Think Tanks in the 1990s,* a special report by the National Committee for Responsive Philanthropy (NCRP) (Washington, D.C.: NCRP, 1999). An excellent up-to-date listing of reference material on think tanks appears in Michael J. Graetz and Ian Shapiro, *Death by a Thousand Cuts: The Fight over Taxing Inherited Wealth* (Princeton, N.J.: Princeton University Press, 2005), 306–12.

4. The centrist Brooking Institute was the most quoted foundation. Michael Dolny, "Spectrum Narrows Further in 2002," *Extra!,* July/August 2003. See also Tom Brazaitis, "Big Think Tanks Lead the Charge in Washington," *Cleveland Plain Dealer,* December 19, 1999, who cites ten think tanks rated for impact.

5. People for the American Way, *Buying a Movement: Right-Wing Foundations and American Politics* (Washington, D.C.: People for the American Way,

1996), 8; Karen Paget, "Lessons of Right-Wing Philanthropy," *American Prospect,* September/October 1998, www.prospect.org/ print/V9/40/ paget-k.html.

6. James Rosenthal, "Heritage Hype: The Second-Generation Think Tank," *New Republic,* September 2, 1985, 17. By 2003, the foundation's budget was $30 million, according to Robert W. McChesney, *The Problem of the Media: U.S. Communication Politics in the 21st Century* (New York: Monthly Review, 2004), 111.

7. Sara Diamond, *Roads to Dominion: Right-Wing Movements and Political Power in the United States* (New York: Guilford, 1995), 199–200.

8. Jerome L. Himmelstein, *To the Right: The Transformation of American Conservatism* (Berkeley: University of California Press, 1992), 150.

9. Sara Diamond, *Facing the Wrath: Confronting the Right in Dangerous Times* (Monroe, Maine: Common Courage Press, 1996), 118.

10. Derrick Wetherell, "The Bush 100: Center Releases Report on Bush's Top Appointees," Center for Public Integrity, 2001.

11. Wetherell, "The Bush 100."

12. Stefancic and Delgado, *No Mercy,* 57.

13. Norman Solomon, "The Manhattan Institute: Launch Pad for Conservative Authors," [1998], http://www.accuracy.org/articles/manhat.htm.

14. Himmelstein, *To the Right,* 150–51.

15. People for the American Way, *Buying a Movement,* 7.

16. Matthew Freeman and Rachel Egen, "Funding the Right," *Freedom Writer* (Institute for First Amendment Studies), January/February 1997, http://www.ifas.org/fw/9701/funding.html.

17. Smith, *Idea Brokers,* 200.

18. See the Web site: http://www.heritage.org/heritage/mission.html.

19. Burton Pines, quoted in Eric Alterman, *What Liberal Media? The Truth about Bias and the News* (New York: Basic Books, 2003), 83.

20. Robert G. Kaiser and Ira Chinoy, "Scaife: Funding Father of the Right," *Washington Post,* May 2, 1996.

21. Freeman and Egen, "Funding the Right."

22. Greg Easterbrook, "'Ideas Move Nations': How Conservative Think Tanks Have Helped to Transform the Terms of Political Debate," *Atlantic Monthly,* January 1986. At this time, the AEI had six hundred corporate sponsors. Himmelstein, *To the Right,* 147.

23. Lewis H. Lapham, "Tentacles of Rage: The Republican Propaganda Mill: A Brief History," *Harper's Magazine,* September 2004, 35.

24. Brian Whitaker, "US Thinktanks Give Lessons in Foreign Policy," *Guardian* (London, U.K.), August 19, 2002, www.guardian.co.uk/Print/0,3858,4484490,00.htm.

25. Domhoff, *Who Rules America?* 136.

26. Deborah Toler, "The Right's 'Race Desk': American Enterprise Institute Finds Profit in Prejudice," *Extra!* March/April 1999.

27. "The purpose of the institution," Hoover stated in 1959, "must be, by its research and publications, to demonstrate the evils of the doctrines of Karl Marx." Quoted in Paul Dickson, *Think Tanks* (New York: Atheneum, 1971), 304.

28. Smith, *Idea Brokers,* 186.

29. Robert Collier, "Group at Hoover Helping to Steer Administration's Drive toward Iraq," *San Francisco Chronicle,* September 15, 2002.

30. Paul Krugman, "Gambling with Your Retirement," *New York Times,* February 4, 2005.

31. For a concise history of this right-wing campaign, see "Naming the Names behind the Grab for Social Security," *The Hightower Lowdown,* April 2005, 1–6.

32. "Naming the Names," 3.

33. Greenspan warned Congress that a failure to cut back on entitlements would create massive federal debt. Four years before, in justifying tax cuts, he had insisted that the government was in danger of paying off too much debt. "By repeatedly shilling for whatever the Bush administration wants, he has betrayed the trust placed in Fed chairmen, and deserves to be treated as just another partisan hack," concludes Paul Krugman, "Three-Card Maestro," *New York Times,* February 18, 2005.

34. Jacob S. Hacker and Paul Pierson, *Off Center: The Republican Revolution and the Erosion of Democracy* (New Haven, Conn.: Yale University Press, 2005), 76.

35. See Susan Q. Stranahan and Bill Hogan, "Way off Target," *AARP Bulletin,* April 2005, 3–4.

36. Joseph F. García, "Rightist Conspiracy? Maybe Not; A Better Word Would Be 'Industry': A Fortune Has Funded Many Conservative Obsessions. Clinton May Simply Be the Latest Scaife-Goat," *Philadelphia Inquirer,* March 7, 1998.

37. Phil Wilayto, "Kenneth Starr, the Bradley Foundation and the Conspiracy to Get President Clinton," http://www.execpc.com/~ajrc/starr.html. Olson is Starr's best friend, according to David Brock, *Blinded by the Right: The Conscience of an Ex-Conservative* (New York: Three Rivers, 2002), 346.

38. See the Federalist Society Web site: www.fed-soc.org.

39. García, "Rightist Conspiracy?"

40. Kevin Phillips, *Wealth and Democracy: A Political History of the American Rich* (New York: Broadway Books, 2002), 337.

41. Phillips, *Wealth and Democracy,* 338.

42. "Court Kills Ban on 'Soft Money,'" *San Francisco Chronicle,* May 3, 2003.

43. Cal Thomas, "Campaign Finance Law Is a Hit on Free Speech," *Contra Costa Times* (Walnut Creek, Calif.), December 14, 2003.

44. For conservative efforts to bring about tort reform, see Stefancic and Delgado, *No Mercy,* chap. 6. Also relevant is the fine work by lawyer Herman Schwartz, *Right-Wing Justice: The Conservative Campaign to Take Over the Courts* (New York: Nation Books, 2004).

45. Michael Scherer, "The Making of the Corporate Judiciary: How Big Business Is Quietly Funding a Legal Revolution," *Mother Jones,* November/December 2003, 74.

46. Howard Zinn, *A People's History of the United States, 1492–Present,* 3d ed. (New York: HarperCollins, 2001), 574. "Since 1968 Republican presidents have made 10 of 12 Supreme Court appointments, along with 65 percent of all federal appeals–court appointments and 62 percent of all district-court appointments," according to Michael Nelson, "How the GOP Conquered the South," *Chronicle of*

Higher Education, October 21, 2005. For GOP designs on the judicial system, see Herman Schwartz, *Packing the Courts: The Conservative Campaign to Rewrite the Constitution* (New York: Scribner, 1988).

47. See "Who's Afraid of the Federalist Society?" *Wall Street Journal,* May 15, 2001.

48. Jeffrey Toobin, *A Vast Conspiracy: The Real Story of the Sex Scandal That Nearly Brought Down a President* (New York: Simon & Schuster, 1999), 77. Charged with finding evidence of financial malfeasance, Starr failed miserably; the best he could do was a morals charge. Based on the flimsiest of pretexts, Republicans howled for impeachment. Where were these guardians of morality during Irangate—"the most blatant violation of constitutional government in American history," according to the historian Theodore Roszak, "Where Did the Middle Go?" *San Francisco Chronicle,* October 10, 2004—when a Republican president wantonly broke the law by trading arms for hostages? Was this not a much more serious transgression than marital infidelity?

49. Bill Clinton, *My Life* (New York: Knopf, 2004), 613.

50. Toobin, *Vast Conspiracy,* 9.

51. See *Bush v. Gore,* 531 U.S. 98 (2000); Haynes Johnson, *The Best of Times: America in the Clinton Years* (New York: Harcourt, 2001), 526.

52. Mark Hertsgaard, *The Eagle's Shadow: Why America Fascinates and Infuriates the World* (New York: Farrar, Straus & Giroux, 2002), 161–62.

53. For the Florida electoral irregularities, see Greg Palast, *The Best Democracy Money Can Buy* (London: Pluto, 2002), 6.

54. Daniel Schorr, "The Supreme Fix Was In," *Christian Science Monitor,* December 15, 2000. See also Kevin Phillips: "George W. Bush is the first president to be chosen by the Supreme Court—by a single vote." "His Fraudulency the Second? The Illegitimacy of George W. Bush," *American Prospect,* January 29, 2001, 4.

55. On the High Court's highly partisan ruling, see chap. 4 in Alan Dershowitz, *Supreme Injustice: How the High Court Hijacked Election 2000* (New York: Oxford University Press, 2001). Even some conservatives were disturbed by the Court's inconsistency. See Gary Rosen, "Reconsidering *Bush v. Gore,*" *Commentary,* November 2001.

56. Johnson, *Best of Times,* 263. One instance where "personal and financial hardship" *has* been the intent of the Republican political machine, apparently, is the persecution of Henry Cisneros, Clinton's housing secretary. In 1995, independent counsel David Barrett was appointed to investigate charges that Cisneros had lied to the FBI about money he paid to a former mistress. Cisneros pled guilty, paid a $10,000 fine, and was later pardoned by President Clinton. Barrett, however, has continued the investigation, and indeed turned up the pressure, spending more than $1.26 million of federal money during the second half of the 2004 fiscal year (long after the independent counsel law had been allowed to lapse by Congress). The total spent on this probe to date is an incredible $21 million. Jonathan Weisman, "Cisneros Probe Has Cost $21 Million for $10,000 Fine," *Washington Post,* March 31, 2005.

57. Johnson, *Best of Times,* 340.

58. Sally Covington, "Right Thinking, Big Grants, and Long-Term Strategy: How Conservative Philanthropies and Think Tanks Transform US Policy," *Co-*

vert Action Quarterly 63 (Winter 1998), http://mediafilter.org/CAQ/caq63/caq63thinktank.html.

59. Godfrey Hodgson, *The World Turned Right Side Up: A History of the Conservative Ascendancy in America* (New York: Houghton Mifflin, 1996), 282. An excellent example of the kind of scholar Hodgson describes is Victor Davis Hanson. A respected classicist, Hanson has been touted as an expert on current Mexican immigration after a right-wing press, Encounter Books, published his book, *Mexifornia: A State of Becoming,* in 2003. Essentially a nativist tract, the book calls for the restriction of Mexican immigration into the United States. Currently a fellow at the Hoover Institution, where he writes op-eds mirroring that organization's views, Hanson has a very superficial knowledge of the vast scholarly work that has been done recently on immigration. *Mexifornia* does not contain a single footnote.

60. The recent disclosure that a senior scholar at the Cato Institute, Doug Bandow, received secret payments from a prominent GOP lobbyist, Jack Abramoff, to write columns favorable to his clients caused general indignation. Anne E. Kornblut and Philip Shenon, "Lobbyist Paid Writer for Columns," *San Francisco Chronicle,* December 17, 2005. The public outrage is perfectly understandable: This must be the first time a think tank fellow has been paid to sustain a partisan position!

61. Barbara Ehrenreich, *Fear of Falling: The Inner Life of the Middle Class* (New York: HarperPerennial, 1990), 155.

62. For corporate threats to individual liberties, see Jamie Court, *Corporateering: How Corporate Power Steals Your Personal Freedom ... and What You Can Do about It* (New York: Tarcher/Putnam, 2003).

63. Dennis Judd, quoted by Robert L. Kaplan, "Was Democracy Just a Moment?" *Atlantic Monthly,* December 1997.

64. The Hoover Institution Web site is www.hoover.org.

65. Brock, *Blinded by the Right,* 125, 127.

66. Brock, *Blinded by the Right,* 79.

67. Joe Conason, *Big Lies: The Right-Wing Propaganda Machine and How It Distorts the Truth* (New York: Dunne, 2003), 141.

68. Adam Shatz, "The Thernstroms in Black and White," *American Prospect,* March 12–26, 2001, 12.

69. Solomon, "Manhattan Institute."

70. People for the American Way, *Buying a Movement,* 15.

71. Diamond, *Facing the Wrath,* 127–28.

72. Diamond, *Facing the Wrath,* 134.

73. CSPC direct mail flyer, quoted in People for the American Way, *Buying a Movement,* 8. Horowitz's tortuous journey across the political spectrum is described in Scott Sherman, "David Horowitz's Long March," *The Nation,* June 19, 2000.

74. Jennifer Jacobson, "What Makes David Run: Mr. Horowitz Demands a Place in Academe for Conservatives Like Himself," *Chronicle of Higher Education,* May 6, 2005. Using tax records, Jacobson shows that Horowitz's activities are heavily subsidized by right-wing foundations.

75. Eric Scigliano, "Naming—and Un-naming—Names," *The Nation,* December 31, 2001.

76. Isaiah Berlin, quoted in Earl Shorris, "Ignoble Liars: Leo Strauss, George Bush, and the Philosophy of Mass Deception," *Harper's Magazine,* June 2004, 70.

77. Peter Hart and Steve Rendall, "Meet the Myth-Makers: Right-Wing Media Groups Provide Ammo for 'Liberal Media' Claims," *Extra!,* July/August 1998.

78. The Media Research Web site (www.mediaresearch.org) has a glowing biography of Bozell, credited with being "lecturer, syndicated columnist, television commentator, debater, marketer, businessman, publisher, and activist."

79. Michael Lind, *Up from Conservatism: Why the Right Is Wrong for America* (New York: Free Press, 1996), 87.

Chapter 4

1. Michael Parenti, *America Besieged* (San Francisco: City Lights, 1998), 149–50.

2. Michael Massing, "The Press: The Enemy Within," *New York Review of Books,* December 15, 2005, http://www.nybooks.com/articles/18555.

3. Cited in Robert W. McChesney, *The Problem of the Media: U.S. Communication Politics in the 21st Century* (New York: Monthly Review, 2004), 21.

4. Republican candidates have "received a majority of newspaper endorsements in all but two presidential elections since 1932," according to Steve Rendall and Peter Hart, *Arizona Republic* (Tucson), January 20, 2002.

5. Joe Conason, *Big Lies: The Right-Wing Propaganda Machine and How It Distorts the Truth* (New York: Dunne, 2003), 40.

6. A relatively complete list of Murdoch holdings is found in Robert W. McChesney, *Rich Media, Poor Democracy: Communication Politics in Dubious Times,* rev. ed. (New York: New Press, 2000), 96–98. For Fox's partisanship, see Seth Ackerman, "The Most Biased Name in News: Fox News Channel's Extraordinary Right-Wing Tilt," *Extra!,* August 2001. News Corp.'s ownership of a major network is not unique: NBC is owned by General Electric, CBS by Westinghouse, ABC by Disney, and CNN by Times Warner (Ted Turner and friends).

7. As of 1999, media companies controlled about twenty-eight major league sports franchises in the United States. McChesney, *Rich Media, Poor Democracy,* 44.

8. Mark Hertsgaard, *The Eagle's Shadow: Why America Fascinates and Infuriates the World* (New York: Farrar, Straus & Giroux, 2002), 93.

9. Jonathan Alter, "Rush, to Judgment," *Newsweek,* October 20, 2003, 50.

10. Arian Campo-Flores, "Rush's World of Pain," *Newsweek,* October 13, 2003.

11. McChesney, *Problem of the Media,* 116.

12. Edward Monks, "The End of Fairness: Right-Wing Commentators Have a Virtual Monopoly When It Comes to Talk Radio Programming," *Register-Guard* (Eugene, Ore.), June 30, 2002.

13. Mary C. Brennan, *Turning Right in the Sixties: The Conservative Capture of the GOP* (Chapel Hill: University of North Carolina Press, 1995), 335. In 2005, Will was awarded a $250,000 prize by the right-wing Bradley Foundation

for outstanding intellectual achievement. Bradley awards were given to Charles Krauthammer and Thomas Sowell the year before. Dave Astor, "Is George Will's $250,000 Prize Yet More Payola?" *Editor and Publisher,* February 25, 2005, http://www.editorandpublisher.com/eundp/news/article_dispay.jsp?vnu_content_id=1000817846.

14. Quoted by Nicholas Lemann, "The Wayward Press," *New Yorker,* February 14, 2005, http://www.newyorker.com/fact/content/?050214fa_fact1.

15. Pew Research Center for the People and the Press, "Pew Research Center Biennial News Consumption Survey," July 8, 2004, http://www.pewtrusts.com/pdf/pew_research_news_060804.pdf. The study also indicated that 25 percent of the public regularly tuned in to Fox News Channel, and the majority of Fox viewers (52 percent) identified themselves as political conservatives.

16. Jeff Cohen, "Television's Political Spectrum," *Extra!,* July/August, 1990. For a relatively comprehensive list of right-wing talking heads, and of the conservative groups that employ them, see Charles L. Klotzer, "How Many Commentators Can You Identify?" *St. Louis Journalism Review,* November 2001, 28-29.

17. McChesney, *Problem of the Media,* 105.

18. According to the Major League Baseball Players Association, the average baseball salary was $31,543 in 1971, $143,756 in 1980, $597,537 in 1990, $1,895,630 in 2000, and $2,372,189 in 2003. *San Francisco Chronicle,* December 25, 2003.

19. McChesney, *Problem of the Media,* 106.

20. Eric Alterman, *What Liberal Media? The Truth about Bias and the News* (New York: Basic Books, 2003), 21. For a good example of a journalist who leads such a privileged life that he is almost completely blind to the problems that beset fellow Americans, see David Brooks, *On Paradise Drive: How We Live Now (and Always Have) in the Future Tense* (New York: Simon & Schuster, 2004). See, too, the devastating critique of the Brooks book by Nicholas von Hoffman, "Don't Worry, Be Happy," *The Nation,* June 21, 2004, 30-32.

21. Alterman, *What Liberal Media?,* 33.

22. Scott Smallwood, "Survey of Ivy League Professors Finds Few Conservatives," *Chronicle of Higher Education,* February 1, 2002. College faculties are in fact more liberal in their politics than the U.S. population at large. A faculty survey by the University of California at Los Angeles Research Institute in 1995-1996 yielded the following results for university professors: far left, 6.4 percent; liberal, 44.8 percent; moderate, 35.2 percent; conservative, 13.4 percent; and far right, 0.3 percent. The totals for professors at other four-year colleges: far left, 4.8 percent; liberal, 37.5 percent; moderate, 37.8 percent; conservative, 19.5 percent; and far right, 0.4 percent. *Chronicle of Higher Education,* August 28, 1998.

23. According to Arianna Huffington, Cheney's staff met "with executives from Exxon Mobil, ChevronTexaco, ConocoPhillips—and yes, Halliburton—to discuss who would get what in a post-Hussein Iraq." "Profiting from Iraq," *San Francisco Chronicle,* February 21, 2003.

24. As CEO of Halliburton, Cheney had no qualms about doing illegal business with rogue nations like Iran, Iraq, and Libya. "Richard B. Cheney," Paul Begala charges, "is a poster boy for all that is wrong with the Bush Republican economic philosophy." *It's Still the Economy, Stupid: George W. Bush, The GOP's CEO* (New York: Simon & Schuster, 2002), 143-44. Arianna Huffington's assessment

of Cheney is even more severe: "The vice president is one of those ideological purists who never let little things like logic, morality or mass murder interfere with the single-minded pursuit of profitability." "Profiting from Iraq." Tom DeLay's ethical conduct has been so reprehensible (fund-raising improprieties and expensive junkets financed by lobbyists, among many other transgressions) that even staunch right-wing journalists like Debra Saunders, "DeLavish, DeLoutish, DeLayly," *San Francisco Chronicle,* March 25, 2005, are critical. DeLay himself dismisses public criticism as part of a liberal conspiracy to destroy the conservative movement. R. Jeffrey Smith and James V. Grimaldi, "Lobbyists Allegedly Paid for DeLay Trip to Russia," *San Francisco Chronicle,* April 6, 2005.

25. Senator Alan Simpson, quoted in Bill Clinton, *My Life* (New York: Knopf, 2004), 692.

26. Media coverage of the 2000 presidential race was overwhelmingly pro-Bush, according to a Brookings Institution study released immediately after the election. This study is cited by Mark Crispin Miller in J. H. Hatfield, *Fortunate Son: George W. Bush and the Making of an American President,* 2d ed. (New York: Soft Skull, 2001), xii. Bush collected more than $193 million and Gore just over $133 million, according to the Center for Responsive Politics. Of course, four years later, running against John Kerry, Mr. Bush easily topped his previous record, collecting $367,228,801, http://www.opensecrets.org/presidential/index.asp.

27. Eric Alterman, "Corrupt, Incompetent & Off Center," *The Nation,* November 7, 2005, 12; Paul Krugman, "Questions of Character," *New York Times,* October 14, 2005.

28. Bernard Goldberg, *Bias: A CBS Insider Exposes How the Media Distort the News* (Washington, D.C.: Regnery, 2002). See, too, Ann Coulter, *Slander: Liberal Lies about the American Right* (New York: Crown, 2002).

29. McChesney, *Problem of the Media,* 102.

30. Alterman, *What Liberal Media?* 10–11.

31. Michael Parenti, *Democracy for the Few,* 4th ed. (New York: St. Martin's, 1983), 189.

32. McChesney, *Problem of the Media,* 115.

33. Steve Rendall, "Fox's Slanted Sources: Conservatives, Republicans Far Outnumber Others," *Extra!,* August 2001. Of the fifty-six partisan guests, fifty were Republicans and six were Democrats.

34. Hertsgaard, *Eagle's Shadow,* 16.

35. McChesney, *Problem of the Media,* 122.

36. One of the few major journals to categorically reject the war was the *New York Review of Books.* See Scott Sherman, "The Rebirth of the NYRB," *The Nation,* June 7, 2004. Though hardly considered "mainstream," being a progressive journal, *The Nation,* too, refused to join the misguided crusade.

37. See Evan Derkacz, "Voice of America," *AlterNet.org,* February 14, 2005, http://www.alternet.org/mediaculture/21250/.

38. William D. Hartung, *How Much Are You Making on the War, Daddy? A Quick and Dirty Guide to War Profiteering in the Bush Administration* (New York: Nation Books, 2003), xxii.

39. McChesney, *Problem of the Media,* 123.

40. Eric Alterman, "Hawks Eating Crow," *The Nation,* June 7, 2004, 10.

41. See Seymour M. Hersh, "Torture at Abu Ghraib," *New Yorker,* May 10, 2004.

42. During the war, "Fox TV openly discarded traditions of journalistic impartiality and, like right-wing radio talk shows, acted as a cheerleader for conservative and chauvinistic attitudes," Godfrey Hodgson, *More Equal Than Others: America from Nixon to the New Century* (Princeton, N.J.: Princeton University Press, 2004), 238–39.

43. Ed Bark, "TV War Coverage Was More Show Than Tell," *Contra Costa Times* (Walnut Creek, Calif.), May 1, 2003.

44. For numerous examples, see Daniel Benaim and Priyanka Motaparthy, "TV's Conflicted Experts," *The Nation,* April 21, 2003, 6–7.

45. Hertsgaard, *Eagle's Shadow,* 106.

46. See Mark Hertsgaard, *On Bended Knee: The Press and the Reagan Presidency* (New York: Farrar, Straus & Giroux, 2002). The failure of the Democrats to challenge Reagan is one of the major reasons the media followed suit, according to Hertsgaard, "News Media Were Willingly Seduced by Reagan's Charm," *San Francisco Chronicle,* June 13, 2004.

47. William Safire, quoted in Bill Clinton, *My Life,* 698.

48. Clinton, *My Life,* 531.

49. Christopher Marquis, "U.S. Considers Charging Aristide with Corruption," *Contra Costa Times,* April 6, 2004.

50. Bill Moyers, "This Is Your Story—The Progressive Story of America," text of a speech to the Take Back America conference sponsored by the Campaign for America's Future in Washington, D.C., on June 4, 2003, http://www.commondreams.org/views03/0610-11.htm.

51. A Pew Research Center survey on campaign news and political communication, released on January 11, 2004, indicated that 21 percent of people ages 18 to 29 regularly turn to television comedy shows for their presidential campaign coverage. See Cameron Jan, "Cable TV's 'Daily Show' Catches Politicos off Guard," *Contra Costa Times,* June 21, 2004.

52. Doyle McManus and Bob Drogin, "Speculation Rages over Who Leaked Agent's Name," *Contra Costa Times,* October 1, 2003; James Risen, "Leak Shows CIA, White House Strains," *San Francisco Chronicle,* October 2, 2003.

53. Tony Norman, "Why Isn't Bob Novak Going to Jail?" *Pittsburgh Post-Gazette,* February 18, 2005.

54. Anna Quindlen, "Free Pass for the President," *Newsweek,* October 6, 2003. Some journalists may have gone overboard in accommodating the president; in early 2005, it came out that prominent conservative columnists Armstrong Williams, Maggie Gallagher, and Karen Ryan were paid "consultants" for the Bush White House (one of them, Williams, was paid $240,000 to plug the No Child Left Behind Act).

55. Jim Hightower, *Thieves in High Places* (New York: Viking Penguin, 2003), 35.

56. McChesney, *Rich Media, Poor Democracy,* xiv.

57. Fairness & Accuracy in Reporting, "FAIR Issues New Study on PBS's *MacNeil/Lehrer* and ABC's *Nightline,*" May 21, 1990, http://www.fair.org/reports/macneil-study.html.

58. People for the American Way, *Buying a Movement: Right-Wing Foundations and American Politics* (Washington, D.C.: People for the American Way, 1996), 12.

59. Blaine Harden, "Religious Broadcasters Pushing Public Radio off Air," *San Francisco Chronicle,* September 15, 2002.

60. Steve Rendall and Daniel Butterworth, "How Public Is Public Radio? A Study of NPR's Guest List," *Extra!,* June 2004.

61. Michael Hirschorn, "Little Men on Campus," *New Republic,* August 5, 1985.

62. Jean Stefancic and Richard Delgado, *No Mercy: How Conservative Think Tanks and Foundations Changed America's Social Agenda* (Philadelphia: Temple University Press, 1996), 110.

63. Bill Berkowitz, "Movement Building on the Internet: Christian Right and 'Free Market' Think Tanks Collaborate in Cyberspace," *Media Alliance* media file, http://www.media-alliance.org/mediafile/19-3/rightwing.html.

64. Berkowitz, "Movement Building on the Internet."

65. Peter Hartlaub, "Guilty or Not, Here She Comes—Nancy Grace Brings Mob Justice to CNN," *San Francisco Chronicle,* May 20, 2005.

Chapter 5

1. See Paul Krugman, "Design for Confusion," *New York Times,* August 5, 2005, who disparages "supply-side economics, a doctrine whose central claim—that tax cuts have such miraculous effects on the economy that they pay for themselves—has never been backed by evidence."

2. Cornel West, "Exiles from a City and a Nation," *Observer* (London, U.K.), September 11, 2005.

3. West, "Exiles from a City and a Nation." See also David Leonhardt, "U.S. Poverty Rate Was up Last Year," *New York Times,* August 31, 2005.

4. Micki McGee, "Belabored: The Cult of Life as a Work of Art," *Chronicle of Higher Education,* September 16, 2005, http://chronicle.com/weekly/v52/i0404601701.htm.

5. Lawrence Mishel and Ross Eisenbrey, "The Economy in a Nutshell: Wages & Incomes Down, Poverty & Debt Up," *Counterpunch,* December 23, 2005, http://www.counterpunch.org/mishell12232005.html. Surveying the period from the Clinton administration to the end of 2005, Mishel and Eisenbrey see the acceleration of five major trends: (1) the rise of corporate profits and the decline of workers' wages, (2) the increase both in the number of Americans burdened by debt and in the amount they owe, (3) the failure of job creation to keep up with population growth, (4) the growth of the poverty rate, and (5) the escalation of health care costs.

6. On the role of conservative organizations such as the American Enterprise Institute in the "Constitution in Exile" movement, which emphasizes total deregulation, see Jeffrey Rosen, "The Unregulated Offensive," *New York Times Magazine,* April 17, 2005.

7. Nicholas D. Kristoff, "The Larger Shame," *New York Times,* September 6, 2005.

8. E. Digby Baltzell, *The Protestant Establishment: Aristocracy and Caste in America* (New York: Random House, 1964), 334.

9. Quoted in Barbara Ehrenreich, *Fear of Falling: The Inner Life of the Middle Class* (New York: HarperPerennial, 1990), 128.

10. As social critic Kevin Baker has aptly observed, "one is struck by nothing so much as how utterly dismal modern conservative thought has been." "Up from Extremism: Getting It Wrong about the American Right," *Harper's Magazine,* August 2001, 65. Baker's uncharitable view of the conservative intellectual tradition is shared by many scholars, including Ehrenreich, *Fear of Falling,* 160.

11. Michael Lind, *Up from Conservatism: Why the Right Is Wrong for America* (New York: Free Press, 1996), 88–89.

12. George H. Nash, *The Conservative Intellectual Movement in America, since 1945* (New York: Basic Books, 1979), 335–40. W. Wesley McDonald, another sympathetic student of the Right, concurs: "Conservative thought is really suffering because it lacks substance and direction." Quoted in Scott McLemee, "A Conservative of the Old School," *Chronicle of Higher Education,* May 7, 2004.

13. Roger Kimball, "Retaking the University: A Battle Plan," *New Criterion,* May 11, 2003, http://www.newcriterion.com/archive/23/may/05/universe.com.

14. The president's anti-intellectualism, machismo, and emphasis on religion are the basis for his enormous appeal among Texans, claims Molly Ivins. "Texas: Texas on Everything," in *These United States: Original Essays by Leading American Writers on Their State within the Union,* ed. John Leonard (New York: Thunder's Mouth Press/Nation Books, 2003), 423–25.

15. The book to read: Max Weber, *The Protestant Ethic and the Spirit of Capitalism,* trans. Talcott Parsons (New York: Scribner's, 1958).

16. Robert D. Putnam, *Bowling Alone: The Collapse and Revival of American Community* (New York: Simon & Schuster, 2000), 65.

17. Materialism is inevitable given a commercial culture that constantly hammers home the same message: "all our most treasured values—democracy, freedom, individuality, equality, education, community, love, and health—are reduced in one way or another to commodities produced by the market." Robert W. McChesney, *The Problem of the Media: U.S. Communication Politics in the 21st Century* (New York: Monthly Review, 2004), 166.

18. Morris Berman, *The Twilight of American Culture* (New York: Norton, 2000), 52–54.

19. Andrew Hacker, *Money: Who Has How Much and Why* (New York: Scribner's, 1997), 41.

20. Mark Hertsgaard, *The Eagle's Shadow: Why America Fascinates and Infuriates the World* (New York: Farrar, Straus & Giroux, 2002), 128.

21. Mary Leonard, "Rich Getting Richer Faster Than Ever," *Contra Costa Times* (Walnut Creek, Calif.), July 29, 1997.

22. Leonard Peikoff, "Christmas Should Be More Commercial," *San Francisco Chronicle,* December 25, 2003.

23. David Kay Johnston, "At the Very Top, a Surge in Income '03," *New York Times,* October 5, 2005.

24. Robert J. Samuelson, "America the Open," *Newsweek,* July 31, 1995, 48.

25. Lind, *Up from Conservatism,* 248. This wealth, almost exclusively the patrimony of the truly privileged in U.S. society, white people, as social justice

advocate Tim Wise reminds us, is gigantic: "the current baby-boomer generation of whites is currently in the process of inheriting between $7–10 trillion in assets from their parents and grandparents." "Whites Swim in Racial Preference," *AlterNet.org,* February 20, 2003, http://www.alternet.org/story/15223.

26. Baker, "Up from Extremism," 65.

27. Molly Ivins, "The Uncompassionate Conservative," *Mother Jones,* November/December 2003, 47.

28. Michael Kinsley, "How Affirmative Action Helped George W.," *Time,* January 27, 2003.

29. The United States has the highest poverty level among the major industrial nations, according to a recent United Nations state-of-the-art world report, United Nations Development Programme, *Human Development Report 2001: Making New Technologies Work for Human Development* (New York: Oxford University Press, 2001), 153.

30. *The Hightower Lowdown,* February 2003, 3.

31. Hertsgaard, *Eagle's Shadow,* 149.

32. Robert Kuttner, "Top-Down Class Warfare," *American Prospect,* October 23, 2000, http://www.prospect.org/V11/22/kuttner-r.html.

33. Mark Zepezauer and Arthur Naiman, *Take the Rich off Welfare* (Tucson, Ariz.: Odonian, 1996), 6.

34. Barbara Ehrenreich, *Nickel and Dimed: On (Not) Getting By in America* (New York: Holt, 2001), 201.

35. Hacker, *Money,* 53–54.

36. Michael Parenti, *The Terrorism Trap: September 11 and Beyond* (San Francisco: City Lights, 2002), 5.

37. Zepezauer and Naiman, *Take the Rich off Welfare,* 22, 25, 33.

38. Chalmers Johnson, *Blowback: The Costs and Consequences of American Empire* (New York: Holt, 2000), 10.

39. Zepezauer and Naiman, *Take the Rich off Welfare,* 17.

40. Paul Rockwell, "Who Armed Iraq?" *San Francisco Chronicle,* March 2, 2003.

41. Johnson, *Blowback,* 222.

42. David Wallechinsky, "Where Does Your Tax Money Go?" *Parade,* April 10, 2005, 5.

43. Hertsgaard, *Eagle's Shadow,* 96.

44. Jerome L. Himmelstein, *To the Right: The Transformation of American Conservatism* (Berkeley: University of California Press, 1992), 247.

45. "Since September 11," reports Michael Scherer, "the Bush administration has awarded the world's second-largest oil-services company at least $2.2 billion in defense-related business, mostly to support military operations overseas." "The World According to Halliburton," *Mother Jones,* July/August 2003, 24.

46. Arianna Huffington, "This Is What Happens When Crony Capitalism Goes to War," *Contra Costa Times,* April 24, 2003.

47. *Contra Costa Times,* June 19, 2002.

48. Jason Vest, "The Men from JINSA and CSP," *The Nation,* September 2, 2002.

49. "Clark Reports Income Zoomed to $1.6 Million," *San Francisco Chronicle,* December 13, 2003.

50. Amy Ross, "Truth or Dare—Confronting 9/11," *San Francisco Chronicle,* April 8, 2004. In fact, Kissinger has business interests throughout the globe. Scott Sherman, "Kissinger's Shadow over the Council of Foreign Relations," *The Nation,* December 27, 2004, 24.

51. Joseph L. Galloway, "Air Force Bid Fitted to Boeing," *Contra Costa Times,* March 28, 2004.

52. Paul Krugman, "For Richer: How the Permissive Capitalism of the Boom Destroyed American Equality," *New York Times Magazine,* October 20, 2002, 77.

53. Robert L. Borosage, "Sacrifice Is for Suckers," *The Nation,* April 28, 2003, 4.

54. Michael J. Graetz and Ian Shapiro, *Death by a Thousand Cuts: The Fight over Taxing Inherited Wealth* (Princeton, N.J.: Princeton University Press, 2005), 134–36.

55. E. J. Dionne Jr., "Taxing Wealth, Not Death," *San Francisco Chronicle,* June 14, 2002.

56. Wallechinsky, "Where Does Your Tax Money Go?" 5.

57. A point made cogently by David Broder, "Dumbfounded by Death Tax Plans," *Contra Costa Times,* June 16, 2002, and seconded by Ellen Goodman, "Optimistic Americans in for a Big Shock on Estate Tax," *Contra Costa Times,* June 18, 2002, who explains that repealing the estate tax permanently would cost the government an estimated $740 billion in revenues in the decade after 2010, the peak baby boomer retirement years.

58. These tax dodges are the subject of a fine study by William Brittain-Catlin, *Offshore: The Dark Side of the Global Economy* (New York: Farrar, Straus & Giroux, 2005).

59. Arianna Huffington, *Pigs at the Trough: How Corporate Greed and Political Corruption Are Undermining America* (New York: Crown, 2003), 13.

60. Borosage, "Sacrifice Is for Suckers," 4–5.

61. John D. McKinnon, "60% of U.S. Firms Escaped Taxes during Boom," *Contra Costa Times,* April 7, 2004.

62. David Cay Johnston, "Stroke the Rich: IRS Has Become a Subsidy System for Super-Wealthy Americans," *San Francisco Chronicle,* April 11, 2004. "The wealthy who mine the tax system," Johnston claims, "face little risk of getting caught. Only 1 partnership in 400 gets audited." "How Rich Get Richer: All the Rest Pay More," *San Francisco Chronicle,* April 10, 2005.

63. David E. Rosenbaum, "Unemployment Weighs on Bush's Future," *Contra Costa Times,* September 28, 2003.

64. Andrew J. Cherlin, "Ends Don't Meet for Hard-Working, Low-Wage Workers," *San Francisco Chronicle,* September 28, 2003.

65. Alan Sloan, "Bush's Depressing Economy," *Newsweek,* February 10, 2003.

66. Paul Krugman, "The Deficit Spending Con," *San Francisco Chronicle,* January 28, 2004.

67. Paul Krugman, *The Great Unraveling: Losing Our Way in the New Century* (New York: Norton, 2003), 9.

68. Jay Bookman, "Tax Cut a Con Game on Multiple Levels," *Contra Costa Times,* May 4, 2003. The Bush strategy is not new: Increasing the national deficit as a means of justifying the elimination of social programs was a device

employed by Ronald Reagan, according to his budget director, David Stockman, cited in Ehrenreich, *Fear of Falling,* 189.

69. Robert Reich, "Bush Administration Paradox Explained," *San Francisco Chronicle,* September 19, 2005.

70. Robert Scheer, "The Real Costs of a Culture of Greed," *Los Angeles Times,* September 6, 2005.

71. Ronald Reagan, quoted in Zepezauer and Naiman, *Take the Rich off Welfare,* 35.

72. Paul Begala, *It's Still the Economy, Stupid: George W. Bush, the GOP's CEO* (New York: Simon & Schuster, 2002), 15.

73. Sam Zuckerman, "Record Federal Deficit Forecast," *San Francisco Chronicle,* July 16, 2003; Jonathan Weisman, "Federal Debt Will Explode $1.9 Trillion over 5 Years," *Contra Costa Times,* July 16, 2003.

74. Jonathan Weisman, "U.S. Budget Drowning in Red Ink," *San Francisco Chronicle,* August 27, 2003. In fact, the 2004 deficit turned out to be $412 billion, still a record though not as high as anticipated, and 2005's deficit is projected at $427 billion. Molly Ivins, "Between Word and Deed," *San Francisco Chronicle,* February 7, 2005.

75. Floyd Norris, "More Than Ever, the U.S. Spends and the Foreigners Lend," *New York Times,* October 1, 2005.

76. Howard Dean, quoted by Richard W. Stevenson and Edmund L. Andrews, "Debt Grows into Pain for Bush," *Contra Costa Times,* November 30, 2003.

77. Eileen Alt Powell, "We're Good at Spending, Bad at Saving," *San Francisco Chronicle,* January 6, 2004.

78. Foreign governments lent the American treasury $3.5 billion in 2001, $7.1 billion in 2002, and $109 billion in 2003. By mid-2004, Chinese holdings in the United States were about $166 billion. Jonathan Weisman, "Consequences of Deficit on Horizon," *San Francisco Chronicle,* October 9, 2004.

79. Michael Lind, *The Next American Nation: The New Nationalism and the Fourth American Revolution* (New York: Free Press, 1995), 193.

80. Berman, *Twilight of American Culture,* 28. Berman uses Kevin Phillips to back up this assertion.

81. Kevin Danaher, *Corporations Are Gonna Get Your Mama* (Monroe, Maine: Common Courage Press, 1996), 23-24.

82. Noam Chomsky, "Neoliberalism and Global Order: Doctrine and Reality," Alternative Information and Development Centre, Cape Town, South Africa, 1998, http://aidc.org.za/archives/chomsky_01.html.

83. Editorial, *San Francisco Chronicle,* March 9, 2002.

84. Carolyn Lochhead, "Bush's Sop to Swing States," *San Francisco Chronicle,* March 11, 2002.

85. Lind, *Next American Nation,* 93.

86. Daniel Kurtzman, "Learning to Love Big Brother," *San Francisco Chronicle,* July 28, 2002.

87. Kevin Baker, "We're in the Army Now: The G.O.P.'s Plan to Militarize Our Culture," *Harper's Magazine,* October 2003, 38.

88. Jonathan Turley, "New Security's Orwellian Twists," *Contra Costa Times,* November 28, 2002.

89. *The Hightower Lowdown,* September 2003, 3-4.

90. Joe Conason, *Big Lies: The Right-Wing Propaganda Machine and How It Distorts the Truth* (New York: Dunne, 2003), 104.

91. David A. Horowitz and Peter N. Carroll, *On the Edge: The U.S. since 1941,* 2d ed. (New York: West/Wadsworth, 1998), 285.

92. The result, massive corporate corruption, is carefully chronicled in Joseph E. Stiglitz, *The Roaring Nineties: A New History of the World's Most Prosperous Decade* (New York: Norton, 2003). Stiglitz, a 2001 Nobel laureate in economics and a former Clinton economic adviser, is as critical of Democrats as he is of Republicans for their failure to curb corporate avarice.

93. James P. Steyer, "The Stranger in Our House," *San Francisco Chronicle,* June 23, 2002.

94. This entire episode is covered in considerable detail by Gingrich biographer Dick Williams, *Newt! Leader of the Second American Revolution* (Marietta, Ga.: Longstreet Press, 1995), 197–201.

95. Molly Ivins, "Industry Self-Policing Won't Work," *San Francisco Chronicle,* November 13, 2002.

96. Robert L. Borosage, "Blame It on Washington's Conservative Bubble Boys," *San Francisco Chronicle,* July 14, 2002.

97. Eliot Spitzer, quoted in Allan Sloan, "Unfair Fight: The Mutual Fund Scandal," *Newsweek,* December 8, 2003. Molly Ivins has a different take: "Hey, you take away the regulations and *it's all legal!* Just as though you'd repealed the law against sticking up the Jiffy Mart." "Mutual Fund Scandal: The Rich Get Richer and the Rest of Us, Well . . . ," *Contra Costa Times,* November 14, 2003.

98. Zachary Coile, "Business Scandals Could Help Democrats, GOP Fears," *San Francisco Chronicle,* June 27, 2002. The Arthur Andersen firm, which did the accounting for both Enron and WorldCom, was one of Pitt's clients.

99. Begala, *It's Still the Economy, Stupid,* 159.

100. Huffington, *Pigs at the Trough,* 167.

101. Maureen Dowd, "Bush Talks Like a Populist but . . . ," *San Francisco Chronicle,* July 11, 2002.

102. Zepezauer and Naiman, *Take the Rich off Welfare,* 51.

103. Michael Parenti, *Democracy for the Few,* 7th ed. (Boston: Bedford/St. Martin's, 2002), 54.

104. Michael Parenti, *America Besieged* (San Francisco: City Lights, 1998), 45.

105. Vicki Kemper, "Social Security Woes Predicted to Hit in 2052," *Contra Costa Times,* June 15, 2004.

106. Robert Kuttner, "Social Security: Finally, an Honest Debate," *Business Week,* March 15, 2004, 24. Like Kuttner, the economist Jane Bryant Quinn ("Social Security Isn't Doomed," *Newsweek,* March 29, 2004, 47) agrees that "Social Security is basically sound."

107. Jane Bryant Quinn, "Medicare's in Good Health," *Newsweek,* May 24, 2004, 41.

108. For more on private contractors doing government work, see Michael Scherer, "Contracts with America," *Mother Jones,* May/June 2004, 57–61, 92–93.

109. William D. Hartung, "Outsourcing Is Hell," *The Nation,* June 7, 2004, 5. See, too, Nicholas von Hoffman, "Contract Killers: How Privatizing the U.S. Military Subverts Public Oversight," *Harper's Magazine,* June 2004, 79.

110. Molly Ivins, "The Masters of Mean," *Mother Jones,* March/April 2002, 29.

111. David Von Drehle, "Bennett Admits High-Stakes Gaming," *Contra Costa Times,* May 3, 2003; Jonathan Alter and Joshua Green, "Bennett: Virtue Is as Virtue Does?" *Newsweek,* May 12, 2003, 6.

112. Kevin Phillips, "Neil, Prince of Bush," *Harper's Magazine,* May 2004, 79.

113. Conason, *Big Lies,* 153.

114. For a good overview of Bush's sordid business dealings, see Begala, *It's Still the Economy, Stupid,* chap. 8.

115. Randall Balmer, "Bush and God," *The Nation,* April 14, 2003, 7.

Chapter 6

1. Kevin Baker, "We're in the Army Now: The G.O.P.'s Plan to Militarize Our Culture," *Harper's Magazine,* October 2003, 42. It is hard to disagree with the author's somber assessment of the opposition: "The Democratic Party is a cobweb, waiting to be swept away. In a unique disaster, it has been simultaneously de-pedded and beheaded; bereft of a dedicated, activist core and any meaningful leadership" (41).

2. Thomas Frank, "Lie Down for America: How the Republican Party Sows Ruin on the Great Plains," *Harper's Magazine,* April 2004, 33. This is essentially the question posed by a puzzled Godfrey Hodgson in his provocative book, *More Equal Than Others: America from Nixon to the New Century* (Princeton, N.J.: Princeton University Press, 2004), 295–96.

3. Michael Lind, *The Next American Nation: The New Nationalism and the Fourth American Revolution* (New York: Free Press, 1995), 183.

4. Godfrey Hodgson, *The World Turned Right Side Up: A History of the Conservative Ascendancy in America* (New York: Houghton Mifflin, 1996), 282–83.

5. George Lakoff, *Moral Politics: How Liberals and Conservatives Think,* 2d ed. (Chicago: University of Chicago Press, 2002), 416; Jean Stefancic and Richard Delgado, *No Mercy: How Conservative Think Tanks and Foundations Changed America's Social Agenda* (Philadelphia: Temple University Press, 1996), 144–47.

6. "Nothing—not low education, not full-time work, not long commutes in urban agglomerations, not poverty or financial distress—is more broadly associated with civic disengagement and social disconnection than is dependence on television for entertainment." Robert D. Putnam, *Bowling Alone: The Collapse and Revival of American Community* (New York: Simon & Schuster, 2000), 231.

7. Neil Postman, *Amusing Ourselves to Death* (New York: Penguin Books, 1995), 141.

8. Norman Solomon, "The Orwellian Zone," in *Time for Choices: Deep Dialogues for Deep Democracy,* ed. Michael Toms (Gabriola Island, B.C., Canada: New Society, 2002), 52–53.

9. Robert W. McChesney, *The Problem of the Media: U.S. Communication Politics in the 21st Century* (New York: Monthly Review, 2004), 86.

10. Haynes Johnson, *The Best of Times: America in the Clinton Years* (New York: Harcourt, 2001), 215.

11. Morris Berman, *The Twilight of American Culture* (New York: Norton, 2000), 55.

12. Clinton reportedly earned $10 million to $12 million on his book. Sharon Theimer, "Bush Cabinet Members Should Land on Their Feet," *Contra Costa Times* (Walnut Creek, Calif.), January 10, 2005.

13. The best examples of firms using celebrities to endorse their products without public awareness of the fact that these are paid advertisements are drug companies, who are known to shell out between $20,000 and $2 million for the service. Jeff Stryker, "Behind Celebrity Endorsements," *San Francisco Chronicle*, November 7, 2004.

14. Postman, *Amusing Ourselves to Death*, 132.

15. Postman, *Amusing Ourselves to Death*, 135.

16. Lewis H. Lapham, "Buffalo Dances," *Harper's Magazine*, May 2004, 10.

17. For the actor's campaign strategy, see Tim Goodman, "Schwarzenegger's Snug Union of Showbiz, Politics a Scary but Inevitable Next Step," *San Francisco Chronicle*, October 2, 2003.

18. Dion Nissenbaum, "Schwarzenegger's Donors Test His Image as Ethical Outsider," *Contra Costa Times*, April 5, 2004.

19. Carla Marinucci and John Wildermuth, "Lockyer's Shocking Choice in Recall," *San Francisco Chronicle*, October 19, 2003.

20. Mike Davis, "Recall Spun out of Thin Air," *San Francisco Chronicle*, October 19, 2003.

21. E. J. Dionne Jr., *Why Americans Hate Politics* (New York: Touchstone, 1991), 15.

22. Molly Ivins, "The Uncompassionate Conservative," *Mother Jones*, November/December 2003, 47.

23. David Corn, *The Lies of George W. Bush: Mastering the Politics of Deception* (New York: Crown, 2003), 1. For a lengthy catalogue of misrepresentations associated with the president, see Jerry "Politex" Barrett, ed., *Big Bush Lies* (Ashland, Ore.: River Wood Books, 2004).

24. Coulter is undoubtedly the most successful graduate of the National Journalism Center (NJC). Based in Herndon, Virginia, the NJC was established in 1977 by Stanton Evans to train a cadre of right-wing journalists.

25. Susan Rasky, quoted by Edward Guthmann, "An Outbreak of Partisan Warfare on the Best-Seller List Is Encouraging Authors to Stoke the Fires of Readers Hungry for Political Squabbles—and the Bay Area Is Fertile Ground for Bush-Whackers," *San Francisco Chronicle*, December 2, 2003.

26. The president, in fact, carefully avoids the citizenry—except for military audiences. "Bush," it has been observed, "may be the most isolated president in modern history, at least since the late-stage Richard Nixon." Evan Thomas and Richard Wolffe, "Bush in the Bubble," *Newsweek*, December 19, 2005, 33.

27. Berman, *Twilight of American Culture*, 61.

28. Mark Hertsgaard, *The Eagle's Shadow: Why America Fascinates and Infuriates the World* (New York: Farrar, Straus & Giroux, 2002), 20.

29. Putnam, *Bowling Alone*, 222. Moreover, what mesmerizes the youth is not C-SPAN but MTV, or worse still, ESPN. Spectator sports are truly the opium of this particular generation. Nor are they alone. As a society, we are so enamored with this kind of entertainment that we're more willing to pay a professional

baseball player, Alex Rodriguez—an adult human being playing what is essentially a children's game—$25 million a year for ten years rather than provide a $100,000 salary for a schoolteacher. Moreover, the head football coach of the leading state-supported university is probably the highest-paid public employee in most states of the Union, making more even than the governor—which tells us volumes about our value system.

30. Barbara Ehrenreich, *Nickel and Dimed: On (Not) Getting By in America* (New York: Holt, 2002), 210.

31. Ruth Rosen, "The Right to Be Ordinary," *San Francisco Chronicle,* December 8, 2003.

32. Morris Berman, *booktv.org,* March 25, 2001.

33. Alan B. Kruger, "Tax Cuts Confuse Americans," *Contra Costa Times,* October 16, 2003.

34. Robert D. Kaplan, "Was Democracy Just a Moment?" *Atlantic Monthly,* December 1997.

35. C. Wright Mills, *The Power Elite* (New York: Oxford University Press, 1959), 10.

36. David Cay Johnston, "Lower Income, Lower Taxes for the Wealthy," *San Francisco Chronicle,* September 28, 2003. This figure was down from the $313,500 of the previous year. (Sociologists generally define class on the basis of income since wealth, a more accurate barometer of class, is much more difficult to assess.)

37. Barbara Ehrenreich, *Fear of Falling: The Inner Life of the Middle Class* (New York: Pantheon Books, 1989), 199–200. During this period, according to Ehrenreich, managers and professionals constituted about one-fifth of the U.S. population.

38. Robert B. Reich, "As the World Turns," *New Republic,* May 1, 1989, 28.

39. Lewis Lapham, *Money and Class in America: Notes and Observations on Our Civil Religion* (New York: Weidenfeld & Nicolson, 1988), 6.

40. George Lakoff, quoted in Rick DelVecchio, "Berkeley: Why Would 1,000 People Crowd into a Church to Hear a Talk by a Linguist?" *San Francisco Chronicle,* June 18, 2004.

41. See Arthur M. Schlesinger Jr., *The Disuniting of America: Reflections on a Multicultural Society* (New York: Norton, 1992), and Samuel P. Huntington, *Who Are We? The Challenges to America's National Identity* (New York: Simon & Schuster, 2004).

42. This argument is well articulated by Amy Goodman, *The Exception to the Rulers: Exposing Oily Politicians, War Profiteers, and the Media That Love Them* (New York: Hyperion, 2004), who concludes that George W. Bush "has used the war on terror as its rationale for the biggest crackdown on civil liberties since the McCarthy era of the 1950s" (10).

43. Leonie Huddy, Stanley Feldman, Charles Taber, and Gallya Lahav, "Threat, Anxiety, and Support of Antiterrorism Policies," *American Journal of Political Science,* July 2005, http://www.blackwell-synergy.com/doi/toc/ajps/49/3; Noam Chomsky, "Resort to Fear," *Z Net,* July 21, 2005, http://www.zmag.org/content/showarticle.cfm?ItemID=8347.

44. Joseph E. Stiglitz, *The Roaring Nineties: A New History of the World's Most Prosperous Decade* (New York: Norton, 2003), x.

45. William C. Berman, *America's Right Turn: From Nixon to Clinton,* 2d ed. (Baltimore: Johns Hopkins University Press, 1998), 3.

46. Kevin Phillips, *The Politics of Rich and Poor: Wealth and the American Electorate in the Reagan Aftermath* (New York: Random House, 1990), 8.

47. See, for example, Thomas Edsall, with Mary Edsall, *Chain Reaction: The Impact of Race, Rights, and Taxes on American Politics* (New York: Norton, 1991), 28, 254.

48. Berman, *Twilight of American Culture,* 28.

49. Naomi Klein, *No Logo: Taking Aim at the Brand Bullies* (New York: Picador, 2000), 242.

50. Klein, *No Logo,* 242.

51. Klein, *No Logo,* 247.

52. Lind, *Next American Nation,* 202.

53. Named the most admired firm by *Forbes* magazine in 2003, the Arkansas-based chain is "the darling of Wall Street," according to Elizabeth DiNovella, "The True Costs of Low Prices," *The Progressive,* January 2005, 45. For the utterly dismal working conditions at this much maligned enterprise (by liberals), see Liza Featherstone, *Selling Women Short: The Landmark Battle for Workers' Rights at Wal-Mart* (New York: Basic Books, 2004), which is reviewed by DiNovella above.

54. David Gates, "The Pop Prophets," *Newsweek,* May 24, 2004, 46.

55. According to pollsters Marc Sapir and Mickey Huff, "U.S. citizens have existed under a cloud of media and government induced fear" since the Creel Commission at the start of the First World War. "The Public Opinion Polling Fraud," *Z Magazine,* October 2003, 43.

56. William Greider, *Who Will Tell the People: The Betrayal of American Democracy* (New York: Simon & Schuster, 1992), 275.

57. Greider, *Who Will Tell the People,* 275.

58. Joe Conason, *Big Lies: The Right-Wing Propaganda Machine and How It Distorts the Truth* (New York: Dunne, 2003), 8.

59. Ehrenreich, *Fear of Falling,* 163, 183.

60. David Brock, *Blinded by the Right: The Conscience of an Ex-Conservative* (New York: Three Rivers, 2002), 67.

61. Larry Everest, *Oil, Power and Empire: Iraq and the U.S. Global Agenda* (Monroe, Maine: Common Courage Press, 2004), 298.

62. George Soros, "America's Global Rule," *American Prospect,* June 1, 2003, http://www.prospect.org/web/page.ww?section=root8name=ViewPrint8 articleId=6807.

63. Thomas L. Friedman, "Learning to Listen," *San Francisco Chronicle,* October 17, 2003.

64. See, for example, Noam Chomsky, *Hegemony or Survival: America's Quest for Global Dominance* (New York: Metropolitan, 2003), chap. 4.

65. Greider, *Who Will Tell the People,* 276.

66. Michael Omi and Howard Winant, *Racial Formation in the United States: From the 1960s to the 1990s,* 2d ed. (New York: Routledge, 1994), 123.

67. See, particularly, *Chain Reaction,* 148, 158.

68. Southern electoral votes in the 2004 presidential election went 153–0 for Bush. Michael Nelson, "How the GOP Conquered the South," *Chronicle of Higher Education,* October 21, 2005.

69. Eric Foner, "Shedding Lincoln's Mantle," *The Nation,* August 7, 2000, 5.

70. Diane McWhorter, "Dixiecrats and the GOP," *The Nation,* January 27, 2003.

71. David R. Roediger, *Colored White: Transcending the Racial Past* (Berkeley: University of California Press, 2002), 24.

72. Hodgson, *World Turned Right Side Up,* 123.

73. Hodgson, *More Equal Than Others,* 213.

74. For the competition between new white suburbs and older suburbs inhabited by people of color, see chap. 7, "Beyond Blade Runner," in Mike Davis, *Ecology of Fear: Los Angeles and the Imagination of Disaster* (New York: Vintage Books, 1998).

75. Andrew L. Barlow, *Between Fear and Hope: Globalization and Race in the United States* (Lanham, Md.: Rowman & Littlefield, 2003), 38.

76. Omi and Winant, *Racial Formation,* 100. An indispensable guide to an understanding of racial attitudes in the South is still W. J. Cash's timeless classic, *The Mind of the South* (New York: Vintage Books, 1941).

77. George Wallace, quoted in Dan T. Carter, *From George Wallace to Newt Gingrich: Race in the Conservative Counterrevolution, 1963-1994* (Baton Rouge: Louisiana State University Press, 1996), 2.

78. Andrew Hacker, *Two Nations: Black and White, Separate, Hostile, Unequal* (New York: Scribner's, 1992), 206.

79. John A. Andrew III, *The Other Side of the Sixties: Young Americans for Freedom and the Rise of Conservative Politics* (New Brunswick: Rutgers University Press, 1997), 217.

80. Carter, *From George Wallace to Newt Gingrich,* 30.

81. Barlow, *Between Fear and Hope,* 48.

82. Edsall, *Chain Reaction,* 164. "Reagan was not racist in the narrow meaning of the term," according to Michael Schaller and George Rising, *The Republican Ascendancy: American Politics, 1968-2001* (Wheeling, Ill.: Harlan Davidson, 2002), 95. Rather than being overtly racist, the Teflon President was the kind of person who simply did not *see* minorities even when they were present; people of color were practically nonexistent in his universe. (Nixon at least had his Bebe Rebozo, who was in fact his best friend.) "Ronald Reagan," journalist Joe Conason recalls in *Big Lies,* "once greeted his own black Secretary of Housing and Urban Development as 'Mr. Mayor,' because he didn't have any idea who the man was" (129). Yes, President Reagan was a great patriot, but one gets the distinct impression that his America was the one he nostalgically recalled from his midwestern boyhood, the lily-white America of Norman Rockwell.

83. Carter, *From George Wallace to Newt Gingrich,* 55.

84. Roger Wilkins, "Smiling Racism," *The Nation,* November 3, 1984, 437.

85. Haynes Johnson, *Sleepwalking through History: America in the Reagan Years* (New York: Anchor Books/Doubleday, 1991), 50.

86. Harold Bloom, "How to Read and Write," *Booknotes,* September 3, 2000, interview with Brian Lamb.

87. Carter, *From George Wallace to Newt Gingrich,* 68; *New York Times,* January 19, 1986. Robert C. Smith, professor of political science at San Francisco State University and the author of the *Encyclopedia of African American Politics,*

ranks Reagan as the second worst U.S. president, right behind Andrew Johnson. Mark Simon, "Seeds of Discontent Sown in Bay Area," *San Francisco Chronicle,* June 11, 2004.

88. "Republican Group Wants to Review Reagan Film," *Contra Costa Times,* November 1, 2003.

89. David Greenberg, "Everybody Loves Reagan: How a Divisive President Became an American Idol," *Slate,* November 13, 2003, http://slate.msn.com/id/2091175/. Gallup polls indicate that Reagan's job approval rating during his eight years in office averaged 53 percent, slightly below average for all presidents Gallup monitored. Tony Hicks, "Outpouring of Praise Overlooks Problems," *Contra Costa Times,* June 10, 2004.

90. The relative merits of the two presidents, however, is not in doubt among most scholars, although few would go so far as ex-conservative pundit Michael Lind, who, writing in 1995, concluded, "Our only four-term president looms above the other American statesmen of the century, including his cousin Theodore, like a whale above porpoises. Truman and Johnson were footnotes to the testament of FDR; Reagan, a quibble in the margin." *Next American Nation,* 377. The illustrious historian Arthur M. Schlesinger Jr., writing a week after Reagan's death, gives this terse summation of our nation's fortieth president: "He had 'the vision thing' in abundance—alas, not too much else." "'He Knew How to Lead a People': The Dean of American Historians Assesses President Reagan's Faults and Virtues," *Newsweek,* June 14, 2004, 44.

91. Not all anxieties manipulated by the Bush team in 1988 were racial in nature. In fact, one observer feels that "George Bush managed to win the presidency by spreading alarm about flag-burning, a nonexistent threat that older voters remembered with horror from twenty years before." Thomas Frank, *One Market under God: Extreme Capitalism, Market Populism, and the End of Economic Democracy* (New York: Doubleday, 2000), 27.

92. Robert B. Reich, "The Rove Machine Rolls On," *American Prospect,* February 1, 2003, http://www.prospect.org/web/page.wwfsection=root8name=ViewPrintsarticleID=6689. See, too, Lou Dubose, Jan Reid, and Carl M. Cannon, *Boy Genius: Karl Rove, the Brains Behind the Remarkable Political Triumph of George W. Bush* (New York: Public Affairs, 2003), 142. "Rove's record has been consistent. Over 35 years, he has been a master of dirty tricks, divisiveness, innuendo, manipulation, character assassination, and roiling partisanship." "Rove's Role," *Boston Globe,* August 28, 2005.

93. "Chavez," *hispanicvista.com,* "Anti-Immigration: Hate in CAPS & Gowns, Part II: The Web of Hate," October 24, 2003, http://www.hispanicvista.com/html3/102403comm.htm.

94. David Montejano, *Chicano Politics and Society in the Late Twentieth Century,* ed. David Montejano (Austin: University of Texas Press, 1999), 242.

95. Montejano, *Chicano Politics,* 246.

96. Stefancic and Delgado, *No Mercy,* 24, 36. For the Pioneer Fund, see Chip Berlet, "Into the Mainstream," *Intelligence Report,* Summer 2003, 57–58.

97. Janet L. Abu-Lughod, *New York, Chicago, Los Angeles: America's Global Cities* (Minneapolis: University of Minnesota Press, 1999), 383.

98. See Rachel L. Swarns, "Capitol's Pariah on Immigration Is Now a Power," *New York Times,* December 21, 2005.

99. David G. Gutierrez, *Between Two Worlds: Mexican Immigrants in the United States,* ed. David G. Gutierrez (Wilmington, Del.: Scholarly Resources, 1996), xv. On Mexican immigration into the United States, see Manuel G. Gonzales, *Mexicanos: A History of Mexicans in the United States* (Bloomington: Indiana University Press, 1999), 224–31.

100. For anti-Mexican sentiment in the United States during the past generation, see Rodolfo Acuña, *Occupied America: A History of Chicanos,* 5th ed. (New York: Pearson Longman, 2004), chap. 15.

101. Lawrence (Larry) Pratt, quoted in Stefancic and Delgado, *No Mercy,* 17. Pratt founded English First, another highly financed English-only organization, in 1986.

102. See Huntington, *Who Are We? The Challenges to America's National Identity* (New York: Simon & Schuster, 2004).

103. "*Who Are We?* is Patrick Buchanan with footnotes," comments religious scholar Alan Wolfe, "Native Son: Samuel Huntington Defends the Homeland," *Foreign Affairs,* May/June 2004, 121.

104. Abu-Lughod, *New York, Chicago, Los Angeles,* 425.

105. Davis, *Ecology of Fear,* 405–11. The suburbs east of Los Angeles are a good example. See David Holthouse, "California Conflict: As Minorities Move into the Region Known as the Inland Empire, White Supremacists Unleash a Hate Crime Backlash," *Intelligence Report,* Fall 2005.

106. Marcelo M. Suárez-Orozco, *Crossings: Mexican Immigrants in Interdisciplinary Perspectives,* ed. Marcelo M. Suárez-Orozco (Cambridge, Mass.: Harvard University Press, 1998), 7. Linda Chavez argues that most Latinos are middle-class, in *Out of the Barrio: Toward a New Politics of Hispanic Assimilation* (New York: Basic Books, 1991), 102; but, given the modest skill and educational levels of Latino immigrants, this conclusion seems highly unwarranted.

107. "Latinos Rise Nationwide," *National Geographic,* November 2003.

108. Abu-Lughod, *New York, Chicago, Los Angeles,* 548.

109. Stefancic and Delgado, *No Mercy,* 22.

110. Omi and Winant, *Racial Formation,* 118.

111. Roediger, *Colored White,* 40.

112. Carter, *From George Wallace to Newt Gingrich,* 120.

113. Kevin Canfield, "Profit Motive Propels Publishers to the Right," *Contra Costa Times,* August 10, 2003.

114. Stephen Jay Gould, quoted by Hodgson, *World Turned Right Side Up,* 343.

115. Barlow, *Between Fear and Hope,* 10.

116. Omi and Winant, *Racial Formation,* 132.

117. "Limbaugh Quits as NFL Analyst over Race Remarks," *San Francisco Chronicle,* October 2, 2003.

118. Columnist Cynthia Tucker reflects what most blacks feel about the man: "Bush has never been willing to rein in the racists in his party. That's because he needs them; their dirty work helps to ensure GOP victories. The president may not be a bigot, but if you stand on bigots' shoulders, what does that make you?" "Bush's Rapport with Racists," *San Francisco Chronicle,* November 28, 2005.

119. Lind, *Next American Nation,* 161.

120. Linda Chavez and Daniel Gray, *Betrayal: How Union Bosses Shake Down Their Members and Corrupt American Politics* (New York: Crown Forum, 2004).

121. Navarrette's political orientation is not consistent, but anyone who seriously argues, as Navarrette does in "Bush the Moderate Emerging," *San Francisco Chronicle,* December 1, 2004, that George W. Bush is actually a misunderstood political moderate has to be categorized as a strong conservative.

122. For an overview of black conservatism, see Deborah Toler, "Black Conservatives," *The Public Eye* (Web site of Political Research Associates), September 1993, http://www.publiceye.org/magazine/v07n3/Blackcon.htm.

123. Chavez, *Out of the Barrio,* 91–92; Berlet, "Into the Mainstream," 58.

124. Berlet, "Into the Mainstream," 54; Conason, *Big Lies,* 140.

125. Conason, *Big Lies,* 133.

126. Jeff Sharlet, "Big World: How Clear Channel Programs America," *Harper's Magazine,* December 2003, 43. For a perceptive biography of Watts, see Amy Waldman, "The GOP's Great Black Hope: He Talks Like Kemp but Votes with Gingrich. Whose Side Is J. C. Watts On?" *Washington Monthly,* October 1996, http://www.washingtonmonthly.com/features/2001/9610.waldman.html. Apparently, Watts enjoyed scant success in recruiting blacks for state GOP offices: "Out of 218 African-American state legislators, 214 are Democrats." Ellen Goodman, "GOP's 'Ladies First' Strategy Is Clever Political Ploy," *Contra Costa Times,* May 24, 2005.

127. Mark Hosenball, Michael Isikoff, and Evan Thomas, "Cheney's Long Path to War," *Newsweek,* November 17, 2003, 40.

128. Conason, *Big Lies,* 142.

129. Buddy Watts, quoted in Kimberley Wilson, "Thoughts on Republican Outreach," *Enter Stage Right,* June 1999, http://www.enterstageright.com/archive/articles/0699repoutreach.htm.

130. Barlow, *Between Fear and Hope,* 76.

131. Paul Gottfried and Thomas Fleming, *The Conservative Movement* (Boston: Twayne, 1988), 23.

132. Andrew III, *Other Side of the Sixties,* 105.

133. Paul J. Weber, "Catholics and the 2000 Election," *America,* October 28, 2000, http://www.americamagazine.org/articles/weber-catholic-vote.htm.

134. Jon Wiener, "No Success Like Failure," *The Nation,* May 3, 2004, 53.

135. Bush captured 52 percent of the Catholic vote in 2004. Don Lattin, "Christian Strategy: Go Beyond 2004 Election's Hot-Button Issues," *San Francisco Chronicle,* November 7, 2004.

136. William Dinges, quoted by George Gerner, "Catholics and the 'Religious Right': We Are Being Wooed," *Commonweal,* May 5, 1995, 16.

137. Lattin, "Christian Strategy."

138. Fundamentalist Protestants are "historically the most anti-Catholic group in American society," notes Susan Jacoby. "Vatican Makes Common Cause with Fundamentalist Protestants," *San Francisco Chronicle,* May 3, 2004.

139. David Cohen, *Chasing the Red, White, and Blue* (New York: Picador, 2001), 211–12.

140. Molly Ivins, "Our Own Nuremberg," *San Francisco Chronicle,* June 15, 2004.

141. Lakoff, *Moral Politics,* 12.

142. In the aftermath of John Kennedy's election to the White House in 1960, the sociologist E. Digby Baltzell predicted that despite the Democratic victory, Catholics would increasingly abandon the party they had traditionally supported for the Republicans as they achieved middle-class status. *The Protestant Establishment: Aristocracy and Caste in America* (New York: Random House, 1964), 315.

143. Weber, "Catholics and the 2000 Election."

144. Paul Weyrich, quoted by Greider, *Who Will Tell the People,* 278.

145. Erich Fromm, *Escape from Freedom,* rev. ed. (New York: Avon Books, 1965), 236.

146. Ehrenreich, *Fear of Falling,* 10-15, 249.

147. Alan Crawford, *Thunder on the Right: The "New Right" and the Politics of Resentment* (New York: Pantheon Books, 1980), 5.

148. Chip Berlet and Matthew N. Lyons, *Right-Wing Populism in America: Too Close for Comfort* (New York: Guilford, 2000), 7, who quote Jean Hardisty to that effect.

Chapter 7

1. Andrew Hacker, *Money: Who Has How Much and Why* (New York: Scribner, 1997), 105.

2. Charles Derber, *Corporation Nation: How Corporations Are Taking over Our Lives and What We Can Do about It* (New York: St. Martin's, 1998), 18; Arianna Huffington, *Pigs at the Trough: How Corporate Greed and Political Corruption Are Undermining America* (New York: Crown, 2003), 25, 202-3.

3. Derber, *Corporate Nation,* 3.

4. Brian Levack et al., *The West: Encounters and Transformations,* vol. 2: *Since 1550* (New York: Pearson Longman, 2004), 996-97.

5. Ambrose Bierce, quoted in Alan T. Saracevic, "Insightful Books Put Ubiquitous Corporations under a Microscope," *San Francisco Chronicle,* May 30, 2004.

6. Huffington, *Pigs at the Trough,* 60.

7. William Greider, *Who Will Tell the People: The Betrayal of American Democracy* (New York: Simon & Schuster, 1992), 349.

8. Huffington, *Pigs at the Trough,* 134.

9. Robert Sherrill, "Why the Bubble Popped," *The Nation,* May 3, 2004, 60.

10. Critics charged that the legislation was a gift to financial institutions, which "they contend are largely responsible for the high rate of bankruptcies because they heavily promote credit cards and loans that often come with large and largely unseen fees for late payments." Stephen Labaton, "Bankruptcy Bill Set for Passage; Victory for Bush," *New York Times,* March 9, 2005. In 2004, credit card issuers collected $14.8 billion in late fees. *AARP Bulletin,* April 2005, 30.

11. Greider, *Who Will Tell the People,* 105.

12. Elizabeth Drew, *The Corruption of American Politics: What Went Wrong and Why* (Woodstock, N.Y.: Overlook, 1999), 61.

13. Michael Lind, *The Next American Nation: The New Nationalism and the Fourth American Revolution* (New York: Free Press, 1995), 156.

14. Godfrey Hodgson, *More Equal Than Others: America from Nixon to the New Century* (Princeton, N.J.: Princeton University Press, 2004), 31.

15. Warren Buffett, quoted in *Public Citizen News,* September/October 2003, 9.

16. Thomas Edsall, with Mary Edsall, *Chain Reaction: The Impact of Race, Rights, and Taxes on American Politics* (New York: Norton, 1991), 167.

17. For DeLay's ruthless methods of raising campaign funds, see "Tom DeLay Thinks He's God's Man in Congress," *The Hightower Lowdown,* November 2003, 1. Not only did his political action committees solicit money from corporations in Texas to be used to finance a (successful) redistricting effort in the state, an illegal activity, but DeLay also "created a fund for corporate donors to help him pay legal bills related to allegations of improper fund-raising." R. Jeffrey Smith, "Enron Documents Show DeLay's Workmanship," *Contra Costa Times* (Walnut Creek, Calif.), July 12, 2004.

18. Editorial, "The New Money Game," *The Nation,* January 5, 2004, 5. Robert W. McChesney is more specific: "In the election cycle ending in 2002, a mere *one-tenth of one percent* of Americans provided 83 percent of all itemized campaign contributions, and the vast majority of these individuals came from the very wealthiest sliver of Americans." *The Problem of the Media: U.S. Communications Politics in the 21st Century* (New York: Monthly Review, 2004), 131.

19. Charles Lewis, *The Buying of the President 2004* (New York: Perennial, 2004), 10.

20. Lewis, *The Buying of the President 2004,* 236. According to a watchdog group, Texans for Public Justice, the ninety "Pioneers" who were appointed to federal posts by Bush included twenty-one ambassadors. The study is cited in Tim Shorrock and Michael Scherer, "Bundles of Influence," *Mother Jones,* May/June 2004, 15. The Web site motherjones.com contains a complete list of "Pioneer" ambassadors.

21. For a list of Rangers, see WhiteHouseforSale.org, a Web site created by two liberal groups: Public Citizen and Texans for Public Justice.

22. William D. Hartung, *How Much Are You Making on the War, Daddy? A Quick and Dirty Guide to War Profiteering in the Bush Administration* (New York: Nation Books, 2003), 16.

23. Hartung, *How Much Are You Making on the War, Daddy?* 135.

24. Nick Anderson and Janet Hook, "Big Money Thrives Even after Reform," *Contra Costa Times,* December 11, 2003. See, too, Hodgson, *More Equal Than Others,* 57.

25. Ken Silverstein, *Washington on $10 Million a Day: How Lobbyists Plunder the Nation* (Monroe, Maine: Common Courage Press, 1998), 3.

26. Drew, *Corruption of American Politics,* 63.

27. Silverstein, *Washington on $10 Million a Day,* 53.

28. Huffington, *Pigs at the Trough,* 78.

29. Drew, *Corruption of American Politics,* 78.

30. Joseph E. Stiglitz, *The Roaring Nineties: A New History of the World's Most Prosperous Decade* (New York: Norton, 2003), 110–11.

31. McChesney, *Problem of the Media,* 128.

32. Jeffrey H. Birnbaum, "Lobbying Firms Lust after Clout Packed by Retiring Senators," *San Francisco Chronicle,* June 22, 2004.

33. Amy Goldstein, "Medicare Analyst Says Bush Aides Threatened to Fire Him," *San Francisco Chronicle,* March 13, 2004; Robert Pear, "Medicare Official Says White House Knew of Estimate," *San Francisco Chronicle,* March 25, 2004.

34. Robert Pear, "Probe Confirms Withholding of Medicare Data," *San Francisco Chronicle,* July 7, 2004.

35. Ceci Connolly and Mike Allen, "Medicare Drug Benefit Could Cost $1.2 Trillion," *San Francisco Chronicle,* February 9, 2005.

36. Silverstein, *Washington on $10 Million a Day,* 29.

37. Walter F. Roche Jr. and Richard B. Schmitt, "Abramoff Cops Plea, Faces Prison," *San Francisco Chronicle,* January 4, 2006.

38. Quoted by James Harding, "Jack Abramoff: The Friend Tom DeLay Can't Shake," *Slate,* April 7, 2005, http://www.slate.com/id/2116389/. For Abramoff's legal problems, see Barry Yeoman, "The Fall of a True Believer," *Mother Jones,* September/October 2005.

39. Alexander Cockburn, "Bush as Hitler? Let's Be Fair," *The Nation,* January 26, 2004, 8.

40. Howard Dean, quoted by Joe Klein, "The Fire This Time," *Time,* January 12, 2004, 32.

41. Jonathan McLeod, "Write Your Congressman? Don't Even Bother: His Signature Is Phony, So Is His Interest," *San Francisco Chronicle,* January 11, 2004.

42. Silverstein, *Washington on $10 Million a Day,* 37–38.

43. Barbara Ehrenreich, *Fear of Falling: The Inner Life of the Middle Class* (New York: HarperPerennial, 1990), 191.

44. See Keillor, *Homegrown Democrat: A Few Plain Thoughts from the Heart of America* (New York: Viking Books, 2004).

45. Edsall, *Chain Reaction,* 25.

46. Kevin Phillips, *The Politics of Rich and Poor: Wealth and the American Electorate in the Reagan Aftermath* (New York: Random House, 1990), 46.

47. Richard N. Rosenfeld, "What Democracy? The Case for Abolishing the United States Senate," *Harper's Magazine,* May 2004, 40. In the Supreme Court, at least six of the nine justices were millionaires in mid-2005. Hope Yen, "U.S. Supreme Court Justices Mostly Moneyed, Well-Traveled," *Contra Costa Times,* June 11, 2005.

48. Lind, *Next American Nation,* 187. After Bush's 2004 reelection, the Democrats continued to offer weak resistance to GOP initiatives. They basically caved in on the nominations of Alberto Gonzales as attorney general, Condoleezza Rice as secretary of state, and Michael Chertoff as head of the Department of Homeland Security. "Democrats: MIA," *The Nation,* April 11, 2005, 4.

49. Matt Rothschild, "Beyond Patriotism," in *A Time of Choices: Deep Dialogues for Deep Democracy,* ed. Michael Toms (Gabriola Island, B.C., Canada: New Society, 2002), 115.

50. Lind, *Next American Nation,* 187.

51. Huffington, *Pigs at the Trough,* 21.

52. Silverstein, *Washington on $10 Million a Day,* 179.

53. Huffington, *Pigs at the Trough,* 21, 234.

54. Huffington, *Pigs at the Trough,* 107.

55. Eric Alterman, "Washington Goes to War (with Howard Dean)," *The Nation*, January 12/19, 2004, 12.

56. Lieberman's enthusiastic endorsement of Rice as secretary of state prompted one journalist to ask, "Why is this man a Democrat?" Ruth Conniff, "Standing Their Ground," *The Progressive*, March 2005, 12.

57. Nicholas Fraser, "To BBC or Not BBC: Independent Journalism Suffers an Identity Crisis," *Harper's Magazine*, May 2004, 57.

58. Jim Hightower, *If the Gods Had Meant Us to Vote They Would Have Given Us Candidates*, rev. ed. (New York: Perennial, 2001), 291. The U.S. Census Bureau set the figure at 43.6 million for 2002, but a study by Families USA, a private watchdog group, indicates almost 82 million people lacked health coverage at some point from mid-2002 to mid-2004, with most of them uninsured for more than nine months. Mark Sherman, "Study: 82 Million Lack Health Insurance," *Contra Costa Times*, June 16, 2004.

59. Michael Parenti, *America Besieged* (San Francisco: City Lights, 1998), 84–85.

60. Eric Schlosser, *Reefer Madness: Sex, Drugs, and Cheap Labor in the American Black Market* (New York: Houghton Mifflin, 2003), 108.

61. Christopher Lasch, *Revolt of the Elites and the Betrayal of Democracy* (New York: Norton, 1995), 97–98.

62. McChesney, *Problem of the Media*, 159.

63. Hodgson, *More Equal Than Others*, 223.

64. The Enron scandal has, in fact, solicited scattered criticism among liberal commentators. "Enron is a cancer on capitalism ... the disease may be in the nodes of the marketplace, poisoning the rest of the system." Jonathan Alter, "Which Boot Will Drop Next?" *Newsweek*, February 4, 2002, 25. "The individuals involved may have been uniquely greedy and unethical, but they were empowered by a system that exalted greed as it diminished ethics and responsibility. ... Free market mythology is a smoke screen that disguises the real nature of elite power.... It allows elites to run our economy to suit themselves, without interference but with a veneer of legitimacy." Marjorie Kelly, "Waving Goodbye to the Invisible Hand: How the Enron Mess Grew and Grew," *San Francisco Chronicle*, February 24, 2002. "Capitalism doesn't work without regulation. Powerful people will take advantage of their muscle unless someone—like it or not, that usually includes the government—keeps an eye on them." E. J. Dionne Jr., "New Class Politics Is Good for Capitalism," *San Francisco Chronicle*, February 22, 2002.

65. Bertram Gross, *Friendly Fascism: The New Face of Power in America* (Boston: South End, 1980), 267.

66. McChesney, *Problem of the Media*, 145.

67. Mark Hertsgaard, *The Eagle's Shadow: Why America Fascinates and Infuriates the World* (New York: Farrar, Straus & Giroux, 2002), 38.

68. For the relationship between media and hypercommercialism, see chap. 4, "The Age of Hyper-Commercialism," in McChesney, *The Problem of the Media*.

69. See Ken Auletta, *Backstory: Inside the Business of News* (New York: Penguin Books, 2003).

70. Leonard Steinhorn, "Gambling on Capital for Our Wealth," *Contra Costa Times*, June 1, 2003. The *New York Times*, for example, employs about sixty

reporters to cover business and only one to cover labor. Michael Massing, "The Press: The Enemy Within," *New York Review of Books,* December 15, 2005, http://www.nybooks.com/articles/18555.

71. Gregory Mantsios, "Media Magic: Making Class Invisible," in *Race, Class and Gender,* ed. Paula Rothenberg, 3d ed. (New York: St. Martin's, 1995), 410.

72. Lynnley Browning, "Data Show Growing Gap between Rich and Poor," *Contra Costa Times,* September 25, 2003.

73. Kevin Phillips, *Wealth and Democracy: A Political History of the American Rich* (New York: Broadway Books, 2002), 337–38. Statistical averages are quite misleading. Al Franken cogently illustrates this point: "You and Bill Gates probably have an average net worth of $32 billion." *Lies and the Lying Liars Who Tell Them: A Fair and Balanced Look at the Right* (New York: Dutton, 2003), 289.

74. Paul Krugman, "For Richer: How the Permissive Capitalism of the Boom Destroyed American Equality," *New York Times Magazine,* October 20, 2002, 67.

75. Hertsgaard, *Eagle's Shadow,* 139.

76. Gar Alperovitz, "Tax the Plutocrats!" *The Nation,* January 27, 2003, 16.

77. Edward Wolff, "The Wealth Divide: The Growing Gap in the United States between the Rich and the Rest" (an interview with Edward Wolff), *Multinational Monitor,* May 2003, http://multinationalmonitor.org/mm2003/03may/mayo3 interviewswolff.html.

78. Wolff, "The Wealth Divide." An analysis of U.S. census data by the Pew Hispanic Center in 2004 concluded that by that year, white households had a median net worth eleven times greater than Latinos and fourteen times more than blacks. Cited in Genaro C. Armas, "Wealth Gap Widens for Blacks, Latinos Following Recession," *Contra Costa Times,* October 18, 2004. On the wealth disparity between blacks and whites, see Thomas M. Shapiro, *The Hidden Cost of Being African American: How Wealth Perpetrates Inequality* (New York: Oxford University Press, 2005).

79. David R. Roediger, *Colored White: Transcending the Racial Past* (Berkeley: University of California Press, 2002), 11.

80. Kevin Fagan, "The Hard Core Stuck on Street," *San Francisco Chronicle,* November 30, 2003.

81. Hertsgaard, *Eagle's Shadow,* 151.

82. Lind, *Next American Nation,* 14.

83. The foremost champion of this identification is Francis Fukuyama, *The End of History and the Last Man* (New York: Free Press, 1992).

84. See in this regard Paul Kivel, *You Call This a Democracy? Who Benefits, Who Pays and Who Really Decides* (New York: Apex, 2004), who finds few signs of popular sovereignty in the United States.

85. Kevin Baker, "Up from Extremism: Getting It Wrong about the American Right," *Harper's Magazine,* August 2001, 67.

86. Michael Parenti, *Blackshirts and Reds: Rational Fascism and the Overthrow of Communism* (San Francisco: City Lights, 1997).

87. Robert Collier, "U.S. Resists Cleric's Demand for Direct Elections in Iraq," *San Francisco Chronicle,* January 13, 2004. Eventually, in late 2004, succumbing to pressures at home and abroad, the United States was forced to permit Iraqi elections, and the result was indeed the triumph of a Shiite-dominated religious slate. *The Hightower Lowdown,* March 2005, 3.

88. See Amitabh Pal, "Beyond Ukraine Bush Sides with Dictators," *The Progressive,* February 2005, 29–32.

89. Katha Pollitt, "Show & Tell in Abu Ghraib," *The Nation,* May 24, 2004, 9.

90. A moral malaise, incidentally, that right-wingers conveniently blame on the government, when the primary culprit is the out-of-control consumer culture wrought by the very capitalists they lionize. Ehrenreich, *Fear of Falling,* 182; Hodgson, *More Equal Than Others,* 291.

91. Lind, *Next American Nation,* 233.

92. See Greider, *The Soul of Capitalism: Opening Paths to a Moral Economy* (New York: Simon & Schuster, 2003).

93. Gross, *Friendly Fascism,* 112–16.

94. Stiglitz, *Roaring Nineties,* 278–79.

95. *The Hightower Lowdown,* June 2003, 3.

96. Mark Landler, "Italian Economist Goes on a Crusade," *San Francisco Chronicle,* March 25, 2004.

97. William Greider, "The Serpent That Ate America's Lunch," *The Nation,* May 10, 2004, 14.

98. William Kolasky, quoted in Landler, "Italian Economist Goes on a Crusade."

99. Juliet B. Schor, *The Overworked American: The Unexpected Decline of Leisure* (New York: Basic Books, 1992), xviii, 7. For the orthodox view that the free market has provided Americans greater leisure, see the ever dependable capitalist cheerleader, Robert J. Samuelson, "The Afflictions of Affluence," *Newsweek,* March 22, 2004, 45.

100. McChesney, *Problem of the Media,* 125.

101. Nicole C. Wong, "A Third of Staffers Overwork," *Contra Costa Times,* March 16, 2005.

102. Jim Hightower, *Thieves in High Places* (New York: Viking Penguin, 2003), 66.

103. Garry Wills, *Reagan's America: Innocents at Home* (Garden City, N.Y.: Doubleday, 1987), 378–79.

104. Complaining about taxes seems to be the sole function of the taxpayers' associations that are ubiquitous in this country.

105. This point is made forcefully by Peter Singer, *The President of Good & Evil: Questioning the Ethics of George W. Bush* (New York: Plume, 2004), 14–17.

106. Jonathan Weisman, "Taxation, Unemployment Link Absent," *Contra Costa Times,* March 21, 2004.

107. According to Public Citizen, a liberal watchdog organization, Enron and its employees contributed $312,500 to Bush's gubernatorial campaigns and $413,800 to his presidential war chest and inaugural fund prior to 2001. In fact, many members of the first Bush II team, including John Ashcroft and Spencer Abraham, were beneficiaries of Enron largess. See "Enron's Web of Influence: The Political Players," http://www.publiccitizen.org/print_article.cfm?ID=7107.

108. John D. McKinnon, "60% of U.S. Firms Escaped Taxes during Boom," *Contra Costa Times,* April 7, 2004.

109. Scherer, "Make Your Taxes Disappear," *Mother Jones,* March/April 2005, 75. From 2000 to 2005, Scherer claims, Wall Street's tax bills dropped by a third (74).

110. Michael Parenti, *Democracy for the Few,* 7th ed. (Boston: Bedford/St. Martin's, 2002), 110.

111. Michael Moore, *Stupid White Men and Other Sorry Excuses for the State of the Nation!* (New York: Regan Books, 2001), 54.

112. As of June 30, 2003, 68 percent of the nation's 2,078,570 prisoners were minorities, according to a press release issued by the U.S. Bureau of Justice Statistics on May 27, 2004, http://www.ojp.usdoj.gov/bjs/press/pjim03pr.htm.

113. Andrew L. Barlow, *Between Fear and Hope: Globalization and Race in the United States* (Lanham, Md.: Rowman & Littlefield, 2003), 122. For an extended discussion of the unequal administration of justice as it relates to blacks, see Earl Ofari Hutchinson, *The Mugging of Black America* (Chicago: African American Images, 1990), chap. 2.

114. Lawrence E. Mitchell, "American Corporations: The New Sovereigns," *Chronicle of Higher Education,* January 18, 2002.

115. Molly Ivins, "What Hath Deregulation Wrought?" *San Francisco Chronicle,* July 24, 2002.

116. McChesney, *Problem of the Media,* 133.

117. Jonathan D. Salant, "Congress' Freshmen Are One Rich Bunch," *San Francisco Chronicle,* December 25, 2002.

118. Robert D. Kaplan, "Was Democracy Just a Moment?" *Atlantic Monthly,* December 1997.

119. This is essentially the thesis proposed by Bill Moyers, "Our Story," *The Progressive,* May 2004, 30.

120. Greider, *Who Will Tell the People,* 31. Godfrey Hodgson, too, maintains great faith in "the essential good sense of the American people." *More Equal Than Others,* 304.

121. *Bartlett's Familiar Quotations,* rev. ed. (Boston: Little, Brown, 1980), 624.

122. Greider, *Who Will Tell the People,* 17.

123. Estimates ran as high as ninety-eight thousand by mid-2005. Jack Epstein and Matthew B. Stannard, "Tally of Civilian Deaths Depends on Who's Counting," *San Francisco Chronicle,* May 12, 2005.

Conclusion

1. See Bertram Gross, *Friendly Fascism: The New Face of Power in America* (Boston: South End, 1980).

2. "Most of which," as Harvard professor Robert Putnam perceptively notes of that decade, "actually happened in the seventies." *Bowling Alone: The Collapse and Revival of American Community* (New York: Simon & Schuster, 2000), 187.

3. Paul Krugman, *The Great Unraveling: Losing Our Way in the New Century* (New York: Norton, 2003), 5-20. "Krugman's primacy is based largely on his dominance of a particular intellectual niche. As major columnists go, he is almost alone in analyzing the most important story in politics in recent years—the seamless melding of corporate, class, and political party interests at which the Bush administration excels." Nicholas Confessore, "Comparative Advantage:

How Economist Paul Krugman Became the Most Important Political Columnist in America," *Washington Monthly,* December 2002, 20.

4. John Nichols, "The GOP Hunts Its Own," *The Nation,* May 3, 2004, 9.

5. The Weyrich quotation, recalled by Richard Viguerie, is found in Chip Berlet and Matthew N. Lyons, *Right-Wing Populism in America: Too Close for Comfort* (New York: Guilford, 2000), 334; the second quotation is in E. J. Dionne Jr., *Why Americans Hate Politics* (New York: Touchstone, 1991), 229. David Grann's article "Robespierre of the Right—What I Ate at the Revolution," *New Republic,* October 27, 1997, precipitated a lawsuit by Weyrich against the journal for defamation. The Court of Appeals of the District of Columbia essentially ruled against Weyrich in 2001. Even his admirers, according to Lewis Lapham, describe Weyrich as "the Lenin of social conservatism." "Tentacles of Rage: The Republican Propaganda Mill: A Brief History," *Harper's Magazine,* September 2004, 35.

6. Eric Foner, "Shedding Lincoln's Mantle," *The Nation,* August 7, 2000, 5.

7. James A. Smith, *The Idea Brokers: Think Tanks and the Rise of the New Policy Elite* (New York: Free Press, 1991), 166.

8. Lou Dubose, Jan Reid, and Carl M. Cannon, *Boy Genius: Karl Rove, the Brains behind the Remarkable Political Triumph of George W. Bush* (New York: Public Affairs, 2003), 129–30.

9. Alistair Cooke, *Alistair Cooke's America* (New York: Knopf, 1980), 144.

10. Ana Radelat, "Up for Grabs: Latinos Are This Election Year's Swing Voters," *Hispanic,* October 2004, 18.

11. "The GOP Seeks a Broader Base: Strategists Advise Wooing Women and Hispanics," *Washington Post National Weekly Edition,* January 6–12, 2003.

12. It is this "political reality," argues Earl Ofari Hutchinson, that has forced the GOP to reverse its traditional stance on minority recruitment. "The GOP's Growing Rainbow Contingent," *San Francisco Chronicle,* September 1, 2004. By the time of the 2004 elections, census figures indicate that in Texas, Bush's home state, minorities had overtaken non-Hispanic whites, who were down to 49.5 percent of the population. *Hispanic Business,* November 2004, 25.

13. Many students of the culture claim that the Latino electorate is at least socially conservative—see Earl Shorris, *Latinos: A Biography of a People* (New York: Norton, 1992), 425–26—a view we share. For a dissenting opinion, see Juan Gonzalez, *Harvest of Empire: A History of Latinos in America* (New York: Viking Books, 2000), 188. Recent publications that illuminate the tradition of *tejano* political activism include Julie Leininger Pycior, *LBJ & Mexican Americans: The Paradox of Power* (College Station: Texas A&M University Press, 1999), and Ignacio M. García, *Hector P. García: In Relentless Pursuit of Justice* (Houston, Tex.: Arte Público, 2002). Also useful is Ignacio M. García, *Viva Kennedy: Mexican Americans in Search of Camelot* (College Station: Texas A&M University Press, 2000), much of which focuses on *tejanos.*

14. Bob Moser, "The Battle of 'Georgiafornia,'" *Intelligence Report,* Winter 2004, 40.

15. Hutchinson, "GOP's Growing Rainbow Contingent."

16. Vicki Haddock, "Politics of Myth: Pre-Election Expectations Fail to Materialize at Polls," *San Francisco Chronicle,* November 7, 2004; Radelet, "Up for Grabs," 18; Gonzalez, *Harvest of Empire,* 186.

17. William D. Hartung, *How Much Are You Making on the War, Daddy? A Quick and Dirty Guide to War Profiteering in the Bush Administration* (New York: Nation Books, 2003), 39.

18. Michael Lind, "The Weird Men behind Bush's War," *New Statesman* (London, U.K.), April 7, 2003.

19. Earl Shorris, "Ignoble Liars: Leo Strauss, George Bush, and the Philosophy of Mass Deception," *Harper's Magazine,* June 2004, 71.

20. Wolfowitz himself mocks the idea that he is a Straussian. Michael Hirsh, "Welcome to the Real World: Neocons on the Line," *Newsweek,* June 23, 2004, 32.

21. Hartung, *How Much Are You Making on the War, Daddy?* 143.

22. Hartung, *How Much Are You Making on the War, Daddy?* 69.

23. Naomi Klein, "Risky Business," *The Nation,* January 5, 2004, 14.

24. Hartung, *How Much Are You Making on the War, Daddy?* 85. For more on Perle's entrepreneurial activities, see Tim Shorrock, "Richard Perle's Corporate Adventures," *The Nation,* April 3, 2003.

25. Stephen Labaton, "Perle Says Hollinger's Ex-CEO Misled Him," *Contra Costa Times* (Walnut Creek, Calif.), September 7, 2004.

26. Peter Steinfels, *The Neoconservatives: The Men Who Are Changing America's Politics* (New York: Simon & Schuster, 1979), 294.

27. Arianna Huffington, *Pigs at the Trough: How Corporate Greed and Political Corruption Are Undermining America* (New York: Crown, 2003), 14. There are over 4.8 million millionaires in the United States.

28. William D. Rohlf Jr., *Introduction to Economic Reasoning,* 5th ed. (Boston: Addison-Wesley, 2002), 449.

29. Jodie T. Allen, "Looking for a Hot New Job of the Future? Think Pizza Delivery ...," *Contra Costa Times,* March 14, 2004.

30. Michael Lind, *The Next American Nation: The New Nationalism and the Fourth American Revolution* (New York: Free Press, 1995), 14.

31. Huffington, *Pigs at the Trough,* 39.

32. Huffington, *Pigs at the Trough,* 207.

33. Elisabeth Bumiller, "Religious Coalition Walks the Halls of Power," *San Francisco Chronicle,* October 26, 2003.

34. Paul Weyrich, quoted by William Greider, *Who Will Tell the People: The Betrayal of American Democracy* (New York: Simon & Schuster, 1992), 279.

35. Haynes Johnson, *Sleepwalking through History: America in the Reagan Years* (New York: Anchor Books/Doubleday, 1991), 69–71; Thomas Edsall, with Mary Edsall, *Chain Reaction: The Impact of Race, Rights, and Taxes on American Politics* (New York: Norton, 1991), 139.

36. *Washington Post,* n.d., quoted by Dan Baum, *Citizen Coors: An American Dynasty* (New York: Morrow, 2000), 236.

37. Edwin J. Feulner, "Coors, R.I.P.," *National Review Online,* March 18, 2003, http://www.nationalreview.com/. See, too, the lofty assessment of Coors at the time of his death by one of his closest collaborators, Edwin Meese III, "The Commitment of a Conservative," *San Diego Union-Tribune,* March 22, 2003.

38. Kevin Phillips, *The Politics of Rich and Poor: Wealth and the American Electorate in the Reagan Aftermath* (New York: Random House, 1990), 76.

39. David A. Horowitz and Peter N. Carroll, *On the Edge: The U.S. since 1945,* 2d ed. (New York: West/Wadsworth, 1998), 262.

40. Edsall, *Chain Reaction*, 193.

41. Hillary Rodham Clinton, *Living History* (New York: Simon & Schuster, 2003), 452.

42. Robert B. Reich, "The Rove Machine Rolls On," *American Prospect,* February 1, 2003, http://www.prospect.org/web/page.ww?section=root8name=ViewPrintsarticleID=6689.

43. John F. Dickerson, "Confessions of a White House Insider," *Time,* January 19, 2004, 36.

44. Michael Tackett, "Speech Gets Points for Simplicity, Gives Fodder to Critics," *Contra Costa Times,* May 25, 2004.

45. William Douglas, "Medicare Reform Could Hurt Bush's Campaign," *Contra Costa Times,* March 21, 2004.

46. Robert C. Cuddy, "Bush Sets Model of Blame Shifting," *Contra Costa Times,* May 15, 2004.

47. For Bush administration efforts to discredit its enemies, see "Unheeded Warnings," *The Progressive,* May 2004, 8–9.

48. Political scientists Jacob S. Hacker and Paul Pierson argue that coordination is the single most important factor in the conservative ascendancy. See *Off Center: The Republican Revolution and the Erosion of American Democracy* (New Haven, Conn.: Yale University Press, 2005), 161.

49. Michael Scherer, "The Soul of the New Machine," *Mother Jones,* January/February 2004, 44. Norquist sits on the boards of directors of both the American Conservative Union and the National Rifle Association. Michael J. Graetz and Ian Shapiro, *Death by a Thousand Cuts: The Fight over Taxing Inherited Wealth* (Princeton, N.J.: Princeton University Press, 2005), 28.

50. Russ Bellant, *The Coors Connection: How Coors Family Philanthropy Undermines Democratic Pluralism* (Boston: South End, 1991), 43.

51. Hirsh, "Welcome to the Real World," 30.

52. Marc J. Ambinder, "Vast, Right-Wing Cabal? Meet the Most Powerful Conservative Group You've Never Heard Of," *ABCNews.com,* May 2, 2002, http://abcnews.go.com/sections/politics/DailyNews/council_020501.html.

53. Barbara Aho, "The Council for National Policy," n.d., http://watch.pair.com/cnp.html.

54. Ambinder, "Vast, Right-Wing Cabal?"

55. Krugman, *Great Unraveling*, 15.

56. Krugman, *Great Unraveling*, 15.

57. Scherer, "Soul of the New Machine," 44.

58. Grover Norquist, quoted by Scherer, "Soul of the New Machine," 44.

59. Bill Moyers, "Our Story," *The Progressive,* May 2004, 34.

SELECTED BIBLIOGRAPHY

Abu-Lughod, Janet L. *New York, Chicago, Los Angeles: America's Global Cities.* Minneapolis: University of Minnesota Press, 1999.

Alba, Richard, and Victor Nee. *Remaking the American Mainstream: Assimilation and Contemporary Immigration.* Cambridge, Mass.: Harvard University Press, 2003.

Alger, Dean. *Megamedia: How Giant Corporations Dominate Mass Media, Distort Competition, and Endanger Democracy.* Lanham, Md.: Rowman & Littlefield, 1998.

Allitt, Patrick. *Catholic Intellectuals and Conservative Politics in America, 1950–1985.* Ithaca, N.Y.: Cornell University Press, 1993.

Alterman, Eric. *What Liberal Media? The Truth about Bias and the News.* New York: Basic Books, 2003.

———. *When Presidents Lie: A History of Official Deception and Its Consequences.* New York: Viking Books, 2004.

Alterman, Eric, and Mark J. Green. *The Book on Bush: How George W. (Mis)leads America.* New York: Viking Books, 2004.

Anderson, Bonnie M. *News Flash: Journalism, Infotainment and the Bottom-Line Business of Broadcast News.* New York: Jossey-Bass, 2004.

Andrew, John A., III. *The Other Side of the Sixties: Young Americans for Freedom and the Rise of Conservative Politics.* New Brunswick, N.J.: Rutgers University Press, 1997.

Ansell, Amy Elizabeth. *New Right, New Racism: Race and Reaction in the United States and Britain.* New York: New York University Press, 1997.

———, ed. *Unraveling the Right: The New Conservatism in American Thought and Politics.* Boulder, Colo.: Westview, 1998.

Askin, Steve. *A New Rite: Conservative Catholic Organizations and Their Allies.* Washington, D.C.: Catholics for Free Choice, 1994.

Auletta, Ken. *Backstory: Inside the Business of News.* New York: Penguin Books, 2003.

———. *Greed and Glory on Wall Street.* New York: Warner, 1987.

Baer, Robert. *Sleeping with the Devil: How Washington Sold Our Soul for Saudi Crude.* New York: Crown, 2003.

Bagdikian, Ben. *The Media Monopoly.* 5th ed. Boston: Beacon, 1997.

Bakan, Joel. *The Corporation: The Pathological Pursuit of Profit and Power.* New York: Free Press, 2004.

Baltzell, E. Digby. *The Protestant Establishment: Aristocracy and Caste in America.* New York: Random House, 1964.

Balz, Dan J., and Ronald Brownstein. *Storming the Gates: Protest Politics and the Republican Revival.* Boston: Little, Brown, 1996.

Barber, Benjamin R. *Jihad vs. McWorld: Terrorism's Challenge to Democracy.* New York: Ballantine Books, 2001.

Barkun, Michael. *Religion and the Racist Right: The Origins of the Christian Identity Movement.* Chapel Hill: University of North Carolina Press, 1994.

Barlow, Andrew L. *Between Fear and Hope: Globalization and Race in the United States.* Lanham, Md.: Rowman & Littlefield, 2003.

Barnet, Richard J., and John Cavanagh. *Global Dreams: Imperial Corporations and the New World Order.* New York: Simon & Schuster, 1994.

Barrett, Jerry "Politex," ed. *Big Bush Lies: 20 Essays and a List of the 50 Most Telling Lies of George W. Bush.* Ashland, Ore.: River Wood Books, 2004.

Barsamian, David. *The Decline and Fall of Public Broadcasting.* Boston: South End, 2003.

Bartlett, Donald, and James Steele. *America: Who Really Pays the Taxes?* New York: Simon & Schuster, 1994.

Baum, Dan. *Citizen Coors: An American Dynasty.* New York: Morrow, 2000.

Beard, Charles A. *An Economic Interpretation of the Constitution of the United States.* 2d ed. New York: Macmillan, 1936.

Begala, Paul. *It's Still the Economy, Stupid: George W. Bush, the GOP's CEO.* New York: Simon & Schuster, 2002.

Bellant, Russ. *The Coors Connection: How Coors Family Philanthropy Undermines Democratic Pluralism.* Boston: South End, 1991.

Bennett, David H. *The Party of Fear: From Nativist Movements to the New Right in American History.* Chapel Hill: University of North Carolina Press, 1988.

Berlet, Chip, and Matthew N. Lyons. *Right-Wing Populism in America: Too Close for Comfort.* New York: Guilford, 2000.

Berman, Morris. *The Twilight of American Culture.* New York: Norton, 2000.

Berman, William C. *America's Right Turn: From Nixon to Clinton.* 2d ed. Baltimore: Johns Hopkins University Press, 1998.

Bernstein, Dennis, and Leslie Kean. *Henry Hyde's Moral Universe.* Monroe, Maine: Common Courage Press, 1999.

Blumenthal, Sidney. *The Clinton Wars.* New York: Farrar, Straus & Giroux, 2003.

———. *The Rise of the Counter-Establishment: From Conservative Ideology to Political Power.* New York: Times Books, 1986.

Bok, Derek. *Universities in the Marketplace: The Commercialization of Higher Education.* Princeton, N.J.: Princeton University Press, 2003.

Bonifaz, John C. *Warrior-King: The Case for Impeaching George W. Bush.* New York: Nation Books, 2003.

Bonillia-Silva, Eduardo. *White Supremacy and Racism in the Post–Civil Rights Era.* Boulder, Colo.: Lynne Rienner, 2001.

Boston, Robert. *Close Encounters with the Religious Right: Journeys into the Twilight Zone of Religion and Politics.* Amherst, N.Y.: Prometheus, 2000.

Boyer, William H. *Myth America: Democracy vs. Capitalism.* Croton-on-Hudson, N.Y.: Apex, 2003.

Brady, John. *Bad Boy: The Life and Politics of Lee Atwater.* New York: Addison-Wesley, 1997.

Brennan, Mary C. *Turning Right in the Sixties: The Conservative Capture of the GOP.* Chapel Hill: University of North Carolina Press, 1995.

Briody, Dan. *The Halliburton Agenda: The Politics of Oil and Money.* New York: Wiley, 2004.

————. *The Iron Triangle: Inside the Secret World of the Carlyle Group.* New York: Wiley, 2003.

Brock, David. *Blinded by the Right: The Conscience of an Ex-Conservative.* New York: Three Rivers, 2002.

————. *The Republican Noise Machine: Right-Wing Media and How It Corrupts Democracy.* New York: Crown, 2004.

Brooks, David. *On Paradise Drive: How We Live Now (and Always Have) in the Future Tense.* New York: Simon & Schuster, 2004.

Brown, Floyd G. *Slick Willie: Why America Cannot Trust Bill Clinton.* Annapolis, Md.: Annapolis-Washington, 1992.

Bruce, Steve. *The Rise and Fall of the New Christian Right: Conservative Protestant Politics in America, 1978-1988.* New York: Oxford University Press, 1988.

Bruce, Tammy. *The Death of Right and Wrong: Exposing the Left's Assault on Our Culture and Values.* Roseville, Calif.: Prima, 2003.

Bruni, Frank. *Ambling into History: The Unlikely Odyssey of George W. Bush.* New York: HarperCollins, 2002.

Buckley, William F., Jr. *God and Man at Yale: The Superstitions of Academic Freedom.* 2d ed. Washington, D.C.: Regnery, 1978.

Carter, Dan T. *From George Wallace to Newt Gingrich: Race in the Conservative Counterrevolution, 1963-1994.* Baton Rouge: Louisiana State University Press, 1996.

————. *The Politics of Race: George Wallace, the Origins of the New Conservatism, and the Transformation of American Politics.* 2d ed. Baton Rouge: Louisiana State University Press, 2000.

Charen, Mona. *Useful Idiots: How Liberals Got It Wrong in the Cold War and Still Blame America First.* Washington, D.C.: Regnery, 2003.

Chavez, Linda. *Out of the Barrio: Toward a New Politics of Hispanic Assimilation.* New York: Basic Books, 1991.

Chavez, Linda, and Daniel Gray. *Betrayal: How Union Bosses Shake Down Their Members and Corrupt American Politics.* New York: Crown Forum, 2004.

Chomsky, Noam. *Hegemony or Survival: America's Quest for Global Dominance.* New York: Metropolitan, 2003.

————. *Manufacturing Consent: The Political Economy of the Mass Media.* New York: Pantheon Books, 2002.

————. *Necessary Illusions: Thought Control in Democratic Societies.* Boston: South End, 1989.

————. *Profit over People: Neoliberalism and the Global Order.* New York: Seven Stories, 1999.

Christopher, Robert C. *Crashing the Gates: The De-Wasping of America's Power Elite.* New York: Simon & Schuster, 1989.

Clarke, Richard A. *Against All Enemies: Inside America's War on Terrorism.* New York: Free Press, 2004.

Clinton, Bill. *My Life.* New York: Knopf, 2004.

Clinton, Hillary Rodham. *Living History.* New York: Simon & Schuster, 2003.

Cohen, David. *Chasing the Red, White, and Blue.* New York: Picador, 2001.

Collier, Peter, and David Horowitz. *Destructive Generation.* New York: Summit, 1990.

Conason, Joe. *Big Lies: The Right-Wing Propaganda Machine and How It Distorts the Truth.* New York: Dunne, 2003.

Conason, Joe, and Gene Lyons. *The Hunting of the President: The Ten-Year Campaign to Destroy Bill and Hillary Clinton.* New York: Dunne, 2000.

Corn, David. *The Lies of George W. Bush: Mastering the Politics of Deception.* New York: Crown, 2003.

Coulter, Ann. *High Crimes and Misdemeanors: The Case against Bill Clinton.* Lanham, Md.: National Book Network, 2002.

———. *Slander: Liberal Lies about the American Right.* New York: Crown, 2002.

———. *Treason: Liberal Treachery from the Cold War to the War on Terrorism.* New York: Crown, 2003.

Court, Jamie. *Corporateering: How Corporate Power Steals Your Personal Freedom ... and What You Can Do about It.* New York: Tarcher/Putnam, 2003.

Covington, Sally. *Moving a Public Policy Agenda: The Strategic Philanthropy of Conservative Foundations.* Washington, D.C.: National Committee for Responsive Philanthropy, 1997.

Crawford, Alan. *Thunder on the Right: The "New Right" and the Politics of Resentment.* New York: Pantheon Books, 1980.

Crenson, Matthew A., and Benjamin Ginsberg. *Downsizing Democracy: How America Sidelined Its Citizens and Privatized Its Public.* Baltimore: Johns Hopkins University Press, 2003.

Critser, Greg. *Generation Rx: How Prescription Drugs Are Altering American Lives, Minds and Bodies.* New York: Houghton Mifflin, 2005.

Croteau, David, and William Hoynes. *By Invitation Only: How the Media Limit Political Debate.* Monroe, Maine: Common Courage Press, 1994.

Danaher, Kevin. *Corporations Are Gonna Get Your Mama: Globalization and the Downsizing of the American Dream.* Monroe, Maine: Common Courage Press, 1997.

———. *Ten Reasons to Abolish the IMF and World Bank.* New York: Seven Stories, 2002.

Danaher, Kevin, and Jason Mark. *Insurrection: Citizen Challenges to Corporate Power.* New York: Routledge, 2003.

D'Antonio, Michael. *Fall from Grace: The Failed Crusade of the Christian Right.* New York: Farrar, Straus & Giroux, 1989.

Davis, Mike. *Ecology of Fear: Los Angeles and the Imagination of Disaster.* New York: Vintage Books, 1998.

———. *Prisoners of the American Dream.* London: Verso, 1986.

Dean, John. *The Rehnquist Choice: The Untold Story of the Nixon Appointment That Redefined the Supreme Court.* New York: Free Press, 2002.

———. *Worse Than Watergate: The Secret Presidency of George W. Bush.* New York: Little, Brown, 2004.

Delbanco, Andrew. *The Death of Satan: How Americans Have Lost the Sense of Evil.* New York: Farrar, Straus & Giroux, 1995.

Delgado, Richard. *Justice at War: Civil Liberties and Civil Rights during Times of Crisis.* New York: New York University Press, 2003.

DeMott, Benjamin. *Junk Politics: The Trashing of the American Mind.* New York: Nation Books, 2003.

Denton, Nancy A., and Douglas S. Massey. *American Apartheid: Segregation and the Making of the Underclass.* Cambridge, Mass.: Harvard University Press, 1993.

Derber, Charles. *Corporation Nation: How Corporations Are Taking Over Our Lives and What We Can Do about It.* New York: St. Martin's, 1998.

Dershowitz, Alan M. *Sexual McCarthyism: Clinton, Starr and the Emerging Constitutional Crisis.* New York: Basic Books, 1998.

———. *Supreme Injustice: How the High Court Hijacked Election 2000.* New York: Oxford University Press, 2001.

De Soto, Hernando. *The Mystery of Capital: Why Capitalism Triumphs in the West and Fails Everywhere Else.* New York: Basic Books, 2003.

Diamond, Sara. *Facing the Wrath: Confronting the Right in Dangerous Times.* Monroe, Maine: Common Courage Press, 1996.

———. *Not by Politics Alone: The Enduring Influence of the Christian Right.* New York: Guilford, 1998.

———. *The Politics of the Christian Right.* Boston: South End, 1989.

———. *Roads to Dominion: Right-Wing Movements and Political Power in the United States.* New York: Guilford, 1995.

———. *Spiritual Warfare: The Politics of the Christian Right.* Montreal: Black Rose Books, 1990.

Didion, Joan. *Fixed Ideas: America since 9.11.* New York: New York Review of Books, 2003.

Diggins, John P. *Up from Communism: Conservative Odysseys in American Intellectual History.* New York: Harper & Row, 1975.

Dionne, E. J., Jr. *Why Americans Hate Politics.* New York: Touchstone, 1991.

Dobbin, Murray. *The Myth of the Good Corporate Citizen: Democracy under the Rule of Big Business.* Toronto: Stoddart, 1999.

Domhoff, G. William. *Bohemian Grove and Other Retreats.* New York: Harper-Collins, 1975.

———. *Changing the Powers That Be: How the Left Can Stop Losing and Win.* Lanham, Md.: Rowman & Littlefield, 2003.

———. *The Higher Circles: The Governing Class in America.* New York: Random House, 1970.

———. *Who Rules America Now?* Englewood Cliffs, N.J.: Prentice Hall, 1983.

———. *Who Rules America? Power and Politics in the Year 2000.* 3d ed. Mountain View, Calif.: Mayfield, 1998.

Dorrien, Gary. *The Neoconservative Mind: Politics, Culture, and the War of Ideology.* Philadelphia: Temple University Press, 1993.

Dowd, Maureen. *Bushworld: Enter at Your Own Risk.* New York: Putnam, 2004.

Downie, Leonard, Jr., and Robert G. Kaiser. *The News about the News: American Journalism in Peril.* New York: Knopf, 2003.

Dubose, Lou, and Jan Reid. *The Hammer: Tom DeLay: God, Money, and the Rise of the Republican Congress.* New York: Public Affairs, 2004.

Dubose, Lou, Jan Reid, and Carl M. Cannon. *Boy Genius: Karl Rove, the Brains behind the Remarkable Political Triumph of George W. Bush.* New York: Public Affairs, 2003.

Dunn, Charles W., and J. David Woodard. *American Conservatives from Burke to Bush: An Introduction.* Lanham, Md.: Madison, 1991.

Drew, Elizabeth. *The Corruption of American Politics: What Went Wrong and Why.* Woodstock, N.Y.: Overlook, 1999.

Easterbrook, Gregg. *The Progress Paradox: How Life Gets Better While People Feel Worse.* New York: Random House, 2003.

Easton, Nina J. *Gang of Five: Leaders at the Center of the Conservative Ascendancy.* New York: Simon & Schuster, 2000.

Eck, Diana L. *A New Religious America: How a "Christian Country" Has Become the World's Most Religiously Diverse Nation.* San Francisco: Harper San Francisco, 2001.

Edsall, Thomas, with Mary Edsall. *Chain Reaction: The Impact of Race, Rights, and Taxes on American Politics.* New York: Norton, 1991.

Edwards, Lee. *The Conservative Revolution: The Movement That Remade America.* New York: Free Press, 1999.

Ehrenreich, Barbara. *Fear of Falling: The Inner Life of the Middle Class.* New York: Pantheon Books, 1989.

———. *Nickel and Dimed: On (Not) Getting By in America.* New York: Holt, 2002.

———. *The Worst Years of Our Lives.* New York: HarperCollins, 1990.

Ehrman, John. *The Rise of Neoconservatism: Intellectuals and Foreign Affairs, 1945-1994.* New Haven, Conn.: Yale University Press, 1995.

Eisendrath, Craig R., and Melvin A. Goodman. *Bush League Diplomacy: How the Neoconservatives Are Putting the World at Risk.* New York: Prometheus, 2004.

Ellsberg, Daniel. *Secrets: A Memoir of Vietnam and the Pentagon Papers.* New York: Viking Books, 2002.

Engler, Allan. *Apostles of Greed: Capitalism and the Myth of the Individual in the Market.* London: Pluto, 1995.

Evans-Pritchard, Ambrose. *The Secret Life of Bill Clinton: The Unreported Stories.* Washington, D.C.: Regnery, 1997.

Everest, Larry. *Oil, Power and Empire: Iraq and the U.S. Global Agenda.* Monroe, Maine: Common Courage Press, 2004.

Faludi, Susan. *Backlash: The Undeclared War on American Women.* New York: Knopf, 1992.

Farley, Reginald, and Walter R. Allen. *The Color Line and the Quality of Life in America.* New York: Oxford University Press, 1989.

Ferguson, Ernest B. *Hard Right: The Rise of Jesse Helms.* New York: Norton, 1986.

Ferguson, Thomas, and Joel Rogers. *Right Turn: The Decline of the Democrats and the Future of American Politics.* New York: Hill & Wang, 1986.

Fitzgerald, Frances. *Way Out There in the Blue: Reagan, Star Wars and the End of the Cold War.* New York: Touchstone, 2001.

Foner, Eric. *The Story of American Freedom.* New York: Norton, 1998.

Fones-Wolf, Elizabeth A. *Selling Free Enterprise: The Business Assault on Labor and Liberalism, 1945–1960.* Urbana: University of Illinois Press, 1994.

Forster, Arnold, and Benjamin R. Epstein. *Danger on the Right.* Westport, Conn.: Greenwood, 1964.

Frank, Thomas. *One Market under God: Extreme Capitalism, Market Populism, and the End of Economic Democracy.* New York: Doubleday, 2000.

———. *What's the Matter with Kansas? How Conservatives Won the Heart of America.* New York: Metropolitan, 2004.

Franken, Al. *Lies and the Lying Liars Who Tell Them: A Fair and Balanced Look at the Right.* New York: Dutton, 2003.

———. *Rush Limbaugh Is a Big Fat Idiot and Other Observations.* New York: Delacorte, 1996.

Fraser, Steve, and Gary Gerstle, eds. *Ruling America: A History of Wealth and Power in a Democracy.* Cambridge, Mass.: Harvard University Press, 2005.

Friedenberg, Daniel M. *Sold to the Highest Bidder: The Presidency from Dwight D. Eisenhower to George W. Bush.* Amherst, N.Y.: Prometheus, 2003.

Friedman, Thomas L. *The Lexus and the Olive Tree.* Rev. ed. New York: Anchor Books, 2000.

Fromm, Erich. *Escape from Freedom.* New York: Holt, Rinehart & Winston, 1941.

Gans, Herbert J. *Democracy and the News.* New York: Oxford University Press, 2003.

Garreau, Joel. *Edge City: Life on the New Frontier.* New York: Doubleday, 1991.

Garrison, Jim. *America as Empire: Global Leader or Rogue Power?* San Francisco: Berrett-Koehler, 2004.

Gates, Jeff. *Democracy at Risk: Rescuing Main Street from Wall Street.* New York: Perseus, 2000.

———. *Democracy under Siege.* New York: Perseus, 2000.

Gates, William H., Sr., and Chuck Collins. *Wealth and Our Commonwealth: Why America Should Tax Accumulated Fortunes.* Boston: Beacon, 2003.

George, John, and Laird Wilcox. *Nazis, Communists, Klansmen, and Others on the Fringe.* New York: Prometheus, 1992.

Gillon, Steven M., and Cathy D. Matson. *The American Experiment: A History of the United States.* New York: Houghton Mifflin, 2002.

Giroux, Henry A. *The Abandoned Generation: Democracy beyond the Culture of Fear.* New York: Palgrave Macmillan, 2003.

———. *Proto-Fascism in America.* Bloomington, Ind.: Phi Delta Kappa Educational Foundation, 2004.

Gitlin, Todd. *Twilight of Our Common Dreams: Why America Is Wracked by Culture Wars.* New York: Metropolitan, 1995.

Glassner, Barry. *The Culture of Fear: Why Americans Are Afraid of the Wrong Things.* New York: Perseus, 1999.

Goldberg, Bernard. *Bias: A CBS Insider Exposes How the Media Distort the News.* Washington, D.C.: Regnery, 2002.

Gonzales, Manuel G. *Mexicanos: A History of Mexicans in the United States.* Bloomington: Indiana University Press, 1999.

Goodman, Amy, and David Goodman. *The Exception to the Rulers: Exposing Oily Politicians, War Profiteers, and the Media That Love Them.* New York: Hyperion, 2004.

Gosse, Van. *The Movements of the New Left, 1950-1975: A Brief History with Documents.* Boston: Bedford/St. Martin's, 2005.

Gottfried, Paul, and Thomas Fleming. *The Conservative Movement.* Boston: Twayne, 1988.

Gould, Lewis L. *Grand Old Party: A History of the Republicans.* New York: Random House, 2003.

Graetz, Michael J., and Ian Schapiro. *Death by a Thousand Cuts: The Fight over Taxing Inherited Wealth.* Princeton, N.J.: Princeton University Press, 2005.

Green, Mark. *Selling Out.* New York: Regan Books, 2002.

Greider, William. *Fortress America: The American Military and the Consequences of Peace.* New York: Public Affairs, 1998.

———. *One World, Ready or Not: The Manic Logic of Global Capitalism.* New York: Simon & Schuster, 1997.

———. *Secrets of the Temple.* New York: Simon & Schuster, 1987.

———. *The Soul of Capitalism: Opening Paths to a Moral Economy.* New York: Simon & Schuster, 2003.

———. *Who Will Tell the People: The Betrayal of American Democracy.* New York: Simon & Schuster, 1992.

Gross, Bertram Myron. *Friendly Fascism: The New Face of Power in America.* Boston: South End, 1998.

Guinier, Lani. *The Tyranny of the Majority: Fundamental Fairness in Representative Democracy.* New York: Free Press, 1994.

Hacker, Andrew. *Money: Who Has How Much and Why.* New York: Scribner, 1997.

———. *Two Nations: Black and White, Separate, Hostile, Unequal.* New York: Scribner's, 1992.

Hacker, Jacob S., and Paul Pierson. *Off Center: The Republican Revolution and the Erosion of Democracy.* New Haven, Conn.: Yale University Press, 2005.

Hadden, Jeffrey K., and Charles E. Swann. *Prime Time Preachers: The Rising Power of Televangelism.* Reading, Mass.: Addison-Wesley, 1981.

Halstead, Ted, and Michael Lind. *The Radical Center.* New York: Anchor Books, 2001.

Hannity, Sean. *Deliver Us from Evil: Defeating Terrorism, Despotism, and Liberalism.* New York: Regan Books, 2004.

———. *Let Freedom Ring: Winning the War of Liberty over Liberalism.* New York: Regan Books, 2002.

Hanson, Victor Davis. *Mexifornia: A State of Becoming.* San Francisco: Encounter Books, 2003.

Hardisty, Jean. *Mobilizing Resentment: Conservative Resurgence from the John Birch Society to the Promise Keepers.* Boston: Beacon, 2000.

Harrigan, John J. *Empty Dreams, Empty Pockets: Class and Bias in American Politics.* New York: Macmillan, 1993.

Hartung, William D. *And Weapons for All.* New York: HarperCollins, 1995.

————. *How Much Are You Making on the War, Daddy? A Quick and Dirty Guide to War Profiteering in the Bush Administration.* New York: Nation Books, 2003.

Hatfield, J. H. *Fortunate Son: George Bush and the Making of an American President.* New York: Soft Skull, 2001.

Herbert, Bob. *Promises Betrayed: Waking Up from the American Dream.* New York: Times Books, 2005.

Herman, Edward S. *Triumph of the Market: Essays on Economics, Politics, and the Media.* Boston: South End, 1995.

Herman, Edward S., and Robert W. McChesney. *The Global Media: The New Missionaries of Global Capitalism.* London: Cassell, 1997.

Hersh, Burton. *The Mellon Family: A Fortune in History.* New York: Harper & Row, 1978.

Hersh, Seymour M. *Chain of Command: The Road from 9/11 to Abu Ghraib.* New York: HarperCollins, 2004.

Hertsgaard, Mark. *The Eagle's Shadow: Why America Fascinates and Infuriates the World.* New York: Farrar, Straus & Giroux, 2002.

————. *On Bended Knee: The Press and the Reagan Presidency.* New York: Farrar, Straus & Giroux, 1988.

Hertz, Noreena. *The Silent Takeover: Global Capitalism and the Death of Democracy.* New York: Free Press, 2001.

Hertzberg, Hendrik. *Politics: Observations and Arguments, 1966–2004.* New York: Penguin Books, 2005.

Hightower, Jim. *If the Gods Had Meant Us to Vote They Would Have Given Us Candidates.* Rev. ed. New York: Perennial, 2001.

————. *Let's Stop Beating around the Bush.* New York: Viking Books, 2004.

————. *Thieves in High Places.* New York: Viking Penguin, 2003.

Himmelstein, Jerome L. *To the Right: The Transformation of American Conservatism.* Berkeley: University of California Press, 1992.

Hitchens, Christopher. *The Trial of Henry Kissinger.* London: Verso, 2001.

Hochschild, Jennifer L. *Facing Up to the American Dream.* Princeton, N.J.: Princeton University Press, 1995.

Hodgson, Godfrey. *More Equal Than Others: America from Nixon to the New Century.* Princeton, N.J.: Princeton University Press, 2004.

————. *The World Turned Right Side Up: A History of the Conservative Ascendancy in America.* New York: Houghton Mifflin, 1996.

Hoeveler, J. David, Jr. *Watch on the Right: Conservative Intellectuals in the Reagan Era.* Madison: University of Wisconsin Press, 1991.

Hoffer, Eric. *The True Believer: Thoughts on the Nature of Mass Movements.* New York: Harper & Row, 1951.

Hofstadter, Richard. *The Paranoid Style in American Politics and Other Essays.* New York: Knopf, 1965.

Horowitz, David A., and Peter N. Carroll. *On the Edge: The U.S. since 1945.* 2d ed. New York: West/Wadsworth, 1998.

Huffington, Arianna. *Fanatics and Fools: The Game Plan for Winning Back America.* New York: Miramax, 2004.

————. *Pigs at the Trough: How Corporate Greed and Political Corruption Are Undermining America.* New York: Crown, 2003.

Huntington, Samuel. *The Clash of Civilizations and the Remaking of World Order.* New York: Simon & Schuster, 1997.

———. *Who Are We? The Challenges to America's National Identity.* New York: Simon & Schuster, 2004.

Ingraham, Laura. *The Hillary Trap: Looking for Power in All the Wrong Places.* New York: Hyperion, 2000.

———. *Shut Up and Sing: How Elites from Hollywood, Politics, and the UN Are Subverting America.* Washington, D.C.: Regnery, 2003.

Isikoff, Michael. *Uncovering Clinton: A Reporter's Story.* New York: Three Rivers, 2000.

Ivins, Molly, and Lou Dubose. *Bushwhacked: Life in George W. Bush's America.* New York: Random House, 2003.

Johnson, Chalmers. *Blowback: The Costs and Consequences of American Empire.* New York: Holt, 2001.

———. *The Sorrows of Empire: Militarism, Secrecy, and the End of the Republic.* New York: Metropolitan, 2004.

Johnson, Haynes. *The Best of Times: America in the Clinton Years.* New York: Harcourt, 2001.

———. *Sleepwalking through History: America in the Reagan Years.* New York: Anchor Books/Doubleday, 1991.

Johnston, David Cay. *Perfectly Legal: The Covert Campaign to Rig Our Tax System to Benefit the Super Rich—and Cheat Everybody Else.* New York: Portfolio, 2003.

Judis, John B. *The Paradox of American Democracy: Elites, Special Interests, and the Betrayal of the Public Trust.* New York: Pantheon Books, 2000.

———. *William F. Buckley, Jr.: Patron Saint of the Conservatives.* New York: Simon & Schuster, 1988.

Kaplan, Esther. *With God on Their Side: George W. Bush and the Christian Right.* New York: New Press, 2005.

Kaplan, Robert D. *Empire Wilderness: Travels into America's Future.* New York: Vintage Books, 1999.

Keillor, Garrison. *Homegrown Democrat: A Few Plain Thoughts from the Heart of America.* New York: Viking Books, 2004.

Kelley, Kitty. *The Family: The Real Story of the Bush Dynasty.* New York: Doubleday, 2004.

Kellner, Douglas. *From 9/11 to Terror War: The Dangers of the Bush Legacy.* Lanham, Md.: Rowman & Littlefield, 2003.

———. *Media Spectacle and the Crisis of Democracy: Terrorism, War, and Election Battles.* Boulder, Colo.: Paradigm, 2005.

Kelly, Charles M. *Class War in America.* Santa Barbara, Calif.: Fithian, 2000.

Kelly, Daniel. *James Burnham and the Struggle for the World: A Life.* Wilmington, Del.: Intercollegiate Studies Institute, 2002.

Kintz, Linda. *Between Jesus and the Market: The Emotions That Matter in Right-Wing America.* Durham, N.C.: Duke University Press, 1997.

Kirk, Russell. *The Conservative Mind: From Burke to Eliot.* 7th ed. Washington, D.C.: Regnery, 2001.

Kirp, David L. *Shakespeare, Einstein and the Bottom Line: The Marketing of Higher Education.* Cambridge, Mass.: Harvard University Press, 2003.

Kivel, Paul. *You Call This a Democracy? Who Benefits, Who Really Decides?* New York: Apex, 2004.

Klein, Naomi. *Fences and Windows: Dispatches from the Front Lines of the Globalization Debate.* New York: Picador, 2002.

———. *No Logo: Taking Aim at the Brand Bullies.* New York: Picador, 2000.

Kolkey, Jonathan Martin. *The New Right, 1960-1968: With Epilogue, 1969-1980.* Washington, D.C.: University Press of America, 1983.

Kolko, Gabriel. *The Triumph of Conservatism.* New York: Free Press, 1977.

———. *Wealth and Power in America.* New York: Praeger, 1972.

Kristol, Irving, and Arving Kristol. *Neo-Conservatism: The Autobiography of an Idea.* Chicago: Ivan R. Dee, 1999.

Krugman, Paul. *Fuzzy Math: The Essential Guide to the Bush Tax Plan.* New York: Norton, 2001.

———. *The Great Unraveling.* New York: Norton, 2003.

Kurtz, Howard. *The Fortune Tellers: Inside Wall Street's Game of Money, Media, and Manipulation.* New York: Simon & Schuster, 2000.

———. *Hot Air: All Talk All the Time.* New York: Times Books, 1996.

Kuttner, Robert. *Everything for Sale: The Virtues and Limits of Markets.* New York: Knopf, 1997.

———. *Revolt of the Haves.* New York: Simon & Schuster, 1980.

Lakoff, George. *Don't Think of an Elephant: Know Your Values and Frame the Debate.* White River Junction, Vt.: Chelsea Green, 2004.

———. *Moral Politics: How Liberals and Conservatives Think.* 2d ed. Chicago: University of Chicago Press, 2002.

Landes, David. *The Wealth and Poverty of Nations.* New York: Norton, 1998.

Lapham, Lewis. *Money and Class in America: Notes and Observations on the Civil Religion.* New York: Ballantine Books, 1989.

———. *Waiting for the Barbarians.* London: Verso, 1997.

Lappe, Anthony, and Stephen Marshall. *True Lies.* East Rutherford, N.J.: Plume Books, 2004.

Lasch, Christopher. *The Revolt of the Elites and the Betrayal of Democracy.* New York: Norton, 1996.

Lemann, Nicholas. *The Big Test: The Secret History of the American Meritocracy.* New York: Farrar, Straus & Giroux, 1999.

LeRoy, Greg. *The Great American Jobs Scam: Corporate Tax Dodging and the Myth of Job Creation.* San Francisco: Berrett-Koehler, 2005.

Levitas, Daniel. *The Terrorist Next Door: The Militia Movement and the Radical Right.* New York: St. Martin's Griffin, 2004.

Lewis, Charles. *The Buying of the Congress.* New York: Avon, 1998.

———. *The Buying of the President 2000.* New York: Avon, 2000.

———. *The Buying of the President 2004.* New York: Perennial, 2004.

Lewis, Charles, and Bill Allison. *The Cheating of America: How Tax Avoidance and Evasion by the Super Rich Are Costing the Country Billions—and What You Can Do about It.* New York: Morrow, 2001.

Lind, Michael. *Made in Texas: George W. Bush and the Southern Takeover of American Politics.* New York: Basic Books, 2002.

———. *The Next American Nation: The New Nationalism and the Fourth American Revolution.* New York: Free Press, 1995.

————. *Up from Conservatism: Why the Right Is Wrong for America.* New York: Free Press, 1996.

Linn, Susan. *Consuming Kids: The Hostile Takeover of Childhood.* New York: New Press, 2004.

Lowenthal, Abraham F., and Katrina Burgess, eds. *The California-Mexico Connection.* Stanford, Calif.: Stanford University Press, 1993.

Lundberg, Ferdinand. *The Rich and the Super-Rich: A Study in the Power of Money Today.* New York: Bantam, 1968.

MacKenzie, Angus. *Secrets: The CIA's War at Home.* Berkeley: University of California Press, 1997.

Maharidge, Dale. *Homeland.* New York: Seven Stories, 2004.

Maher, Bill. *When You Ride Alone You Ride with Bin Laden: What the Government Should Be Telling Us to Help Fight the War on Terrorism.* New York: New Millennium, 2002.

Mailer, Norman. *Why Are We at War?* New York: Random House, 2003.

Mann, James. *Rise of the Vulcans: The History of Bush's War Cabinet.* New York: Viking Books, 2004.

Marshall, Jonathan, Peter Dale Scott, and Jane Hunter. *The Iran-Contra Connection.* Boston: South End, 1988.

Martin, William. *With God on Our Side: The Rise of the Religious Right in America.* New York: Broadway Books, 1996.

Massey, Douglas S., Jorge Durand, and Nolan J. Malone. *Beyond Smoke and Mirrors: Mexican Immigration in an Era of Economic Integration.* New York: Russell Sage Foundation, 2002.

Matalin, Mary, and James Carville. *All's Fair: Love, War, and Running for President.* New York: Random House, 1994.

Matusow, Allen J. *The Unraveling of America: A History of Liberalism in the 1960s.* New York: HarperCollins, 1986.

McCartney, Laton. *Friends in High Places. The Bechtel Story: The Most Secret Corporation and How It Engineered the World.* New York: Ballantine Books, 1989.

McChesney, Robert W. *Corporate Media and the Threat to Democracy.* New York: Seven Stories, 1997.

————. *Rich Media, Poor Democracy: Communication Politics in Dubious Times.* Rev. ed. New York: New Press, 2000.

McGirr, Lisa. *Suburban Warriors: The Origins of the New American Right.* Princeton, N.J.: Princeton University Press, 2001.

McGowan, David. *Derailing Democracy.* Monroe, Maine: Common Courage Press, 2000.

McLean, Bethany, and Peter Elkind. *The Smartest Guys in the Room: The Amazing Rise and Scandalous Fall of Enron.* New York: Portfolio, 2003.

Micklethwait, John, and Adrian Wooldridge. *The Right Nation: Conservative Power in America.* New York: Penguin Books, 2004.

Miles, Michael W. *The Odyssey of the American Right.* New York: Oxford University Press, 1980.

Miller, Mark Crispin. *Cruel and Unusual: Bush/Cheney's New World Order.* New York: Norton, 2004.

Mills, C. Wright. *The Power Elite.* New York: Oxford University Press, 1959.

Montejano, David, ed. *Chicano Politics and Society in the Late Twentieth Century.* Austin: University of Texas Press, 1999.

Moore, James. *Bush's War for Reelection: Iraq, the White House, and the People.* New York: Wiley, 2004.

Moore, James C., and Wayne Slater. *Bush's Brain: How Karl Rove Made George W. Bush Presidential.* New York: Wiley, 2003.

Moore, Michael. *Dude, Where's My Country?* New York: Warner Books, 2003.

———. *Stupid White Men and Other Sorry Excuses for the State of the Nation!* New York: Regan Books, 2001.

Nace, Ted. *Gangs in America: The Rise of Corporate Power and the Disabling of Democracy.* San Francisco: Berrett-Koehler, 2003.

Nader, Ralph. *Crashing the Party: How to Tell the Truth and Still Run for President.* New York: St. Martin's/ Dunne, 2002.

Nash, George H. *The Conservative Intellectual Movement in America, since 1945.* Rev. ed. Wilmington, Del.: Intercollegiate Studies Institute, 1998.

Newhouse, John. *Imperial America: The Bush Assault on the World Order.* New York: Knopf, 2003.

Ngai, Mae M. *Impossible Subjects: Illegal Aliens and the Making of Modern America.* Princeton, N.J.: Princeton University Press, 2004.

Nichols, John. *Dick: The Man Who Is President.* New York: New Press, 2004.

———. *Jews for Buchanan: Did You Hear the One about the Theft of the American Presidency?* New York: New Press, 2001.

Nichols, John, and Robert W. McChesney. *It's the Media, Stupid.* New York: Seven Stories, 2000.

———. *Our Media, Not Theirs: The Democratic Struggle against Corporate Media.* New York: Seven Stories, 2002.

Noonan, Peggy. *The Case against Hillary Clinton.* New York: Regan Books, 2000.

Novak, Michael. *The Catholic Ethic and the Spirit of Capitalism.* New York: Free Press, 1993.

Novick, Michael. *White Lies, White Power: The Fight against White Supremacy and Reactionary Violence.* Monroe, Maine: Common Courage Press, 1995.

Oliver, Melvin L., and Thomas M. Shapiro. *Black Wealth, White Wealth.* New York: Routledge, 1997.

Olson, Barbara. *The Final Days: The Last, Desperate Abuses of Power by the Clinton White House.* Washington, D.C.: Regnery, 2001.

———. *Hell to Pay: The Unfolding Story of Hillary Rodham Clinton.* Washington, D.C.: Regnery, 1999.

Omi, Michael, and Howard Winant. *Racial Formation in the United States: From the 1960s to the 1990s.* 2d ed. New York: Routledge, 1994.

Packer, George. *Blood of the Liberals.* New York: Farrar, Straus & Giroux, 2000.

Palast, Greg. *The Best Democracy Money Can Buy.* London: Pluto, 2002.

Parenti, Michael. *America Besieged.* San Francisco: City Lights, 1998.

———. *Democracy for the Few.* 7th ed. Boston: Bedford/St. Martin's, 2002.

———. *Make-Believe Media: The Politics of Entertainment.* New York: St. Martin's, 1992.

————. *The Terrorism Trap: September 11 and Beyond.* San Francisco: City Lights, 2002.

Patterson, James T. *Restless Giant: The United States from Watergate to Bush vs. Gore.* New York: Oxford University Press, 2005.

Peele, Gillian. *Revival & Reaction: The Right in Contemporary America.* New York: Oxford University Press, 1984.

Perkins, John. *Confessions of an Economic Hit Man.* San Francisco: Berrett-Koehler, 2004.

Perlstein, Rick. *Before the Storm: Barry Goldwater and the Unmaking of the American Consensus.* New York: Hill & Wang, 2002.

Phillips, Kevin. *American Dynasty: Aristocracy, Fortune, and the Politics of Deceit in the House of Bush.* New York: Viking Books, 2003.

————. *Arrogant Capital: Washington, Wall Street, and the Frustration of American Politics.* New York: Little, Brown, 1994.

————. *The Boiling Point: Democrats, Republicans and the Decline of Middle Class Prosperity.* New York: Random House, 1993.

————. *The Politics of Rich and Poor: Wealth and the American Electorate in the Reagan Aftermath.* New York: Random House, 1990.

————. *Post-Conservative America: People, Politics and Ideology in a Time of Crisis.* New York: Random House, 1982.

————. *Wealth and Democracy: A Political History of the American Rich.* New York: Broadway Books, 2002.

Phillips, Peter, ed. *Censored 2003: The Top 25 Censured Stories.* New York: Seven Stories, 2002.

Piven, Frances Fox, and Richard A. Cloward. *The Breaking of the American Social Contract.* New York: New Press, 1997.

————. *Regulating the Poor.* New York: Vintage Books, 1993.

————. *Why Americans Don't Vote.* New York: Pantheon Books, 1988.

Pizzo, Stephen, Mary Fricker, and Paul Muolo. *Inside Job: The Looting of America's Savings and Loans.* New York: HarperCollins, 1991.

Portes, Alejandro, and Rubén G. Rumbaut. *Immigrant America: A Portrait.* Berkeley: University of California Press, 1990.

Postman, Neil. *Amusing Ourselves to Death.* New York: Penguin Books, 1995.

Powers, John. *Sore Winners (and the Rest of Us) in George Bush's America.* New York: Doubleday, 2004.

Prendergast, William. *The Catholic Voter in American Politics: The Passing of the Democratic Monolith.* Washington, D.C.: Georgetown University Press, 1999.

Priest, Dana. *The Mission: Waging War and Keeping Peace with America's Military.* New York: Norton, 2003.

Pycior, Julie Leininger. *LBJ & Mexican Americans: The Paradox of Power.* Austin: University of Texas Press, 1997.

Quadagno, Jill. *The Color of Welfare: How Racism Undermined the War on Poverty.* New York: Oxford University Press, 1994.

Rae, Nicol C. *The Decline and Fall of Liberal Republicans: From 1952 to the Present.* New York: Oxford University Press, 1989.

Rampton, Sheldon, and John Stauber. *Weapons of Mass Deception: The Uses of Propaganda in Bush's War on Iraq.* New York: Tarcher/Penguin, 2003.

Reeves, Richard. *The Reagan Detour.* New York: Simon & Schuster, 1985.

Reich, Robert B. *Reason: Why Liberals Will Win the Battle for America.* New York: Knopf, 2004.

Ricci, David M. *The Transformation of American Politics: The New Washington and the Rise of Think Tanks.* New Haven, Conn.: Yale University Press, 1993.

Roediger, David R. *Colored White: Transcending the Racial Past.* Berkeley: University of California Press, 2002.

———. *The Wages of Whiteness.* London: Verso, 1991.

Rowse, Arthur. *Drive-By Journalism.* Monroe, Maine: Common Courage Press, 2000.

Rubin, Robert E., and Jacob Weisberg. *In an Uncertain World.* New York: Random House, 2003.

Rusher, William. *Rise of the Right.* New York: Morrow, 1984.

Ryscavage, Paul. *Income Inequality in America: An Analysis of Trends.* Armonk, N.Y.: Sharpe, 1999.

Sabato, Larry, and Glenn Simpson. *Dirty Little Secrets: The Persistence of Corruption in American Politics.* New York: Times Books/Random House, 1996.

Saloma, John S., III. *Ominous Politics: The New Conservative Labyrinth.* New York: Hill & Wang, 1984.

Savage, David. *Turning Right: The Making of the Rehnquist Supreme Court.* New York: Wiley, 1992.

Schaller, Michael, and George Rising. *The Republican Ascendancy: American Politics, 1968–2001.* Wheeling, Ill.: Harlan Davidson, 2002.

Scheer, Christopher, Lakshmi Chaudhry, and Robert Scheer. *The Five Biggest Lies Bush Told Us about Iraq.* New York: Seven Stories/Akashic Books, 2003.

Scheer, Robert. *America after Nixon: The Age of the Multinationals.* New York: McGraw-Hill, 1974.

Schell, Jonathan. *A Hole in the World.* New York: Nation Books, 2004.

Schiller, Herbert I. *Culture, Inc.: The Corporate Takeover of Public Expression.* New York: Oxford University Press, 1989.

Schlesinger, Arthur M., Jr. *The Disuniting of America.* New York: Norton, 1992.

Schlosser, Eric. *Fast Food Nation: The Dark Side of the All-American Meal.* New York: Perennial, 2002.

———. *Reefer Madness: Sex, Drugs, and Cheap Labor in the American Black Market.* Boston: Houghton Mifflin, 2003.

Schor, Juliet. *The Overworked American.* New York: Basic Books, 1991.

Schrecker, Ellen. *The Age of McCarthyism.* 2d ed. Boston: Bedford/St. Martin's, 2002.

Schrecker, Ellen, and Maurice Isserman, eds. *Cold War Triumphalism.* New York: New Press, 2004.

Schwartz, Herman. *Packing the Courts: The Conservative Campaign to Rewrite the Constitution.* New York: Scribner, 1988.

———. *Right-Wing Justice: The Conservative Campaign to Take Over the Courts.* New York: Nation Books, 2004.

Sexton, Patricia Cayo. *The War on Labor and the Left.* Boulder, Colo.: Westview, 1991.

Shapiro, Thomas M. *The Hidden Cost of Being African American: How Wealth Perpetuates Inequality.* New York: Oxford University Press, 2004.

Shorris, Earl. *Jews without Mercy: A Lament.* Garden City, N.Y.: Anchor/Doubleday, 1982.

———. *Latinos: A Biography of the People.* New York: Norton, 1992.

———. *A Nation of Salesmen: The Tyranny of the Market and the Subversion of Culture.* New York: Avon, 1994.

Sieber, Sam D. *Second-Rate Nation: From the American Dream to the American Myth.* Boulder, Colo.: Paradigm, 2004.

Siegal, Marc. *False Alarm: The Truth about the Epidemic of Fear.* New York: Wiley, 2005.

Silverstein, Ken. *Washington on $10 Million a Day: How Lobbyists Plunder the Nation.* Monroe, Maine: Common Courage Press, 1998.

Singer, Peter. *The President of Good and Evil: The Ethics of George W. Bush.* New York: Dutton, 2004.

Singer, P. W. *Corporate Warriors: The Rise of the Privatized Military Industry.* Ithaca, N.Y.: Cornell University Press, 2003.

Skrzycki, Cindy. *The Regulators: Anonymous Power Brokers in American Politics.* Lanham, Md.: Rowman & Littlefield, 2003.

Smant, Kevin J. *Principles and Heresies: Frank S. Meyer and the Shaping of the American Conservative Movement.* Wilmington, Del.: Intercollegiate Studies Institute, 2002.

Smith, James A. *The Idea Brokers: Think Tanks and the Rise of the New Policy Elite.* New York: Free Press, 1991.

Soley, Lawrence C. *Leasing the Ivory Tower: The Corporate Takeover of America.* Boston: South End, 1995.

Solomon, Norman. *False Hope: The Politics of Illusion in the Clinton Era.* Monroe, Maine: Common Courage Press, 1994.

———. *War Made Easy: How Presidents and Pundits Keep Spinning Us to Death.* Hoboken, N.J.: Wiley, 2005.

Solomon, Norman, and Jeff Cohen. *Wizards of Media Oz: Behind the Mainstream News.* Monroe, Maine: Common Courage Press, 1997.

Solomon, Norman, and Reese Erlich. *Target Iraq: What the News Media Didn't Tell You.* New York: Context Books, 2003.

Stefancic, Jean, and Richard Delgado. *No Mercy: How Conservative Think Tanks and Foundations Changed America's Social Agenda.* Philadelphia: Temple University Press, 1996.

Stein, Donald G., ed. *Buying In or Selling Out? The Commercialization of the American Research University.* New Brunswick, N.J.: Rutgers University Press, 2004.

Stein, Judith. *Running Steel, Running America: Race, Economic Policy, and the Decline of Liberalism.* Chapel Hill: University of North Carolina Press, 1998.

Steinfels, Peter. *The Neoconservatives: The Men Who Are Changing America's Politics.* New York: Simon & Schuster, 1979.

Steyer, James P. *The Other Parent: The Inside Story of the Media's Effect on Our Children.* New York: Atria Books, 2002.

Stiglitz, Joseph E. *Globalization and Its Discontents.* New York: Norton, 2002.

————. *The Roaring Nineties: A New History of the World's Most Prosperous Decade.* New York: Norton, 2003.

Suskind, Ron. *The Price of Loyalty: George W. Bush, the White House and the Education of Paul O'Neill.* New York: Simon & Schuster, 2004.

Thomas, Cal, and Ed Dobson. *Blinded by Might: Can the Religious Right Save America?* Grand Rapids, Mich.: Zondervan, 1999.

Thorne, Melvin. *American Conservative Thought since World War II: The Core Ideas.* Westport, Conn.: Greenwood, 1990.

Tiefer, Charles. *Veering Right: How the Bush Administration Subverts the Law for Conservative Causes.* Berkeley: University of California Press, 2004.

Tirman, John. *The Maze of Fear: Security and Migration after 9/11.* New York: New Press, 2004.

Toms, Michael, ed. *A Time for Choices: Deep Dialogues for Deep Democracy.* Gabriola Island, B.C., Canada: New Society, 2002.

Toobin, Jeffrey. *A Vast Conspiracy: The Real Story of the Sex Scandal That Nearly Brought Down a President.* New York: Touchstone, 2000.

Twitchell, James B. *Adcult USA: The Triumph of Advertising in American Culture.* New York: Columbia University Press, 1996.

Tyrrell, R. Emmett, Jr. *The Conservative Crack-Up.* New York: Simon & Schuster, 1992.

Unger, Craig. *House of Bush, House of Saud: The Secret Relationship between the World's Two Most Powerful Dynasties.* New York: Scribner, 2004.

Utter, Glenn H., and John W. Storey. *The Religious Right.* 2d ed. Santa Barbara, Calif.: ABC/CLIO, 2001.

Vidal, Gore. *Dreaming War: Blood for Oil and the Cheney-Bush Junta.* New York: Thunder's Mouth, 2002.

————. *Imperial America: Reflections on the United States of Amnesia.* New York: Nation Books, 2004.

Wald, Alan M. *The New York Intellectuals: The Rise and Decline of the Anti-Stalinist Left from the 1930s to the 1980s.* Chapel Hill: University of North Carolina Press, 1987.

Waldman, Paul. *Fraud: The Strategy behind the Bush Lies and Why the Media Didn't Tell You.* Naperville, Ill.: Sourcebooks Trade, 2004.

Walsh, Lawrence. *Firewall: The Iran-Contra Conspiracy and Cover-Up.* New York: Norton, 1997.

Washburn, Jennifer. *University, Inc.: The Corporate Corruption of Higher Education.* New York: Basic Books, 2005.

Weber, Max. *The Protestant Ethic and the Spirit of Capitalism.* Trans. Talcott Parsons. New York: Scribner's, 1958.

Wilcox, William Clyde. *God's Warriors: The Christian Right in Twentieth-Century America.* Baltimore: Johns Hopkins University Press, 1992.

Williams, Dick. *Newt! Leader of the Second American Revolution.* Marietta, Ga.: Longstreet Press, 1995.

Williams, Ian. *Deserter: Bush's War on Military Families, Veterans and His Past.* New York: Nation Books, 2004.

Wills, Garry. *Reagan's America: Innocents at Home.* Garden City, N.Y.: Doubleday, 1987.

————. *Under God: Religion and American Politics.* New York: Simon & Schuster, 1990.

Wilson, Joseph. *The Politics of Truth: Inside the Lies That Led to War and Betrayed My Wife's CIA Identity: A Diplomat's Memoir.* New York: Carroll & Graf, 2004.

Wilson, William Julius. *The Truly Disadvantaged: The Inner City, the Underclass and Public Policy.* Chicago: University of Chicago Press, 1987.

————. *When Work Disappears: The World of the New Urban Poor.* New York: Knopf, 1996.

Winokur, Jon. *The Rich Are Different.* New York: Pantheon Books, 1996.

Witcover, Jules. *Party of the People: A History of the Democrats.* New York: Random House, 2003.

Wolff, Edward. *Top Heavy: A Study of the Increasing Inequality of Wealth in America.* New York: Twentieth Century Fund, 1995.

————. *Top Heavy: The Increasing Inequality of Wealth in America and What Can Be Done about It.* 2d. ed. New York: New Press, 2002.

Woodward, Bob. *Plan of Attack.* New York: Simon & Schuster, 2004.

Zepezaur, Mark, and Arthur Naiman. *Take the Rich off Welfare.* Tucson, Ariz.: Odonian, 1996.

Zinn, Howard. *A People's History of the United States: 1492 to Present.* 3d ed. New York: HarperCollins, 2001.

————. *You Can't Be Neutral on a Moving Train: A Personal History of Our Times.* Boston: Beacon, 1995.

Zweigenhaft, Richard L., and G. William Domhoff. *Diversity in the Power Elite.* New Haven, Conn.: Yale University Press, 1998.

INDEX

Abbott Laboratories, 103
Abraham, Spencer, 31
Abramoff, Jack, 103
Abrams, Elliot, 11
Abu Ghraib prison, 47, 70
Abu-Lughod, Janet L., 90, 91
Accuracy in Academia (AIA), 37–38
Accuracy in Media (AIM), 38, 50
Adolph Coors Foundation, 19
advertising, 103, 108
Afghanistan war, 46, 105
Agnew, Spiro, 55
Ailes, Roger, 46, 89
AIM (Accuracy in Media), 38, 50
Air America, 46
Airbus, 59–61
Alfred A. Regnery (publisher), 92
alienation, 84
Alliance for Retirement Prosperity, 30
All Things Considered (radio show), 50
Alperovitz, Gar, 109
Alterman, Eric, 44, 45
America in Black and White (Thernstrom and Thernstrom), 37
American Association of Retired Persons (AARP), 30
American Center for Law and Justice (ACLJ), 31
American Chiropractic Association, 103
American Conservative Union, 5
American Council of Trustees and Alumni (ACTA), 38
American Enterprise Institute (AEI), 10, 20, 25, 28–29, 49–50, 94

American exceptionalism, 9, 111
Americans for Tax Reform (ATR), 14, 51, 130
American Independent Party, 88
American Legislative Exchange Council (ALEC), 21–22
American Petroleum Institute, 21
American Spectator (magazine), 20, 35
Anderson, Bonnie, 75
Andrew, John A., III, 3
Angeles T. Arredondo Foundation, 94
Ankerberg, John, 131
Annenberg, Walter, 89
anti-intellectualism, 55–56, 78, 85
antimodernizationism, 84
Apocalypse, 84
Aristide, Jean-Bertrand, 48
Arnett, Peter, 47
Arthur Andersen, 106
Aryan Brotherhood, 93, 121
Ashcroft, John, 131
Atlantic Monthly (magazine), 45
Atwater, Lee, 13, 89
Auletta, Ken, 108
authoritarian governments, 110
Aventis, 103
Ayn Rand Institute, 57

Baker, Kevin, 66, 109–10
Bakker, Jim, 8
Baltzell, E. Digby, 55
bankruptcy, personal, 100
Barlow, Andrew, 87, 88, 93, 95, 114
Barnes, Fred, 43
Baroody, William J., 28

207

ABOUT THE AUTHORS

Manuel G. Gonzales is an instructor of history at Diablo Valley College in Pleasant Hill, California, and a visiting lecturer for the Department of History at California State University, East Bay. He has also been a visiting professor for the Department of Ethnic Studies at the University of California, Berkeley. His publications include *Andrea Costa and the Rise of Socialism in the Romagna* (University Press of America, 1980), *The Hispanic Elite of the Southwest* (University of Texas at El Paso, 1989), and *Mexicanos: A History of Mexicans in the United States* (Indiana University Press, 1999).

Richard Delgado is professor of law and Derrick Bell Fellow at the University of Pittsburgh. He is author of *No Mercy: How Conservative Think Tanks and Foundations Changed America's Social Agenda* (Temple University Press, 1996), *How Lawyers Lose Their Way* (Duke University Press, 2005), and *The Rodrigo Chronicles* (NYU Press, 1996). Winner of eight national book awards and a Pulitzer Prize nomination, Delgado teaches and writes in the areas of civil rights and social regulation.